Heart
of the Matter

Daily Reflections
for Changing
Hearts and Lives

Christian Counseling
& Educational Foundation

Nancy B. Winter, editor

New
Growth
Press

www.newgrowthpress.com

New Growth Press, Greensboro, NC 27404
Copyright © 2012
by Christian Counseling & Educational Foundation.

ISBN: 978-1-936768-65-3
ISBN: 978-1-936768-54-7 (eBook)

Library of Congress Cataloging-in-Publication Data

Heart of the matter : daily reflections for changing hearts
and lives / CCEF.
       p. cm.
   Includes bibliographical references and index.
   ISBN 978-1-936768-65-3 (alk. paper)
   1. Devotional calendars. I. Christian Counseling & Educational
Foundation.
   BV4810.H43   2012
   242'.2—dc23

                                              2012027979

Printed in Canada

19 18 17 16 15 14 13 12   1 2 3 4 5

INTRODUCTION

We hope this daily devotional will bless and serve you by being a constant reminder that personal change is centered in the person of Christ. The selections are excerpted from books and other materials written by the experienced counselors at CCEF. Each day's meditation is anchored in Scripture and saturated with Christ's mercies. The suggested Bible reading is meant to complement and enlarge on the themes of the daily reading. Reading the meditations thoughtfully, along with the daily Scripture passages, will encourage you to grow in your walk with the Lord.

We know from years of seeing lives changed that short readings alone are not a "quick fix." But we are convinced that the Spirit is always present and active through God's Word, thoughtful contemplation, prayer, and community within the body of Christ. As you seek to know God personally and be changed by him, our prayer is that he would meet you daily as you reflect on who he is and what he has done for you in Christ.

The Christian Counseling & Educational Foundation (CCEF) exists to teach people how to explore the wisdom and depth of the Bible and apply its grace-centered message to the problems of daily living. Our mission is to restore Christ to counseling and counseling to the church. As a ministry, we seek to do this in a variety of ways:

- We counsel.
- We train ministry leaders and laypeople in counseling through our onsite and distance education courses.
- We write counseling literature for the church and publish numerous resources.
- We partner with churches around the world through training and consultation.

To learn more about the ministry of CCEF and to find many helpful resources, visit our website at www.ccef.org.

January 1

2 Peter 1:3–9

God "has given us everything we need for life and godliness" (2 Peter 1:3). The first few verses of this passage lay out the glories of our identity as God's children that Peter says we must not forget. God has given everything we need, not only for eternal life, but also for the God-honoring life to which we have been called until he returns. Notice the tense of the verb. Peter says God has given us everything we need. It has already happened! This is a fundamental Gospel truth. God will not call us to do anything without providing a way for it to be done. If he calls us to cross the Red Sea, he will enable us to swim, send a boat, build a bridge, or part the waters!

Don't forget who you are. You are the children of God who have inherited riches beyond your ability to conceive. You have been given everything you need to do what God has called you to do. Don't give in to discouragement. Don't quit. Don't run away from your calling. Don't settle for a little bit of faith, goodness, knowledge, self-control, perseverance, brotherly kindness, and love. Get everything that is your inheritance as God's children.

Paul David Tripp

JANUARY 2

1 JOHN 1:5–10

Asking for forgiveness is a war between self-righteousness and unearned grace. Between the rules of my kingdom and the commandments of the King. Between a desire to be served and the call to serve. Between living for my own glory and being consumed by the glory of God. I do not fight this war alone. The King, who has welcomed me into his better kingdom, is a Warrior King who will continue to fight on my behalf until the last enemy is under his feet.

This *is* the battle of battles. His kingdom *will* come. His will *will* be done. He will not sit idly by and permit his kingdom children to live with a greater practical allegiance to the building of their own kingdoms. So he fights for the freedom of our souls. He battles for the control of our hearts. He works to liberate our desires and to focus our thoughts. And as he does this, he calls us to humbly confess that we really do love ourselves more than we love him and others. He invites us to admit how regularly we demand our own way. He welcomes us to own up to our anger, greed, envy, and vengeance. If his kingdom is ever to fully come, it must be a kingdom of forgiveness where rebel citizens can be made right again and again and again.

PAUL DAVID TRIPP

1 KINGS 19:1–8

Elijah had abandoned the job God gave him to do as Israel's prophet. He admitted that he had wrongly given up as he prayed in the desert, "Take my life; I am no better than my ancestors."

When we lose confidence in God, we never do so in the abstract. Rather, our faith dissolves in concrete situations where God doesn't seem up to the job. When Jezebel threatened Elijah he ran, revealing his false faith that she could affect his life more than the Lord. Yet, Elijah felt conviction of sin. He knew he'd sold God out, hence his conclusion that he was no better than anyone else. Life had become a messy, vicious cycle that made it hard even to consider approaching people again.

Remarkably, God did not ridicule or berate him. Nor did he reject him and find someone else to complete the mission. Instead, when Elijah arrived in the desert, God sent an angel to feed and strengthen him. Not only did Elijah's strength revive, so did his faith. Instead of simply running away from the enemy, he ran toward his Lord. Elijah may not have had enough faith to face the queen he had angered, but he learned he could face the God he had failed.

WILLIAM P. SMITH

JANUARY 4

1 PETER 1:3–25

The ending makes all the difference. A tragic story like Shakespeare's *Romeo and Juliet* starts well, with people full of hope and love, but it ends badly. A comedy like *Much Ado About Nothing* opens with dark omens and scheming betrayers. The future looks very uncertain but it turns out wonderfully. It is the ending rather than the humor that makes it a comedy.

You must decide whether you will live life as a tragedy or a comedy. The story that Jesus offers you is a comedy. Scripture tells you the end, and, if you have put your faith in Jesus rather than in yourself, it is your end too. Jesus wins. His justice prevails. His love is seen for what it really is—boundless and irresistible. Our unity with him exceeds our imaginations. We will see that life was much more purposeful than we thought. Everything we ever did by faith—because of Jesus— stands firm and results in "praise, glory and honor when Jesus Christ is revealed" (1 Peter 1:7). Knowing this, of course, does not blot out sorrow. But knowing the end reveals that sorrow and death don't win. For those who know Christ, life and joy are the last word.

EDWARD T. WELCH

JANUARY 5

1 Thessalonians 5:14–18

Taking you out of the center of things, deep and thorough repentance and faith enable you to see those around you. You now see them through eyes cleansed by the forgiving grace of Christ. You begin to see things that, in your sin, you were not able to see. You may not ignore sin if it is there, but you begin to see the person and the struggles, temptations, and weaknesses that are part of his conflict with you. At this point, you can choose to serve and not be served. Christ's massive service for you on the cross gets bigger; it progressively changes your heart and empowers you to serve the other person. In 1 Thessalonians 5:14–18, Paul is giving pastoral instruction to the Thessalonians as they seek to help each other grow in grace.

"Warn the idle." Love warns someone when there are patterns of destructive behavior that involve obvious violations of God's wise and loving commands. Whenever there is a persistent pattern of sin, love requires us to move toward the person with gentle courage and humble resolve. "Encourage the timid." Love comes alongside the fearful and brings encouragement. "Help the weak." The word *help* can be translated: "Hold on to them," or "Put your arm round them." This emphasizes the need for practical guidance and support through the long process of change. They need to be reminded of the gospel's comfort as well as its call.

TIMOTHY S. LANE

JANUARY 6

1 Timothy 1:12–17

Watch God engage people in the Bible, and learn that he really doesn't treat us as our sins deserve (Psalm 103:10). He doesn't pursue us to make us pay him back for all our sins and mistakes. He wants us to turn to him and be reconciled to him (2 Corinthians 5:20–21). He does not engage people with a hidden agenda to make his life easier. He invests himself in relationships that make his life harder!

The apostle Paul was handpicked by Jesus to see his resurrected body; he was used by God to share the gospel all over the known world; and wherever he preached, churches were started. Why then does he keep reminding us of his failings—that he was a blasphemer, a persecutor of Christians, and an enemy of Jesus (1 Timothy 1:12–17)? He doesn't do this just once; he regularly and publicly proclaimed his failings (Acts 22:3–5; 1 Corinthians 15:9; Galatians 1:13; Philippians 3:6). Paul had two reasons for his public confessions: to give glory to God and to give hope to others. His message was, "If Jesus can do this for me, the chief of sinners—a self-righteous, murdering, religious hypocrite—then surely he can do the same for you!" Paul's confession inspires hope.

WILLIAM P. SMITH

JANUARY 7

2 CORINTHIANS 1:3–11

Did Paul forget Jesus' words about worry? He wrote about hardships that were far beyond his ability to endure, "so that we despaired even of life" (2 Corinthians 1:8). These hardships indicate that God does not always satisfy basic human needs; Paul was not expecting God to spare him from death. But Paul writes, "This happened that we might not rely on ourselves but on God, who raises the dead" (2 Corinthians 1:9). Paul was delivered from these hardships, but he did not assume that God guaranteed such deliverance in the future.

How did Paul reconcile Jesus' observation about birds that are fed by the Father with his own history of hunger and near-death experiences? The apostle viewed the world through the defining event of the kingdom of heaven: Christ and him crucified (1 Corinthians 2:2). Jesus Christ was the Word that came from heaven. He was the Bread of Life. When Paul witnessed the King going through hunger, the worst of hardships, and death itself, Paul realized he was witnessing the way of the kingdom. When he was ushered down this path, he welcomed it. What sustained him was spiritual food and drink: "I know what it is to be in need, and I know what it is to have plenty. I have learned the secret of being content in any and every situation. . . . I can do everything through him who gives me strength" (Philippians 4:12–13).

EDWARD T. WELCH

HEBREWS 2:5–18

Suffering does not oppose love; it is a result of it. One of the grand purposes of human existence is to look more and more like Jesus. This is God's plan for us. It is one of the greatest gifts he could give. It is evidence that he has brought us into his family. If Jesus learned obedience through suffering, we will too. A path *without* hardships should cause us to wonder if we really belong to God.

The challenge for us is to think as God thinks. In other words, our present thinking must be turned upside-down. We once thought that suffering was to be avoided at all costs; now we must understand that the path to becoming more like Jesus goes through hardship, and it is much better than the path of brief and superficial comfort without Jesus. When we understand this grand purpose, we discover that suffering does not oppose love; it is a result of it (Hebrews 12:8). We are under the mistaken impression that divine love cannot coexist with human pain. Such thinking is one of Satan's most effective strategies. It must be attacked with the gospel of grace.

EDWARD T. WELCH

JANUARY 9

1 Corinthians 1:18–25

The world bears the mark of sin. Culture provides a way for us to see ourselves and the world. It emerges whenever people gather together. Therefore, families, schools, and church denominations all have particular cultures. Culture oversees the unwritten guidelines for manners, traditions, and relationships: whether or not we have dinner together, how we celebrate our holidays, whether we raise hands in worship or kneel, how we greet each other, and so on.

Infused through culture, however, is what Scripture refers to as the *world*. The world was created by God as the abode of human beings. As created by God it is good, but as our abode it bears the mark of our sin. Therefore, in the New Testament, the term *world* is used to denote the order of things that are alienated from God. In this sense, it is morally corrupt (2 Peter 1:4), peddling foolishness as wisdom (1 Corinthians 1:20) and interpreting God's wisdom as foolishness (1 Corinthians 1:23). Even though we don't need any assistance in sensual indulgence, the world plants the message that unbridled sensuality is good, thus abetting the tendencies of our own hearts.

Recognizing that the world is outside us heightens our awareness of the spiritual battle we must fight. Not only do we have to fight against our own sin, we also have to fight against aspects of the culture that applaud our sinful tendencies rather than rebuke them.

Edward T. Welch

JANUARY 10

2 Samuel 7:5–16

Is God punishing us when we suffer? It's easy to feel like it. So as you think about your life and what God is doing, you need to keep in mind the very important distinction between punishment and discipline. Punishment means someone is trying to extract payment from you for what you owe them. When you think about how much debt you've racked up by sinning against an infinite God, then you quickly realize that it would take eternity to pay it off. God knows that it would be impossible for you to pay for your sins, so he sent Jesus to pay your debts. If you have put your faith in Jesus, then the pain you are experiencing has nothing to do with paying what you owe—Jesus' death paid it all. You have no outstanding debt in your relationship with God. That's why you need to understand that what God is doing in your life is not punishment—it's corrective discipline. Those God loves do experience pain, but the pain is not punishment; it's discipline and it's meant for our good. Even verses that use the word "punish" when discussing God's people have disciplined training in view (2 Samuel 7:14–16; Lamentations 4:22). What you're experiencing is pain that is helping you grow in holiness.

WILLIAM P. SMITH

JANUARY 11

2 Timothy 3:14–4:8

The Bible is God's breathed-out word. "Above all, you must understand that no prophecy of Scripture came about by the prophet's own interpretation. For prophecy never had its origin in the will of man, but men spoke from God as they were carried along by the Holy Spirit" (2 Peter 1:20–21). Because the Bible is God's truthful word and not the flight of human fancy, it has authority for God's people. It is, as Paul goes on to say, "useful for teaching, rebuking, correcting and training in righteousness." Peter puts it this way: "His divine power has given us everything we need for life and godliness through our knowledge of him who called us by his own glory and goodness. Through these he has given us his very great and precious promises, so that through them you may participate in the divine nature and escape the corruption in the world caused by evil desires" (2 Peter 1:3–4). Peter connects the knowledge of God, the Word (promises) of God, and our participation in God's nature or character. Both apostles would affirm that the Bible is a divinely authored means of God's grace to grow us into the likeness of Christ. God speaks to change us.

Michael R. Emlet

JANUARY 12

ACTS 2:14–28

Is death a bad thing? Yes. But Scripture tells us that the brightest of good things can be found in the midst of evil's darkness. The cross most powerfully demonstrates this. On the hill of death outside the city, the best thing ever came out of the worst thing ever. What could be worse than the killing of the Messiah? What could be more unjust than the illegal execution of the one perfect person who ever lived? What could be a greater injustice than the torture of the One who came to free us from death? In Acts 2:23 Peter says that the death of Christ was an evil deed by evil men, but Peter says more. He says that God delivered up Jesus for his own "set purpose." This terrible moment was under God's control. He planned from the beginning to use the ultimate evil to accomplish the ultimate good for humanity. In this dark moment, God conquered sin and death—two enemies we could never defeat on our own. On that cross of death, sin and righteousness met.

In the same way, God often brings the most lasting and wonderful things out of the darkest moments in our lives. Your Lord is present in this darkness. He planned the darkest things to result in redemptive good for his children. He surrendered his Son to death so that you could have life. He will not abandon you now.

PAUL DAVID TRIPP

COLOSSIANS 1:24–29

Your suffering occurs alongside of Christ's. Your life story is embedded in his story. Your suffering, therefore, is actually a participation in the sufferings of Christ (2 Corinthians 1:5; Philippians 3:10; 1 Peter 4:12–13). Consider Paul's amazing statement: "Now I rejoice in what was suffered for you, and I fill up in my flesh what is still lacking in regard to Christ's afflictions, for the sake of his body, which is the church" (Colossians 1:24). Paul is not saying that your sufferings add anything to Christ's work on the cross. There's nothing deficient about Jesus' suffering and death. He is saying that there is a purposeful link between the sufferings of Christ and your own suffering. Your connection with Jesus means that your identity is bigger than what you suffer. Paul says: "If we are children, then we are heirs—heirs of God and co-heirs with Christ, if indeed we share in his sufferings in order that we may also share in his glory" (Romans 8:17). Paul is saying that your suffering actually confirms your identity as a child of God. It does not undermine that identity, even though it sometimes feels that way. This perspective reminds you that as you suffer, you suffer in Christ. Your life (both suffering and, ultimately, glory) is intimately connected with his life.

MICHAEL EMLET

JANUARY 14

DEUTERONOMY 1:19–33

God's instructions were not arbitrary. We realize this when we look at God's call to his children to enter the Promised Land, or to Moses to free his people. God did not order those things as extreme tests to develop his people's faith. Those specific events were necessary to bring about his greater purposes of redemption. His people had to be freed from the bondage of slavery (Egypt) so that they could obey him. They had to actively fight against influences (Canaanites) that would tempt them, lead them astray, and re-enslave them. Anything short of these goals would distract his people from serving and enjoying him, ultimately ending up in their rejecting him. His commands furthered his plan to establish a holy people for himself that would bless the whole earth. When he promised to go with them, he gave them an ironclad guarantee that his plans would not fail.

Yet his promised presence came with the expectation that his people were moving in his direction. Often when I think God has failed me—that his presence wasn't enough—I find upon reflection that I've tried to force him to go along with my agenda.

WILLIAM P. SMITH

JANUARY 15

PSALM 121

The peace of God guarding and watching over us is a theme that runs through the entire Bible. In Psalm 121, for example, David says seven different times that God is watching over you. Who is watching you? The Lord, the Creator of the whole universe, and the one who has ultimate power over every circumstance. And when is he watching? By day and by night. Nothing that happens during the day or the night can harm you, because the Lord, your Good Shepherd, is on guard. When the Good Shepherd is present, his peace is present. Paul says, "The God of peace will be with you" (Philippians 4:9). When you read about David in the Bible, the constant refrain is that the Lord was with him. His life was blessed because the Lord was with him. He failed, he sinned big, he often blew it, and yet the Lord was with him. He grew very frail, and yet the Lord was with him. His life was a picture of living faith—a faith that faced trouble squarely and still knew the peace of God because he knew that God was with him.

DAVID POWLISON

JANUARY 16

PSALM 146

Why doesn't God just make your relationships better overnight? We often think that if God really cared for us, he would make our relationships easier. In reality, a difficult relationship is a mark of his love and care. We would prefer that God would just change the relationship, but he won't be content until the relationship changes us too. This is how God created relationships to function.

What happens in the messiness of relationships is that our hearts are revealed, our weaknesses are exposed, and we start coming to the end of ourselves. Only when this happens do we reach out for the help God alone can provide. Weak and needy people finding their hope in Christ's grace are what mark a mature relationship. The most dangerous aspect of your relationships is not your weakness, but your delusions of strength. Self-reliance is almost always a component of a bad relationship. While we would like to avoid the mess and enjoy deep and intimate community, God says that it is in the very process of working through the mess that intimacy is found.

TIMOTHY S. LANE AND PAUL DAVID TRIPP

JANUARY 17

PSALM 34

God's Word invites change. In the Bible's vivid picture, we "turn" to our Father, Savior, and Comforter. He works in us toward one goal: change. The central dynamic of the Christian life has this FROM…TO… movement. Repentance is not only how we start the Christian life; it *is* the Christian life. Faith does new transactions and conversations with God. Love does new actions and choices on the stage of life. When God calls, you listen. When he promises, you trust and talk back to him in your need. When he loves, you love. When he commands, you obey. You aim your life in a new direction by the power of the Holy Spirit. In every case, you turn.

The patterns, themes, and tendencies of our lives are what we see when, figuratively, we view our lives from the observation deck of the Empire State Building. From one hundred floors up, Manhattan and the Hudson River spread serenely before you. But the action and noise of life happens at the corner of Fifth Avenue and 34th Street, and when we take the Lincoln Tunnel home to Hoboken. The big stories of our lives are worked out in a running series of small scenes. This is how God has made it to be. He works for a turn-the-world-upside-down reorientation and redirection. Change takes place in the watershed moments and decisive incidents of everyday life.

DAVID POWLISON

JANUARY 18

ECCLESIASTES 12:1–14

He is God and we are not. When you observe life and listen to wise people, you will quickly find that we simply can't invest our hopes, dreams, and love in the self because it was never intended to carry such freight. For that matter, there is *nothing* created that was intended to sustain such hopes. Creation is to be enjoyed, but we don't put our trust in it. The only alternative is God himself.

The Teacher in the book of Ecclesiastes tries to save us time in our search for meaning and purpose. He tells us that he tried learning, laughter, great projects, unbridled sexual pleasure, money, music, and children. None of them, when they were elevated to his life's purpose, led to anything but despair. He could not find his purpose in the created world. After briefly envying an ordinary life of honest toil, good friends, food, moderate drink, and doing right, he comes to his answer—his purpose. "Now all has been heard; here is the conclusion of the matter: Fear God and keep his commandments, for this is the whole duty of man" (Ecclesiastes 12:13).

The fear of God is how we respond to the fact that God is greater than we are—different from us—in all things. His beauty is greater. His wisdom is greater. His love is greater. And, yes, his anger is greater. Simply put, he is God and we are not.

EDWARD T. WELCH

JANUARY 19

Ephesians 1:15–23

Glorify. Since Scripture has so much to say about our purpose, it has a rich vocabulary for it. One particularly fine word is the word *glorify*. We are created to glorify God. In the book of Ephesians, Paul reminds us three times in his introduction that we live "to the praise of his glory" (Ephesians 1:6, 12, 14). When we think of glory, we think of something big, beautiful, and obvious. "What a glorious sunset this evening!" "Her aria was simply glorious." To glorify God means to have our lives make him obvious and beautiful. We want him to be famous. We want to draw attention to the glorious God who loved us, and we do that by trusting him and loving others.

In 1646 over one hundred clergymen met, at the request of the English king, to develop a summary of biblical teaching that would be suitable to guide the church. In the children's catechism (which is a series of questions and answers), the first question had to do with our purpose: "What is the chief end of man? Man's chief end is to glorify God and enjoy him forever" (The Westminster Shorter Catechism). They are right. This is our purpose. It is not about us; it is about God and his purposes. What could be bigger and grander than that?

Edward T. Welch

January 20

Exodus 16:1–12

"If only we had died by the Lord's hand in Egypt! There we sat around pots of meat and ate all the food we wanted, but you have brought us out into this desert to starve this entire assembly to death."

This is not exactly a model prayer. There is complaining, grumbling, self-pity—all the things that can drive us crazy about other people. Given such self-centered insolence, you would at least expect God to say, "I'm not listening until you ask nicely." But this is not an invented story where the god is like us. This is *the* God. "The Lord said to Moses, 'I have heard the grumbling of the Israelites. Tell them, "At twilight you will eat meat, and in the morning you will be filled with bread. Then you will know that I am the Lord your God"'" (Exodus 16:9–12).

This response goes against all our expectations. God truly is not like us. It is as if God says to us, "Let me remind you of how I listen and see if you think I could listen even to you." Then he recounts stories of adulterers like King David, murderers like the apostle Paul, and grumblers like newly delivered Israel. If he hears and loves them, he will hear and love us. The lesson is clear: He doesn't hear because of *us* and the quality of our prayers. He hears because he is the God Who Hears.

Edward T. Welch

GALATIANS 1:6–9

Self-focus is dangerous. The most dangerous kinds are those that take on the form of the good things of the kingdom of God. Christ warns: "Watch out for false prophets. They come to you in sheep's clothing, but inwardly they are ferocious wolves" (Matthew 7:15). Paul writes: "Such men are false apostles, deceitful workmen, masquerading as apostles of Christ. . . . Satan himself masquerades as an angel of light. It is not surprising, then, if his servants masquerade as servants of righteousness. Their end will be what their actions deserve" (2 Corinthians 11:13–15). In Galatians 1:6–7, Paul warns against a false gospel that wears the costume of the true gospel. Notice the strong language: "I am astonished that you are so quickly deserting the one who called you by the grace of Christ and are turning to a different gospel—which is really no gospel at all. Evidently some people are throwing you into confusion and are trying to pervert the gospel of Christ."

The kingdom of self is most dangerous when it takes on the contours of the kingdom of God. It is possible for you to be convinced that you are living for the transcendent glories of the kingdom of God when you are, in fact, living for yourself. The most dangerous idols are those that are easily Christianized. Selfishness is most dangerous when it masquerades as service. Self-focus is most powerful when it dons the costume of love.

PAUL DAVID TRIPP

JANUARY 22

GENESIS 1

God created the universe to display his glory, to make visible his invisible qualities—his eternal power and divine nature. What you see in nature tells you something about him. When you look at a tree's countless leaves, you're meant to understand something about God's infinity, his beauty, his creativity, and his abundant life. And then you are meant to bow in worship as you imagine what God conveys to you through an entire forest!

In Genesis 1, we witness the unfolding of his glory. God says, "Let there be light," and the angels gasp, not just because they see light, but because the existence of light reveals God more clearly. God separates the waters and the gasps grow louder as more of their Maker is revealed. At each successive stage, the angels see more and more of their God, and they praise him with greater knowledge and insight. And then, at the pinnacle of creation, to reveal himself most clearly and brightly, God makes humans in his image. The angels simply marvel. Here, among all the wonders and majesty of the universe, stand the best reflection of who and what God is. Here was glory so real, so tangible, that the inconsequential planet floating in the heavens blazed like a beacon across the universe, proclaiming not humanity's worth and value, but the Holy Creator's.

WILLIAM P. SMITH

HEBREWS 1:1–14

This is not a distant, indifferent God. There is a strange split we sometimes make between Jesus and God the Father. The Father is always a little testy and picky with our faults; Jesus is always kind and forgiving. The triune God, however, is one God, and he has chosen to most fully reveal himself in Jesus. Jesus is God's summary of himself. "The Son is the radiance of God's glory and the exact representation of his being" (Hebrews 1:3). Jesus is the most complete expression of God's person to us. In him you can take your pick of what is surprising. Here is one: Jesus shared in our sufferings.

If you invented a religious system, it's unlikely that you would imagine a god who became like the people he created. But God did even more. He became like his creatures and willingly suffered a horrifying death so that they could be spared. Even the men and women who studied Scripture didn't anticipate that God would come this close. They never guessed that the Messiah, God himself, would suffer in the way he did. If you think God is far away and indifferent, here is the surprising revelation. From the foundation of the world, God knew your sufferings and declared that he himself would take human form and participate in them (which means that we too could share in his).

EDWARD T. WELCH

PSALM 130

Love produces hope. If we, in our misery, are absolutely persuaded of God's love, we will be confident that he will deliver us. Therefore, we hope in him. We can wait as long as it takes, because we are sure that he hears us and loves us. He *will* come. He *will* deliver. In fact, he is on the move right now. God's love inspires both an eagerness to be with him and a confidence that he is true to his word, so we know he will come. It is these two—eagerness and confidence—that combine to form hope.

The reality is that we are the watchmen on the last watch of the night. It is 4:30 a.m. We have seen the sunrise many times, and we are eager for it and confident it will come. What is the sunrise we are waiting for? In Psalm 130, the morning sun is a person. In that person are many benefits such as healing, deliverance, and love, but, make no mistake, it is a person. We wait for *him* more than for his gifts. We are like married lovers whose spouse is soon to return after a long trip. Just seeing the person is enough, whether he or she bears gifts or not.

EDWARD T. WELCH

PSALM 96

Joy takes practice. Study joy in the Psalms. Psalmists didn't even know the details of Jesus' love but, with their glimpses of God's love, they had joy and gladness. If you are willing to look for joy, the psalmists can lead you to it. The goodness of God is shot through creation and the church, so joy is always possible. When you can't see it, return to the cross and appreciate the beauty of what Jesus did. Appreciate the beauty of his sacrifice—his willingness to become like us and give up everything. Appreciate the beauty of his love. Just behold it. Admire it.

God's splendor ascends over the sorrow of life. Joy is possible. Choose to become an expert in it. After all, joy is not something evanescent. What you will taste is "everlasting joy" (Isaiah 35:10). It is here to stay, and the day is coming when those who know Jesus will be known by their joy. Believe it or not, you are becoming a joyous person. You will be a joyous person. Some say that joy is the serious business of heaven. But don't think that this is just for the sweet by-and-by. The kingdom of heaven began with power when Jesus came, so you can get into the family business even now.

EDWARD T. WELCH

JANUARY 26

ISAIAH 1:10–20

God never loses his temper. When we think of anger, we usually picture someone losing his temper. That can never be the picture of God's anger. Instead, when he reveals his anger, he leaves it on simmer (Exodus 32:9–10, 14). He invites his people to return and reason with him (Isaiah 1:18), and he can quickly be persuaded to turn from his anger. For now, God has chosen to place his anger within limits. "'In a surge of anger I hid my face from you for a moment, but with everlasting kindness I will have compassion on you,' says the LORD, your Redeemer" (Isaiah 54:8).

This sounds wonderful when it is applied to us, but it sounds like God could be a pushover as a judge when it comes to our enemies. We like mercy for ourselves and justice for others. To be merciful and just is a tricky combination. If you think about it without divine guidance, you will begin to think that mercy is unjust and justice is unmerciful.

The cross ultimately solves this dilemma. The reason God extends such mercy and patience is because his anger with our rebellion is ultimately poured out on Jesus. His justice is fully satisfied by the very costly price of his Son's death. Meanwhile, his mercy and love are fully expressed to us as he gives us true life through Jesus' death and resurrection.

EDWARD T. WELCH

JAMES 1:1–18

Joy and suffering are wedded together. It is in the context of desert trials that the book of James says, "Consider it pure joy, my brothers, whenever you face trials of many kinds, because you know that the testing of your faith develops perseverance. Perseverance must finish its work so that you may be mature and complete, not lacking anything" (James 1:2–4). At first glance it looks like an impossible marriage, but James is not the only one to speak about hardships with a hint of a smile on his face. Other Scriptures concur, for example: "Now for a little while you may have had to suffer grief in all kinds of trials. These have come so that your faith—of greater worth than gold . . .—may be proved genuine and may result in praise, glory and honor when Jesus Christ is revealed" (1 Peter 1:6–7).

Before Jesus came, wise people willingly endured difficulties because they knew God was with them. After the cross everything was transformed, including perspectives on suffering. Pilgrim travelers still encounter suffering as much as ever, but suffering is now viewed as the pains of childbirth rather than pain that is purposeless and random—mere accidents. Since Jesus came, suffering is redemptive. When we keep Jesus in view, the one who "learned obedience from what he suffered" (Hebrews 5:8), we can begin to understand how James could encourage us to have joy in the desert trek.

EDWARD T. WELCH

JANUARY 28

JEREMIAH 17:5–10

Life in a desert is hard and brutal. Yet, "Blessed is the man who trusts in the LORD. . . . He will be like a tree planted by the water that sends out its roots by the stream. It does not fear when heat comes; its leaves are always green. It has no worries in a year of drought and never fails to bear fruit" (Jeremiah 17:7–8). The desert in the Bible is the place of death. There's no water, no food. It's hot. There are dangerous predators and poisonous snakes. It is the place where your faith is tested. Yet, it is also the place where faith flourishes.

Do you feel that your sufferings have brought you into a spiritual desert? As you deepen your trust in God, your desert will become the place where you find God's living water of hope, mercy, and blessing. God's living water is his presence. He says, "I am with you." He is the only person who can profoundly reassure your heart. His presence means that even in the darkest of circumstances you can be unafraid. Let me say it again. He is with you. Because God is with you, you will be fruitful, even in the midst of suffering. You must remind yourself many times that the eternal God is with you. He promises that one day death will be ended, and all sorrow, pain, and tears will be wiped away (Revelation 21:4).

DAVID POWLISON

JOB 38:1–7; 42:1–6

God is God. Although Scripture reveals that there are multiple causes of suffering, and that multiple causes can be at work at any one time, it is less forthcoming about diagnosing the precise causes of particular hardships. Of course, there are times when the causes of our hardships are obvious. For example, if a woman leaves her spouse because she simply prefers her freedom, she is the cause of her suffering (and his). But even in this case, we can't always discern the other factors that played a part, such as the woman's mother, who casually divorced her husband and abandoned her family, thus modeling an option that the woman may have never considered otherwise.

The reason Scripture doesn't give clear guidelines for assigning responsibility is that it is not essential for us to know precise causes. Job is the model. Although we know that Satan caused Job's suffering, Job did not. Even after his fortunes were restored, he never knew why he suffered and the only thing God revealed was that he is God and Job was not. Yet this more than satisfied all of Job's why questions. Can you see a picture emerging? We might uncover some of the reasons for our suffering but we might never find them all. There is a mystery in suffering, just as there is ultimate mystery at the end of all human investigations.

EDWARD T. WELCH

JANUARY 30

JOHN 14

Rest rather than work. Trust in another rather than independence. But trust might be the last thing you want to do. You have limits on how much you will trust God. You insist on having an out when you need it; you believe if you abandon your secret behaviors you will not have any resources to deal with life.

The only way you could trust God is to be absolutely certain that he is trustworthy. And he is. How do you know that? Find out for yourself by looking at what God did when he came to earth as a man. Pick up a Bible, and read a little bit every day from the Gospel of John. Underline everything you read that shows you how trustworthy Jesus is. Notice especially how he treated people; think about why he died, and what his resurrection means for you. Jesus gave up his life for you. You can trust him with your life today. You can follow him. You can "cast all your anxiety on him because he cares for you" (1 Peter 5:7).

EDWARD T. WELCH

JANUARY 31

LUKE 11:1–13

God's renown is our first concern. Our task is to be an expert in "hallowed be your name" and "your kingdom come." "Hallowed" means to be known and declared as holy. Our first desire is that God would be known as he truly is, the Holy One. Implicit in his name being hallowed is that his glory or fame would cover the earth. This takes us out of ourselves immediately. Somehow, we want God's glory to be increasingly apparent through the church today. If you need specifics, keep your eyes peeled for the names God reveals to us. For example, we can pray that he would be known as the Mighty God, the Burden-Bearer, and the God who cares.

"Your kingdom come" overlaps with our desire for his fame and renown. It is not so much that we are praying that Jesus would return quickly, though such a prayer is certainly one of the ways we pray. Instead, it is for God's kingdom to continue its progress toward world dominion. The kingdom has already come and, as stewards of the kingdom for this generation, we want it to grow and flourish. The kingdom of heaven is about everything Jesus taught: love for neighbors and even enemies, humility in judgment, not coveting, blessing rather than cursing, meekness, peacemaking, and trusting instead of worrying. It is a matter of "righteousness, peace and joy in the Holy Spirit" (Romans 14:17).

EDWARD T. WELCH

February 1

Matthew 18:21–35

People mistreat us, sometimes in horrific ways. Spouses cheat. Children rebel. Bosses fire. Friends lie. Pastors fail. Parents abuse. Hurts are real. But how do all these one hundred denarii (about $6,000) offenses against us compare to the ten thousand talent (multimillion-dollar) debt we owed God, which he mercifully canceled? Since birth, and for all our lives, we have failed to love the Lord our God with all our heart, soul, mind, and strength, and our neighbor as ourselves (Matthew 22:37–39). But in one fell swoop—by the death and resurrection of Jesus—God wiped our records clean. Through the cross of Jesus and our faith in him, God removed our transgressions from us "as far as the east is from the west" (Psalm 103:12); he hurled "all our iniquities into the depths of the sea" (Micah 7:19).

Could it be that one reason you find it so hard to forgive is because you have never received God's forgiveness by repenting of your sins and believing in Jesus as your Savior? Or maybe you have yet to grasp the enormity of God's forgiveness of all your many sins. If you dwell on your offender's $6,000 debt against you, you will be trapped in bitterness until you die. But if you dwell on God's forgiveness of your multimillion-dollar debt, you will find release and liberty.

Robert D. Jones

FEBRUARY 2

MATTHEW 4:1–11

Suffering tests us and reveals our hearts. This principle appears throughout Scripture. You first see it when the Israelites leave Egypt. Here God demonstrated that he was not simply a local tribal god. To emphasize this point, God used Moses, an unqualified orator, as his representative, and delivered Israel from Egyptian bondage without a warrior unsheathing a sword. Before the people were given access to the land God promised them, Moses led them across a desert wilderness. It was not an easy trek, but God's purpose was to reveal his patience, kindness, and care. He also intended to test them, to see—or have them see—what was in their hearts.

From then on, the wilderness or desert theme recurs in Scripture as part of the journey through which God guides nearly all his people. The desert biographies of Scripture climax when "Jesus was led by the Spirit into the desert to be tempted by the devil" (Matthew 4:1). Regardless of the physical pain or the temptations before him, Jesus trusted in his Father to deliver him. In doing so, he becomes our model, our hope, and our power when we are in the desert. When we fail in our desert trials, we can point to Jesus' success in his. His victories are ours through faith, so his story becomes our own when we trust him.

EDWARD T. WELCH

FEBRUARY 3

PSALM 22

The Psalms all point to Jesus. When you hear the words of Psalm 22, "My God, why have you forsaken me?" you might think about your own experience. Depression, for example, feels like being forsaken. But you also remember that these were Jesus' words on the cross. They point to the fact that when you read these liturgical prayers, you are not alone. David composed many of them, the Israelites sang them, the church has recited them, and they all point to Jesus.

What these psalms do is straighten the trajectory of our lives. Using the words he gives us, God gently turns our hearts toward him. Instead of everything bending back into ourselves, we are able to look straight, outside of ourselves, and fix our eyes on Jesus (Hebrews 12:2). Keep this pattern in mind. It is the path of hope. The fact that all your thoughts turn back on yourself is oppressive. The self cannot carry the load. The way we were intended to function was to be able to look outward, toward God and other people. As you say the Psalms and remember that Jesus said them first, you will gradually find your focus changing.

EDWARD T. WELCH

FEBRUARY 4

PSALM 25

God's love for you in Christ: when you are most conscious of this fact, you are most willing to look at the false love that has replaced your love for him. You are ready to ask specific questions about why you are in conflict with another person—specific questions about your motivation and behavior. Looking inward moves you outward to see Christ and his grace. The more dazzling his grace becomes, the less attractive your god replacements seem. You begin repenting of what has dislodged God from his rightful place in your life. You also believe and grasp how great Christ's grace is. This is the dynamic that leads to lasting change. James 4:7–10 outlines what it looks like to repent of sin (heart and hands/motivation and behavior) and believe in Christ. It is a battle cry to wage war by the Spirit against the world, the flesh, and the devil. As you do, you will be lifted up. God loves humble people and he loves to shower his grace on the humble of heart. Ask yourself, What specifically do I need to repent of? What do I need to ask for in terms of grace? What has hijacked my heart, and what do I need to see and believe about Christ?

TIMOTHY S. LANE

February 5

Romans 3:10–18

Minimizing the doctrine of sin is something we all tend to do even though it is said that it is the one doctrine you can prove empirically. The struggle to accept our exceeding sinfulness is everywhere in the church of Christ. We accept the doctrine of total depravity, but when we are approached about our own sin, we wrap our robes of self-righteousness around us and rise to our own defense.

Scripture challenges this self-righteousness with clarity and power: "The Lord saw how great man's wickedness on the earth had become, and that every inclination of the thoughts of his heart was only evil all the time" (Genesis 6:5), and "There is no one righteous, not even one" (Romans 3:10). The effects of sin twist every thought, motive, desire, word, and action. This disease has infected us all, and the consequences are severe.

Why is this perspective so essential? Only when you accept the bad news of the gospel does the good news make any sense. The grace, restoration, reconciliation, forgiveness, mercy, patience, power, healing, and hope of the gospel are for sinners. They are only meaningful to you if you admit that you have the disease and realize that it is terminal.

Timothy S. Lane and Paul David Tripp

FEBRUARY 6

ZEPHANIAH 3:14–17

God sings with enthusiasm because he delights in his people. He *delights* in his sacrificial love toward us (Zephaniah 3:14–17). Nothing delightful about yourself? That is the point. This is not about you, it's about God. He is the one who takes away our punishment. He is the one who gives us new hearts. His singing comes from the work he has done in us. All we do is bring nothing. No righteousness in ourselves. No ability to pay him back for our sins. No boasting that we were better than other people. God simply asks us to come with nothing.

Too good to be true? If that is how it seems, then we are on track. Even our confession of sin is a delight to him. "There will be more rejoicing in heaven over one sinner who repents than over ninety-nine righteous persons who do not need to repent" (Luke 15:7).

Do you believe that the Father loved the Son? When you acknowledged that Christ alone was your Deliverer, you were brought into the kingdom of Christ. When you come into the kingdom, you don't come as a slave but as a royal child. You receive all the benefits of the King's family. Included in those benefits is the love of the Father. Everything the Son has is yours. The Son has the exuberant love of the Father, so you have that love too.

EDWARD T. WELCH

FEBRUARY 7

1 CORINTHIANS 10:1–13

Every day brings difficulties or blessings. Our hearts are always interacting with situations and relationships. We are always thinking and desiring, trying to make sense of what is happening. There are always things we want. Those thoughts and desires shape the way we respond to what is going on. Because we are sinners, we tend to respond sinfully. Everything we say and do has some result or consequence. We harvest what we plant and every day we plant seed we will harvest in the future. But the Bible's big picture doesn't leave us with the difficulty and the consequences. In 1 Corinthians 10:1–4 we see the cross. Paul speaks of God's presence with Israel in the wilderness, his faithful provision, and the exercise of his power on their behalf.

The hope of the Israelites and the Corinthians is our hope too. The hope Paul talks about is a person. His name is Christ! He is the spiritual food that gives you health and vitality to face difficulties. He is the spiritual drink that quenches the thirst that the heat in your life produces. Christ sustains me so that I can live with him and for him even when I struggle. His grace not only forgives, it enables and delivers. It endows me with wisdom, character, and strength. And all this is at the heart of what God is seeking to produce in me.

TIMOTHY S. LANE AND PAUL DAVID TRIPP

FEBRUARY 8

1 JOHN 2:15–29

Our fickle hearts wander away and so easily give our affection to another. The Bible calls this "love of the world." And the Bible tells us that if we love the world, the love of the father is not in us. James says that we get angry with one another because we are spiritual adulterers, and the person next to us gets in the way of what we love (James 4:1–4). The world is so attractive to our eyes and so seductive to our hearts. The creation can seem so much more real than the Creator. The sights, sounds, touches, and tastes of the world can seem to make us more alive than the purposes, promises, presence, and provisions of a God who can neither be seen nor heard. This is a battle you do not win once. It is a battle that you must face every day. You must tell yourself that in this world you are surrounded by other lovers who will seek to woo you away from the one grand romance that is to be the core of your existence. You must prepare for this seduction and you must steel yourself against the temptation to spiritual adultery. And you must do it again and again and again, or your heart will be stolen away.

PAUL DAVID TRIPP

FEBRUARY 9

1 KINGS 3:16–28

Hope was enough. When God uses prostitutes to illustrate Israel's unfaithfulness to him, he's showing you yourself. One of your primary identities is "unfaithful." Sexual immorality as a metaphor is not confined to the Old Testament. James also uses the image to illustrate the heart of our spiritual problems when he calls believers spiritual adulterers. Like paid professionals, we too are repeatedly and intentionally faithless, bearing the consequences in destroyed relationships, both human and divine.

Do you see yourself creating many of your deepest problems while at the same time eliminating any hope for their resolution? Do you realize that, before God, you don't deserve help? It's miserable to realize that the train wrecks of your life are mostly of your own making. And yet, the woman in Solomon's court did something different. She hoped. She believed. She had faith. And that faith changed her life.

She had the courage to believe that she could be heard and helped despite who she was and what she had done. She had the heart to believe that she would be received, and she was right. Her hope was not disappointed. Hope was the only thing she had going for her and, mercifully, hope was enough.

WILLIAM P. SMITH

FEBRUARY 10

1 PETER 2:1–12

Identity and worship—the two stones in the foundation of good relationships. Your identity is how you define yourself—your talents, qualities, experiences, achievements, goals, beliefs, relationships, and dreams. When we talk about worship, what we are getting at is that, because you are a human being, there is always something you are living for; always some desire, goal, treasure, purpose, value, or craving that controls your heart. The Bible reminds us that God wants—and deserves—to be the defining center of both these things.

When I live out of a biblical sense of who I am (identity) and rest in who God is (worship), I will be able to build healthy relationships. These are not abstract theological concepts. We're talking about the content and character of our hearts. These foundational issues of identity and worship are an inescapable part of your nature as a human being. What you believe and do about these two things will shape the way you live with the people God has placed in your life. For this reason we can say that we all live theologically; that is, the things we believe about God and ourselves are the foundation for all the decisions we make, all the actions we take, and all the words we speak. The theology you live out is much more important to your daily life than the theology you claim to believe.

TIMOTHY S. LANE AND PAUL DAVID TRIPP

FEBRUARY 11

2 CORINTHIANS 11:30–12:10

Whom will I worship? A well-known sufferer was the apostle Paul. His troubles were often caused by other people, but he realized that God authored these sufferings to allow him to walk in the footsteps of Jesus and *his* sufferings. Among the more difficult trials was one he called his "thorn in the flesh" (2 Corinthians 12:7). Although we never learn the precise nature of this malady, Paul identified at least three causes: his own pride, a messenger from Satan, and God—three causes for one hardship.

Instead of teaching us how to identify the causes of suffering, Scripture directs us to the God who knows all things and is fully trustworthy. In other words, Scripture doesn't give us knowledge so that we will have intellectual mastery of certain events; it gives us knowledge so that we would know and trust God. Somehow, turning to God and trusting him with the mysteries of suffering is the answer to the problem of suffering. You might be able to discern some obvious causes of suffering, and knowing those causes might help alleviate the pain. But all suffering is intended to train us to fix our eyes on the true God. Therefore, regardless of the causes, suffering is an opportunity to answer the deepest and most important of all questions: Whom will I trust? Whom will I worship?

EDWARD T. WELCH

February 12

2 Corinthians 5:11–21

You are hard to love too. Understanding this is the start of learning to love difficult people. Just like those difficult people, you and I sin and go astray (Isaiah 53:6; Romans 3:22–23). It took Jesus' sacrifice on the cross for God to welcome you into his family. God doesn't love you because you make such a wonderful addition to his family; he loves you in spite of what you are like. And through his love for you, he changes you to be like himself. He makes you lovely, even though you didn't start out lovely (2 Corinthians 5:17, 21). You need exactly the same things from God—grace, mercy, kindness, and welcome—that others need from you.

If deep down you know you are unlovable and God's acceptance of you is completely undeserved, then you will have a welcoming attitude toward other unlovely people. But if you believe you're basically a decent person who anyone would be privileged to know, then you won't welcome others until they get their act together and become decent . . . just like you! Learning the difficult skill of loving difficult people starts by asking God to show you how hard you are to love. When he answers your prayer, ask him to forgive you. Then because you have been forgiven for so much, you will be able to share the grace you have received with others (Luke 7:47).

WILLIAM P. SMITH

FEBRUARY 13

HEBREWS 11

Have you made mistakes so big that the promises of God can't hold for you any longer? If you think so, focus on God's response to his people's multiple failures. He gives Isaac, the child of promise, to Abraham despite Abraham's faithlessness. He remains faithful to Isaac, giving him offspring to continue the promise. God never abandons Jacob. He sends Joseph to Egypt ahead of his murderous brothers to provide for them during a famine that would have killed them all and ended the promise. God never gives up on the first families he chose. He remains faithful despite their faithlessness.

The Old Testament doesn't tell stories of perfect people who are blessed for their goodness. They're just as much a mess as most of us. God exposes all of the sordid things his people do to give you hope. He is not only the author of their faith but the finisher as well. He overwrites their failings—and overwrites yours as well.

The golden thread running through Scripture does not belong to any faith-filled, loyal human. It belongs to our fiercely faithful God, who towers benevolently above the mess of his people's lives. See beyond the flawed people in the foreground to a gracious God behind them, a God who continues to reconcile and redeem, creating a family for himself, a family of faith.

WILLIAM P. SMITH

FEBRUARY 14

1 JOHN 2:28–3:3

No human being was ever meant to be the source of personal joy and contentment for someone else. Your spouse, your friends, and your children cannot be the sources of your identity. When you seek to define who you are through those relationships, you are asking another sinner to be your personal messiah, to give you the inward rest of soul that only God can give. Only when I have sought my identity in the proper place (in my relationship with God) am I able to put you in the proper place as well. When I relate to you knowing that I am God's child and the recipient of his grace, I am able to serve and love you.

However, if I am seeking to get identity from you, I will watch you too closely. I will become acutely aware of your weaknesses and failures. I will become overly critical, frustrated, and angry. I will be angry not because you are a sinner, but because you have failed to deliver the one thing I seek from you: identity.

When I remember that Christ has given me everything I need to be the person he has designed me to be, I am free to serve and love you. When I know who I am, I am free to be humble, gentle, patient, forbearing, and loving as we navigate the inevitable messiness of relationships.

TIMOTHY S. LANE AND PAUL DAVID TRIPP

FEBRUARY 15

PSALM 103

The Bible is realistic about forgiveness. It does not imply that if you forgive someone, you will forget his sin against you. That is unbiblical. Many people cite Jeremiah 31:34 and conclude that since God forgets my sins when he forgives me, I must forget the sins that others have committed against me. But the omniscient God does not have amnesia when it comes to our sins. The word "remember" in this passage does not refer to "memory" but to "covenant." A covenant is a promise. When God forgives our sins, he does not forget them. Rather, he makes a promise not to treat us as our sins deserve (Psalm 103:10). He chooses to absorb the cost himself in the person and work of our Redeemer, Jesus Christ. Forgiveness is not peace at all costs. Misunderstandings and wrong attitudes and actions can result from wrong views of forgiveness. One such misconception is that forgiveness puts me in a vulnerable position: if I forgive those who sin against me, I will wind up a doormat. But Scripture does not tell us to make it easy for people to sin against us. It calls us to love them well by challenging their actions. We may be called to suffer in a godly way when options for godly confrontation are not available (see 1 Peter 3), but godly confrontation is important. In fact, a failure to confront appropriately shows a lack of love!

TIMOTHY S. LANE

FEBRUARY 16

PROVERBS 3:1–12

Where are you going with your life? Whose dream shapes the decisions that you make and the actions that you take? Who sets the agenda for a given day, week, month, or year? Christ calls us to the death of self-rule. He calls us to submit all that we do to his purpose for our lives. As his children, no longer are we to live as little self-lords, exercising sovereignty over our own lives. No, we are called to something bigger than anything we would plan for ourselves. Everything we think, desire, say, and do must fit within the new identity that we have been given. We have been chosen and called to be *followers*. That means we no longer live with a *master* mentality. We have been bought and paid for by his blood, and our lives no longer belong to us.

Which identity shapes your actions, reactions, and responses to life? Do you walk through your life like a mini-king? Do you try to squeeze the call of Christ into the contours of your self-designed master plan?

PAUL DAVID TRIPP

FEBRUARY 17

PSALM 16

The experience of joy is something to which C. S. Lewis gave considerable thought. He found it in small, good things such as apples, fresh air, seasons, and music. He spoke of "reading" the hand of God in our little pleasures. Like Augustine, Lewis also wanted to make it clear that joy could not rest in those things, however good. "The books or the music in which we thought the beauty was located will betray us if we trust in them; it was not in them, it only came through them, and what came through was a longing. . . . For they are not the thing itself; they are only the scent of a flower we have not found, the echo of a tune we have not heard, news from a country we have never yet visited." [C. S. Lewis, "The Weight of Glory" in *The Weight of Glory and Other Addresses* (New York: Macmillan, 1980), p. 7.]

This longing is joy. It is a longing for glory, heaven, and, especially, God himself. Joy is the natural response when we behold God. What does it have to do with boredom? Joyful people are mobilized. They delight in doing small obediences. They are pleased to serve God in any ordinary way he sees fit. They also know that an army of people taking small steps of obedience is what moves the kingdom of God forward in power.

EDWARD T. WELCH

FEBRUARY 18

PSALM 28

He will not turn a deaf ear to your cries. Your Lord is an adoptive Father who welcomes you into his family, even though you did nothing to deserve his love and welcome. He loves you faithfully, even though you mess up again and again. Your adoptive heavenly Father knows exactly what you need. He knows the size and significance of your trial, and he is aware of your limits and weaknesses. The apostle Paul tells us how God helps those who are weak: "But [God] said to me, 'My grace is sufficient for you, for my power is made perfect in weakness.' Therefore I will boast all the more gladly about my weaknesses, so that Christ's power may rest on me" (2 Corinthians 12:9).

God's grace is most powerfully present when you are at your weakest. Life's trials will take you beyond the borders of your natural wisdom, love, patience, and strength. But you are not without resources. In your weakness you are the moment-by-moment recipient of the powerful grace of a loving Lord who understands exactly what you are going through.

PAUL DAVID TRIPP

FEBRUARY 19

PSALM 88

Feelings of separation and alienation accompany grief. Yet the sadness of losing a loved one is a universal experience. A company of mourners surrounds you. Their lives have also been touched by the pain of death.

Yet there is an even more powerful way in which you are not alone. Your Savior has taken the name Emmanuel, "God with us"—when you came to Christ, you literally became the place where God dwells. You have a powerful Brother, Savior, and Friend who not only stands beside you, but resides within you. That hope will help you make it through your pain. Psalm 88:18 says, "You have taken my companions and loved ones from me; the darkness is my closest friend." Psalm 88 begins and ends in darkness and isolation. Where is hope in the hopeless cry of this psalm? Psalm 88 gives us hope in our grief precisely because it has no hope in it! It means that God understands the darkness we face. He is right there in it with us, "an ever-present help in trouble" (Psalm 46:1). The Lord of light is your friend in darkness. The Lord of life stands beside you in death. The Lord of hope is your companion in your despair. The Prince of Peace supports you when no peace can be found. The God of all comfort waits faithfully near you. The source of all joy is close by when loss has robbed you of joy.

PAUL DAVID TRIPP

FEBRUARY 20

ROMANS 7

Paul continued to struggle with loving and obeying Christ throughout his life (Romans 7). Notice that Paul's struggles moved him closer to Christ and closer to other believers. The Christian life is lived in community. If your struggle with temptation is moving you in these two directions, God will change your desires. You might not notice this from one day to the next, but over the years you will look back and be thankful for the work the Spirit has done in you. The Spirit is the one who is able to fix our eyes on Jesus instead of on our own desires and/or failings. Paul closes Romans 7 by saying, "What a wretched man I am! Who will rescue me from this body of death? Thanks be to God—through Jesus Christ our Lord!" (Romans 7:24–25).

Don't lose hope. You and your sin are no match for God's goodness, power, holiness, and grace! The promise of the gospel is that God moved toward you before you wanted a relationship with him. Paul says, "For while we were still weak, at the right time Christ died for the ungodly" (Romans 5:6 ESV). This is your comfort and your motivation in your daily fight against temptation. Don't lose heart; look to Jesus, the author and finisher of your faith (Hebrews 12:2).

TIMOTHY S. LANE

FEBRUARY 21

ROMANS 8:18–39

Remember what you already know. It is hard to argue when we are reminded that Jesus shared in our sufferings and has compassion for those who suffer. It is easier to protest, however, when we hear the proposition that God is both good and generous. At this moment in your life, it would seem that goodness and generosity, especially from the all-powerful God, could only be demonstrated by a removal of the depression. If he takes it away, you are persuaded. If not, you remain a doubter.

But remember what you already know. First, Jesus suffered, and Jesus was dearly loved as the only Son of the Father. When we suffer what seems like endless pain, it is hard to believe that God loves us, but Jesus' suffering proves that it can be true. Second, "he who did not spare his own Son, but gave him up for us all—how will he not also, along with him, graciously give us all things?" (Romans 8:32). The cross is the only evidence that can fully persuade you that God is, at all times, good and generous. If someone gives his only child for you, you can't doubt that person's love. Our God says, "If I have sacrificed my Son for you, do you really think I am going to be stingy and withhold my love now?"

EDWARD T. WELCH

FEBRUARY 22

1 CORINTHIANS 3:10–23

God has been revealed in Christ, and when someone becomes a Christian, all that fullness dwells in him. We don't need anything else to fill us up—we have Christ. This is staggering when you consider the greatness of our glorious, mighty, gracious and holy God. Notice, too, that Paul says that this is true of you now. It is who you really are. You are the temple of God. God has chosen to reside in you by the Holy Spirit. You are his and he is yours! Second Peter 1:4 says that believers "participate in the divine nature and escape the corruption in the world caused by evil desires." We do not become divine, but we have the Divine One living in us from the moment we trust in Christ. We have everything we need to live in godly ways. There is no need to be seduced by deceptive and hollow promises of change that lead us away from Christ. These promises will prove to be forms of bondage that enslave us to ourselves and our self-sufficiency. They "protect" us from giving up control and wind up enslaving us to our own agendas.

TIMOTHY S. LANE AND PAUL DAVID TRIPP

FEBRUARY 23

2 Corinthians 10:1–5

The gospel gap doesn't stay empty. If we do not live with a gospel-shaped, Christ-confident, and change-committed Christianity, that hole will get filled with other things. I like the term Paul uses for these counterfeits in 2 Corinthians 10:5. He calls them "pretensions."

Not every lie is a pretense. A pretense is a plausible lie. I could tell you that I was a female Olympic gymnast. That would be a lie, but it would not be a pretense because it would lack plausibility. But if I dressed in a suit and stood in front of an office with a briefcase and a set of architectural drawings, I could probably fool you into thinking I was a building contractor.

The most dangerous pretensions are those that masquerade as true Christianity but are missing the identity-provision-process core of the gospel. They have their roots in the truth, but they are incomplete. The result is a Christianity that is mere externalism. Whenever we are missing the message of Christ's indwelling work to progressively transform us, the hole will be filled by a Christian lifestyle that focuses more on externals than on the heart. I believe that a war for the heart of Christianity is raging all around us, seeking to draw us away from its true core toward the externals.

Timothy S. Lane and Paul David Tripp

FEBRUARY 24

1 TIMOTHY 1:12–17

It all sounds so biblical! "You can't love God or others if you don't first love yourself." But this theory assumes that our hearts are empty and need to be filled. The Bible does not say that we are empty. Rather, it says that we are a cauldron of desires for everything but the true and living God. We are rebels against God. This view is deceptive because it seems to capture how we feel inside, but it makes us look far more passive and innocent than we really are. The Bible describes us as defectors and enemies of God who want to fill ourselves with things in creation rather than the Creator (see Romans 1:21–25).

Scripture calls us to forsake the things we have sought to fill our emptiness. Before we can be filled with God's grace, we must engage in intelligent, honest repentance. We have to forsake and demolish the god-replacements that have supplanted the true God in our lives. Repentance is a form of emptying the heart. James 4:1 says that we fight with others, not because we are empty, but because we are full of desires that battle within us. Along with deep repentance, Scripture calls us to faith that rests and feeds upon the living Christ. He fills us with himself through the person of the Holy Spirit and our hearts are transformed by faith.

TIMOTHY S. LANE AND PAUL DAVID TRIPP

February 25

Hebrews 3

"I would never do to someone else what he did to me!" When we are sinned against by others, we can easily forget that we too are sinners and apart from grace we are no better than our offenders. In our resentment against others we forget that our own hearts are "deceitful above all things and beyond cure" (Jeremiah 17:9). The writer of Hebrews reminds us, "See to it . . . that none of you has a sinful, unbelieving heart that turns away from the living God. But encourage one another daily . . . so that none of you may be hardened by sin's deceitfulness" (Hebrews 3:12–13).

A hardened heart expresses sentiments like "I can't believe he did that; I would never do that to him!" Are we so sure that we couldn't do that? How do we know that, given the same circumstances and environment, and the same temptations and provocations, we would not commit the same hurtful act? Proverbs 16:18 alerts us to our danger: "Pride goes before destruction, a haughty spirit before a fall." The apostle Paul warns, "If you think you are standing firm, be careful that you don't fall!" (1 Corinthians 10:12).

Few have captured this concept better than the English Reformation pastor and martyr, John Bradford (1510–55). From his prison cell in the tower of London he saw a criminal being led to execution for his crimes and said, "There but for the grace of God goes John Bradford."

ROBERT D. JONES

FEBRUARY 26

MARK 12:28–34

Heart, mind, soul, and strength obviously overlap. God uses these overlapping terms so that there can be no mistaking that he requires from us an all-consuming love. Is there any part of life that falls outside of your heart, mind, soul, and strength? We're accustomed to dividing life into the spiritual and nonspiritual, handing the spiritual things over to God and managing the rest by ourselves. There are certain areas that we like to consider outside God's control. But this command makes clear that God should be at the center of it all. All barriers between the spiritual and nonspiritual are broken down.

The Bible has a word for this kind of all-consuming love, a devotion that shapes and directs every area of life: *Worship*. That may surprise you since we often use the word *worship* in a very limited sense. We think of worship as a set of specific activities that we perform on one day of the week. We go to a special place, sing songs, pray, listen to a message, stand, kneel, etc. We then leave that special place and worship is over. It is true that God tells us to worship him that way, but the command to love God with our whole being teaches that every aspect of our lives is an act of worship. *Everything* we do is guided by our love of God, our every act one of devotion to him.

WINSTON T. SMITH

FEBRUARY 27

LUKE 17:20–21

Do you live in a kingdom of one? Like the big kingdom of God, the little kingdom isn't a location, but a commitment of the heart. Little kingdom living turns life into an endless search for earthly treasure and an unending focus on personal need. No matter how relational and active I may seem, it is all by me and for me. For all the appearance of community in the way I live, there is only room for one person in it. Wherever I am and whatever I am doing, if the things that I am seeking are not to be found, it will be very hard for me to continue to participate. The little kingdom is always a kingdom of one.

The sales pitch of the Serpent is, "You can have your own way!" Somewhere deep within our sinful hearts, this is what we all want. And this is the thing that the Redeemer has come to rescue us from. He came to pry us from the confines of our little kingdoms and welcome us to the expansive glories of a better kingdom. Yet, even in the face of his grace, I will try to employ his wisdom principles and gracious promises to make my little kingdom work. You can't squeeze the large-vision lifestyle of the kingdom of God into the small-vision confines of the kingdom of self. It will simply never fit.

PAUL DAVID TRIPP

FEBRUARY 28

PHILIPPIANS 2:1–11

The knowledge of Christ revealed most fully at the cross is the thing of first importance. It is no surprise that the knowledge of Christ is central to God's plan for everything. God has exalted Christ over all things. When we know and honor Jesus, God is pleased to bless us with more: more knowledge, more faith, more love, more hope. We are thus better equipped to fight. Another reason it is so important to know Jesus is that one of the grand purposes of human existence is to look more and more like him. This is God's plan for us. It is one of the greatest gifts he could give. It is evidence that he has brought us into his family. If Jesus learned obedience through suffering, we will too. A path *without* hardships should cause us to wonder if we really belong to God.

The challenge for us is to think as God thinks. We once thought that suffering was to be avoided at all costs; now we must understand that the path to becoming more like Jesus goes through hardship, and it is much better than the path of brief and superficial comfort without Jesus. When we understand this grand purpose, we discover that suffering does not oppose love; it is a result of it (Hebrews 12:8). We are under the mistaken impression that divine love cannot coexist with human pain. Such thinking is one of Satan's most effective strategies. It must be attacked with the gospel of grace.

EDWARD T. WELCH

FEBRUARY 29

PSALM 139

Worry and fear always look ahead. When the thing we dread is upon us, we usually do well. Anticipation is the killer. God tells us that there is nothing in the future that can interfere with our kingdom mission. If you get in the car accident you dread, you will have grace to know that God is with you, and you will have grace to bear fruit even in that difficult situation. If your loved one dies before you, you will have grace to know God's comfort and to shine brightly as you reflect your Father's glory. If poverty knocks on your door, you will have grace to trust your King and know that poverty cannot detract from your privilege of being an ambassador who blesses others in his name. As children and stewards who aren't in control but trust the one who is, the assurance of such grace is a blessing.

Keep the manna story in mind. Remember that God gave the Israelites grace to trust and obey him when they left Egypt, just as we are given even more grace for faith and obedience when the wilderness is ahead. But they were also given more unexpected grace than they could have predicted or imagined. Your future includes manna. It *will* come. There is no sense devising future scenarios now because God will do more than you anticipate.

EDWARD T. WELCH

MARCH 1

PSALM 130

Remember, Scripture beseeches us. Before Jesus came, Scripture offered many mnemonic devices, such as yearly feasts that celebrated God's deliverance and Scripture that could be read daily. Since Jesus' death and resurrection, God is willing to jog your memory day after day. Scripture is more accessible, we celebrate the Lord's Supper, and we are given the Holy Spirit, who testifies as an eyewitness and continually points us to Christ. God, apparently, is happy to repeat himself.

For some people, repetition becomes a been-there-done-that, and they check out until there is something new. For the wise, however, remembering is essential to the human soul. It is part of that forsaken art of meditating. It is critical to the process of change, and a prominent means of doing spiritual battle. Psalm 130 begins with sufferings that have pulled the psalmist into the vortex of death itself. This is what he means when he cries, "out of the depths." We don't know how this happened or why, but we do know that he feels close to the grave. In other words, the psalmist understands suffering. While teetering on the edge of the abyss, the psalmist has a choice: he can mourn his fretful condition or he can cry out to the Lord. Of course, as both our voice and our guide, he leads us in crying out.

EDWARD T. WELCH

MARCH 2

PSALM 27

David remembers the God of Moses, who promised the Hebrews his Presence and his rest (Exodus 33:14). Moreover, David recalled how God was pleased with Moses and allowed him to be a witness to his glory (Exodus 33:18). David knew that all the beauty of creation pointed to the Creator, and when Moses saw the glory, it was the beauty of God.

While all Israelites knew the presence of God, most were kept at a safe distance. Priests were given greater access to God's presence than the people, and the High Priest was given access to the Holy of Holies itself. But only Moses was close enough to witness God's back as his glory passed before him.

David wanted more than God's veiled and safe presence. He knew God's forgiving love and he knew that God would not deny needy people access to his throne room. The image is that you are in the presence of the King. When you are in his presence—in his temple, dwelling, or tabernacle—you are kept safe. Whenever you were invited into an ancient Near East home, the host was responsible for your protection. In the home of a powerful king, you could rest secure. This was more than enough to counterbalance David's fears. On one side enemies wanted to kill him, on the other was the protective custody of the King.

EDWARD T. WELCH

MARCH 3

REVELATION 21:1–6

For our good and for his glory, God has chosen to have us remain where grief will touch us all. But believers grieve in a way different from those who do not know the Lord. In times of death, Christians should be sadder than anyone else. We know how sin brought death into the world. We mourn not only for the loved one we have lost, but also for the fact that death continues to destroy. We live in a place where something that was never meant to be has become a common experience. We know how wonderful life on earth could have been.

Yet we should also be the most hopeful of any who mourn. Even in the darkest moments, we are never alone. The death and resurrection of Christ stand as a sure and reliable promise that someday death will die. God doesn't call you to stifle your grief or put on a happy face when you are crushed. He doesn't expect you to hide behind religious clichés and theological platitudes. God approves of your tears! But he welcomes you to look at death through the eyes of Christ. The comfort and hope he provides does not remove your grief, but they allow you to grieve in a brand-new way. And he promises one day to take you to a place where you will never cry again.

PAUL DAVID TRIPP

MARCH 4

ROMANS 5:1–11

Your hope is attached to what kingdom you are serving. If your life is defined by how many of your little kingdom purposes you can realize, you will tend to be stressed, controlling, anxious, disappointed, and fearful. You have defined your life by what you cannot control and by what God has not promised. But if your hope no longer rests on your personal wisdom, strength, and character; if it no longer rests on the acceptance and performance of other people; and no longer rests on the belief that circumstances, institutions, and situations will not fail you, then you are beginning to move toward reliable hope.

Big kingdom hope rests on one place and one place alone—God. It is the deeply held and daily acted-upon trust that God is the ultimate source of all that is wise, true, loving, and good, that what he is doing is best, and that what he has promised is reliable. The only hope that will not disappoint is hope in a Person. Big kingdom hope is about entrusting my past, present, and future, my identity, meaning, and purpose, and my motivation for daily functioning to God and resting unafraid in him. I will still face the disappointments of life in this fallen world. But, I will not panic, I will not run, and I will not quit, because my God is present even in my disappointment, and he will never change!

PAUL DAVID TRIPP

MARCH 5

ROMANS 8:18–39

God has come, in the person of Jesus, and entered into the difficulties, the sufferings, the sins, and the disappointments of this life. Jesus bore your weakness. He was tempted as you are. He triumphed. Now he comes near to you with promises of mercy and goodness. "He who did not spare his own Son, but gave him up for us all—how will he not also, along with him, graciously give us all things?" (Romans 8:32). As you read through Romans 8, notice that Paul doesn't say that we won't have hardships. Instead he acknowledges that there will be "trouble . . . hardship . . . persecution . . . famine . . . nakedness [and] danger" (Romans 8:35). But he does promise that none of these things "will be able to separate us from the love of God that is in Christ Jesus our Lord" (Romans 8:39). Cling to this promise. Cling to Jesus. Invite him into your struggles, your sorrows, and your questions. When you read the Gospel of Luke, notice that Luke doesn't talk much about smart, successful people. He focuses on people who are powerless, bereaved, ignored, and neglected. Watch Jesus in action. Notice how he treats people with wisdom, love, and tenderness; how he's content to do and say only one thing, or a few things. This is also the way he treats you. Pour out your heart to Jesus. He promises to answer (Psalm 86:7). He promises to never leave you or forsake you (Hebrews 13:5).

DAVID POWLISON

MARCH 6

TITUS 2:11–15

God has blessed you with his grace, gifted you with his presence, strengthened you with his power, and made you the object of his eternal love. Because we belong to him, we live for his agenda. And if change is his agenda, then repentance and faith is the lifestyle to which we have been called.

Near the end of his career, Michael Jordan was asked why he always came early to practice before a game, even before the rookies. He was already being called the greatest basketball player of all time. He replied that his shooting percentage was just over 50 percent, which meant that over his career, he had failed almost as much as he had succeeded. He was committed to keep on practicing as long as there was room for him to improve.

There are always new sins for the Christian to address and new enemies to defeat. The Christian life makes God's work of change our paradigm for living, while we celebrate the grace that makes it possible. "For the grace of God that brings salvation has appeared to all men. It teaches us to say 'No' to ungodliness and worldly passions, and to live self-controlled, upright and godly lives in this present age, while we wait for the blessed hope—the glorious appearing of our great God and Savior, Jesus Christ" (Titus 2:11–13).

TIMOTHY S. LANE AND PAUL DAVID TRIPP

March 7

1 Corinthians 15:12–28

Every time someone dies, it reminds those watching that God's work is not yet complete. Because of sin, death entered the world. Only when sin is completely defeated will death cease to be part of the equation. Paul says about Christ's present ministry: "For he must reign until he has put all his enemies under his feet. The last enemy to be destroyed is death" (1 Corinthians 15:25–26). Christ died so that we would no longer have to die. He rose again so that death would be put to death.

Every time someone dies, it reminds us that death still lives. But every death also points us to the promise that Christ brings a resurrection once and forever. Through Christ, death has been defeated. One day, life will no longer give way to death. Children will not mourn their parents. Parents will not mourn their children. There will be no widows or grieving friends. Yes, death is an enemy, but this enemy will die. Christ's present reign guarantees this. One day, life will give way to life in eternity. As you weep, know this: the One who weeps with you is not content for things to stay as they are. His death was a cry and his resurrection a promise. The living Christ will continue to exert his power and you will grieve no more.

Paul David Tripp

MARCH 8

1 John 4:7–21

How does God treat difficult and prickly people? He pursues his people much more earnestly than they have ever pursued him. He isn't put off by their difficult and prickly natures. And when he captures our hearts, he transforms us to be like himself.

It is now our privilege and calling to imitate God by pursuing others so they too will know God's love. This means adopting God's goals for your difficult relationships. If your goal in pursuing others is that, at some point, they will be nicer to you or easier to be around, then your relationships are already on shaky ground. Trying to get someone to treat you the way you want to be treated makes manipulation the foundation of your relationship. Your goal for difficult people should be the same as God's goal: that they become all that God wants them to be. When you do this, you are pursuing them in the same way God does. You are siding with God in what he is doing in his universe. The results may not be exactly what you'd like, but there is no better person to work with and for!

WILLIAM P. SMITH

MARCH 9

EPHESIANS 4:17–25

"Putting on and putting off" is how Paul describes the process of maturing into the image of Christ. We put off all of the sinful and useless ways of thinking and acting that have corrupted our lives before we knew Jesus, and we put on all of the new truths and ways of living that Jesus has taught us.

Paul's instruction to "put off falsehood and speak truthfully," is not just helpful advice on communication, but a product of being connected to Jesus. It is the fruit of growing and maturing in him. It is a change that results from being in relationship with Jesus. Rescued and redeemed by Christ, you no longer have to live a life of inward shame and fear. Remembering that God knows you and loves you and that you no longer have to hide who you are, can be the difference between communication that is an expression of sincere love and communication that is manipulative and self-centered.

In the first half of Ephesians 4, Paul explains how Jesus has equipped us with everything we need to grow and mature in his love. In particular, Paul writes, "speaking the truth in love, we will in all things grow up into him who is the Head, that is, Christ" (Ephesians 4:15). In other words, our willingness to speak truth to one another is part of how we help others to grow in love and maturity in Jesus as well.

WINSTON T. SMITH

MARCH 10

GALATIANS 5:13–6:10

As we say yes to the Holy Spirit, his living water produces new fruit in our hearts: love, joy, peace, patience, kindness, goodness, faithfulness, gentleness, and self-control. These character qualities aren't an ideal standard that God holds over us. They are gifts the Spirit produces in us. This change within us changes the way we respond to the things around us. And this is the fruit that results: Kind people look for ways to do good. Patient and faithful people don't run away when people mess up. Loving people serve even when sinned against. Gentle people help a struggler bear his burden. Galatians 5 and 6 are filled with hope.

We must reject a view of the Christian life that emphasizes what we should do more than what God is doing in us by his Spirit. We should reject any view of the Christian life that says that the change God calls us to is impossible, or only takes place in eternity. We should reject any perspective on the Christian life that minimizes the war that rages in our hearts every day—or ignores the fact that God is fighting it for us and with us! The biblical picture is that God meets us in the trials of life, and he doesn't just give us rules—he gives us his Son!

TIMOTHY S. LANE AND PAUL DAVID TRIPP

MARCH 11

GENESIS 3

See their profound shame. After Adam and Eve sinned, they scrambled to cover their nakedness and they hid in the garden to conceal themselves from God. They had realized they were morally filthy. Try to imagine that first horrifying moment of realizing that you are a sinner, deserving judgment, and living in the world of a holy and just God.

Sinners have been looking for ways to cover themselves ever since. We will do anything to prove that we are making a contribution, that we are good, that we don't deserve God's disapproval. How much of our busyness is really an effort to prove our worth?

When God confronted Adam and Eve, he cursed the very things in which men and women would seek to find their worth—their labor (Genesis 3:16–19). The very things we would hope to give us meaning and worth have been cursed so that to be "fruitful" in them will require extreme effort. You may try to take pride in your work; you may try to find life and meaning in your children, but God isn't going to make it easy for you. God wants us to find our rest in him, not in our own proud efforts. He won't allow us to successfully cover ourselves. He faithfully and lovingly steers us away from trusting in our own efforts so that we can find true rest in the work he has done.

WINSTON T. SMITH

MARCH 12

ISAIAH 49:13–26

We are going to struggle with fear rather than have it instantly disappear. Anticipating this, God reminds us that he will never leave us. "Do not be afraid, for I am with you" (Genesis 26:24). "Do not be afraid or terrified because of them, for the LORD your God goes with you; he will never leave you nor forsake you" (Deuteronomy 31:6). "Do not fear, for I am with you; do not be dismayed, for I am your God" (Isaiah 41:10).

Imagine the presence of one who deeply loves you and is powerful enough to deal with the things you fear. It turns fear into confidence. But, like all spiritual growth, this change only comes with practice. It comes when you say, "Amen—I believe" when you hear or read the promises of God. It comes through meditation on God's words. It comes when the cross of Jesus Christ assures you that God is faithful. These words to the fearful are so important that Jesus makes them his final words on earth: "And surely I am with you always, to the very end of the age" (Matthew 28:20). The resurrection is God's answer to fear. Jesus is alive.

EDWARD T. WELCH

MARCH 13

PSALM 46

How do you seek intimacy with God? Meditate on the way he treats you. God's love for us is the most wonderful thing in this world—it's at the core of what makes life bright and hopeful. Read these Bible verses and make them your own. You are never out of sight or out of mind to God (Psalm 139:7–10). He creates intimacy with you by the way he treats you (Isaiah 42:3). He notices and cares about everything that happens to you (Luke 12:6–7). He speaks openly about himself (John 15:15). He listens to you (Psalm 6:8–9). He is a refuge in the midst of your sufferings (Psalm 46). He hangs in there over the long haul (Isaiah 49:14–16). He laid down his life for you (John 3:16; Romans 5:6–8). He forgives all of your sins (Psalm 103:1–5). His mercies are new every morning (Lamentations 3:21–24).

God wants you to respond to his love by trusting him with your whole life. He has bridged the distance between you and him through the life, death, and resurrection of his Son. Now he is making you like him and walking with you every step of the way.

DAVID POWLISON

MARCH 14

PSALM 95

Real love is persistent. We are called to be longsuffering with the idle, timid, and weak. That means we are to warn, encourage, and help one another for a really, really long time! Change does not happen in us or others overnight. Most of the time, it is a slow, progressive process with many ups and downs. With whom are you in conflict? Have you ever been tempted to say, "I have done all these things and nothing has changed"? Then keep on doing those things. If the person has not changed due to hard-heartedness and clear rejection of the truth, it will be appropriate for the church to assist you and the other person in light of Matthew 18:15–20. But even this is to be done with great care and love.

How is all this possible? Paul brings us full circle in 1 Thessalonians 5:16–17 by calling us to worship! This is a call to first commandment reorientation. Because we are always tempted by ungodly ruling desires, our worship of God must be regular. To engage in godly conflict, I must be captivated by the grace of Christ. This will lead to joy, spontaneous and persistent prayer, and an ability to give thanks in all circumstances—even the circumstance of conflict!

TIMOTHY S. LANE

MARCH 15

REVELATION 7:9–17

We all know that life is sloppy, hard, messy, shameful, and boring. We often deal with things that are out of our control. Good things tend to go bad and bad things tend to seduce us. People leave us hurt and disappointed. Change is often much, much slower than we want it to be. God's Word is full of powerful life principles, but applying them to life is not always an easy task. We tend to encounter the same problems again and again. It is easy to believe that we are powerless to change and that all our effort is meaningless.

The gospel calls us to look at the messiness of life in a radically different way. The good news of the gospel is that Christ has conquered sin and death, and with them every meaningless and destructive end. Our final destination infuses every word, action, desire, and response with meaning and purpose. There are no completely hopeless situations. The gospel welcomes us to a hopeful realism. We can look life in the face and still be hopeful because of who Christ is and where he is taking us. Everything God has brought into your life has been brought with your destination in view. God is moving you on, even when you think you are stuck.

TIMOTHY S. LANE AND PAUL DAVID TRIPP

MARCH 16

1 CORINTHIANS 12:12–27

Jesus has turned the tide on loneliness. Look at Genesis 2 through the lens of Jesus' work on the cross. It's wonderful that a husband and wife become one flesh; but even more wonderful that Christians comprise the body of Christ, so connected with each other that if one part suffers we all suffer. It's incredible for a husband and wife to be fruitful and multiply, but even more incredible that Christ multiplies his kingdom by sending flawed people to "go and make disciples of all nations" (Matthew 28:19). Adam and Eve were naked yet unashamed with each other; but Jesus has washed away our sin, and we now stand clothed in his righteousness! We don't need to hide when our sin is exposed.

Jesus went to the cross, betrayed and deserted. As he hung there, saturated with our sin, even his Father turned away from him. Adam and Eve hid among the trees because of their sin, but Jesus hung naked and exposed on a tree because of our sin. Adam and Eve were guilty, yet tried to pass the blame. Jesus was completely innocent, yet he took our blame on himself. Jesus was rejected by his Father so we could be accepted. He gave up everything so God might lavish his blessings on us. Out of love for us Jesus hung on the cross until he died. By paying the penalty for our sin, he reversed the effects of the fall and turned the tide on loneliness.

JAYNE V. CLARK

MARCH 17

1 PETER 5:1–11

Is there a bull's-eye on your chest? If you knew an enemy was in hot pursuit, you would be on guard, especially if that enemy specialized in guerrilla tactics. During times of suffering and difficulty, spiritual warfare is virtually guaranteed. We watch Satan seize what he thought was his golden opportunity when Jesus was led into the desert to endure physical suffering and spiritual isolation (Matthew 4). The Bible depicts Satan as a lion, lurking in the tall grass, patiently waiting to devour those who are susceptible (1 Peter 5:8). Yes, you are an intended casualty, but you are not the primary target of his lies. Instead, the volleys are aimed especially at the character of God. Their goal is to raise questions about God. Specifically, they question God's love and power.

Our suffering may come from many different places, but, regardless of its origin, Satan ultimately is a player. Suffering is the ideal time for him to raise questions about God, because we ourselves are already asking them. Suffering raises spiritual questions that cannot be ignored. The apostle Paul underscores this when he reminds us that, during suffering, demonic warfare "sets itself up against the knowledge of God" (2 Corinthians 10:5).

EDWARD T. WELCH

MARCH 18

GENESIS 3:1–7

The Serpent offered Eve "more." What he offered Eve was transcendence, but it had a fatal flaw. It wasn't connected to God! Here was an offer of an "above and beyond" glory, but it was a replacement for the transcendent glory that can only be found in God. Notice the thundering implication of these five simple words, "You will be like God." The Serpent was saying, *You know, Eve, there is a greater, more satisfying glory than anything you have yet experienced. Your life can be much, much more than it has already been. Why, Eve, you can have it all. If you would just be willing to step outside of God's narrow boundaries, you wouldn't need to be connected to him, because you would be like him.*

The glory that the Serpent holds out is no glory at all. Essentially Satan is saying, *Eve, you can live for a greater and more satisfying kingdom than the kingdom of God. If you do this one thing, you can have a kingdom where you are central and where you rule unchallenged.* Here we have recorded the very first time in human history when a person was willing to restrict her living to the size of her life. We have been paying the price ever since.

PAUL DAVID TRIPP

MARCH 19

JAMES 3:1–12

The world of talk is a world of trouble. Nobody articulates this more powerfully than James: "If anyone is never at fault in what he says, he is a perfect man, able to keep his whole body in check" (James 3:2b). Who can honestly say that all his words are well-intentioned and appropriately spoken? Who has not hurt someone with words or used words for a selfish purpose? Who hasn't used words as a weapon of anger rather than an instrument of peace? Don't let yourself back away from the troubles. If you are honest, you have to admit that your relationships have been troubled by words as much as they have been helped. James calls us to admit that our words are the most powerful and consistent indicators of our need for the grace of Christ. James says that if we were without fault in this area, we would be perfect in every way. So listen to your words. Don't they expose how deep your need is for God's forgiving grace? We stain our relationships with thoughtless and evil words. We are guilty of turning this gift into a weapon. We need forgiveness and we need help.

TIMOTHY S. LANE AND PAUL DAVID TRIPP

MARCH 20

JOHN 6:1–58

God's stories keep getting better. It is as if we are given small doses of reality when we are very young and can't grasp God's sophisticated love and care. When we are older and have witnessed more of God's ways, we are prepared to hear it all. When we were young he gives us manna; when we are old he gives his life. We get him.

Jesus retold the story of manna by feeding five thousand people from five barley loaves and two small fish. This becomes the background for his public announcement: The words of God you have anticipated since the days of Moses are now revealed to you in the flesh. Come and eat (John 6:26–27). We get food by believing that Jesus is the King sent by the Father. We declare our allegiance to him and acknowledge that we belong to him, not ourselves.

What will you do with Jesus, the better manna? That has been the question all along. The focal point is not us and our needs; it is the King, as it should be (John 6:48–58). The pattern is this: The Father genuinely cares about the daily needs of his children, and he is constantly caring for us, but he wants this to point us to something better. If we don't find our life and strength in Jesus Christ, we will go from one worry to the next.

EDWARD T. WELCH

MARCH 21

LUKE 4:14–30

What are you living for? Is there a place in your life where your little kingdom purposes have been masquerading as the kingdom of God? What in your life right now really excites you? What things do you find fulfilling and satisfying? What has become your treasure, and how do you define your needs? Is there a place where selfishness wears the mask of godliness? Is your little kingdom so well costumed that no one around you would ever recognize it for what it really is?

You are not alone in this battle to unmask and dismantle the little kingdom in your life. Your Messiah gives you just what you need for this battle. The little kingdom leaves you poor, so he offers you the good news of the eternal riches of his grace. The little kingdom enslaves you, so he endured the cross to set you free. The little kingdom leaves you blind, so he places hands of grace on you to restore your sight. The little kingdom has left you oppressed, so he purchased your release. Your hope and mine will not be found in another kingdom. What we all desperately need is a King who will liberate us from the kingdoms we build to ourselves. That King has come for you and for me, and Emmanuel, the Lord Jesus Christ, is his name. Seek him! There is help to be found!

PAUL DAVID TRIPP

MATTHEW 13:24–33

The King has made extravagant promises to us—promises of protection, liberation, and peace. We respond with our allegiance—faith or trust. The essence of faith is not that we trust without evidence but that we choose sides: In whom do we trust? Our allegiance to the kingdom of God is nurtured by the very words of God, and it is demonstrated in our obedience.

God's kingdom has been moving forward since the beginning of creation, but its inaugural moment was the resurrection of Jesus. The resurrection was the Father's confirmation that this was indeed his Son, the only one worthy to sit on the throne. It announced the inauguration with fanfare. But since then, as is characteristic of God's ways, the actual building of the kingdom is gradual. It moves forward by small, individual acts of our obedience.

Does that seem somehow disappointing? This gradual growth of the kingdom is the way of God. Miracles happen, but God's favored method is to bring change with less fanfare. The kingdom is a field that grows, the tiniest mustard seed that becomes the largest of all the garden plants, the yeast that gradually but thoroughly permeates the loaf and transforms it. The kingdom unfolds this way in our own personal lives and in history. So, when in doubt about how to seek first the kingdom, choose the path of persistence and endurance.

EDWARD T. WELCH

MARCH 23

MATTHEW 6:25–34

Will we trust him? That's the obvious question after God reveals himself to fearful people. Whose kingdom are you seeking? Do you trust the King who is also your Father? Dangers abound, and life is comprised of hourly risks, but the real issue behind worry is that of spiritual allegiances. Our answer? "Sort of…a little…usually." We *sort* of want the kingdom, and we sort of want to trust the King—until life gets precarious. When everything is going well and the storehouses are full, we trust him. But when there is nothing for tomorrow, we panic and track down the address of another god who can give us enough for tomorrow and the next day too.

Whom do I trust? Where is my faith? Those are the questions that all worriers must ask, yet all of us already know the answer. Our trust is divided. We don't put all our eggs in one basket—even God's—because that's too risky. Our trust might not pay off the way we hope. We are reluctant to simply say to our Father, "I am yours," and stop worrying. Jesus knows this. Fear and worry reveal that our faith is indeed small. If you are looking to plumb the depths of worry, you can find it in your mixed allegiances. You trust God for some things but not others. You trust him for heaven but not for earth.

EDWARD T. WELCH

MARCH 24

PSALM 18

To be used by God in difficult relationships, you need to understand how he pursues people. How is it that the all-powerful God of the universe doesn't terrify us when he comes looking for us? Why don't we run the other way? Part of the reason is that God has an established track record of being involved in his people's lives for their good. God responded to Adam and Eve's rebellion by promising a Deliverer who would free us from our slavery to sin (Genesis 3:15). God remembered that promise for thousands of years and never turned his back on his people, even though they turned away from him many times. Instead, he continued to move all history toward the point when, at just the right time, Jesus stepped onto center stage (Galatians 4:4).

Jesus literally went to hell and back for you. His death guarantees your forgiveness; his resurrection guarantees your new life; and his Spirit guarantees that he will never leave you. Jesus has remained faithful to you, even through the many times you have not loved him with all your heart, soul, mind, and strength. He is committed to you for the long haul. He invites you to run to him to find safety. He is your rock, fortress, refuge, stronghold, shield, and strong tower (Psalms 9:9; 18:2; 94:22; 144:2). He invites you to find safety in him.

WILLIAM P. SMITH

PSALM 130

The news can't be contained. When you receive something wonderful, you talk about it. In this psalm, what began as the cry of an isolated man becomes a shout to the community. "If I have found hope and love in the Lord, then you can too. If I have found joy in forgiveness, you can too." Or, to paraphrase, "If I, an Old Testament psalmist who hasn't seen the coming of Jesus, can speak with this kind of hope, how much more can you, who have witnessed the cross—the unmistakable evidence of forgiveness of sins?"

Granted, this may still seem like an impossible dream, but remember that God himself is giving you this psalm. He is rewriting your story. You might feel like you are doing very well to repeat the cries of the first two verses, but the Spirit of God wants you to have the entire story.

This is just one psalm of many you could own. It can belong to you and be your future. Think about it. You feel like you have no purpose. Think of what it would be like to be an ambassador of hope to hopeless people. Those who suffer are credible because of their suffering; their hope is tried and genuine. When *you* speak hope to another, it is persuasive and attractive.

EDWARD T.

PSALM 4

Good relationships are always built on the foundation stones of identity and worship. Even though these ideas may seem distant from our daily struggles, nothing can shelter our relationships from difficulty if we aren't building community on this foundation. We often mistakenly think that our relationships are difficult because, like a child learning to walk, we simply lack the skills and experience not to fall. This may be true in part, but the greater problem is the foundation we are walking on. For our relationships to be what God designed them to be, the rebuilding, restoring, and reconciling must start with a solid new foundation.

This foundation is not what we do and say. It begins in the heart, the source of the thoughts and motives that shape what we do and say. Your heart is always with you, and in profound ways it shapes your interactions with others. If our heart's foundation is solid, based on God's truth, design, and purpose for us, we will be able to build healthy, God-honoring relationships even though we are flawed people living in a broken world. By contrast, broken community is always the result of broken foundations.

TIMOTHY S. LANE AND PAUL DAVID TRIPP

MARCH 27

PSALM 71

Because your Lord is with you, your faith and love will operate right up to the end of your life. Psalm 71 is written from the perspective of an elderly person whose strength is failing, but three things are still true about him: (1) He has faith. God is still his refuge, rock, and fortress. He pleads with God to not forsake him in his old age. He honestly faces the fragility of life and puts his faith in God and the resurrection. (2) Because he knows where he's going, he has a reservoir of fundamental, honest joy. You cannot pretend when you are facing death. Either you're anchored in the certainty of the resurrection and full of joy, or you're not anchored and full of fear. (3) He has love. Faith expresses itself in love. Love for God is always expressed in love for others. He says, "Since my youth, O God, you have taught me, and to this day I declare your marvelous deeds" (Psalm 71:17). He has a sense of legacy; he's proclaiming to those he loves that he is dying in hope. You also are called to love others by leaving them a legacy of hope.

There is nothing more powerful as you face death than faith, joy, and love. By faith you look right through death to Jesus, your anchor, and you will be full of joy. And as long as you live, your faith and joy will overflow in love to others.

DAVID POWLISON

MARCH 28

2 CORINTHIANS 4:1–6

The Word or personal experience? Which do you allow to dictate your perception of God? If you look at God only through the lens of your human experience, you misunderstand him. But when you listen, the Holy Spirit speaks through the Word to reinterpret your life experiences. This truth then goes on to shape your perceptions of future experience.

What is the typical human experience of "God"? Depending on who you listen to, God is a philosophical abstraction, your higher power, an idol, an experiential high during meditation, a remote tyrant, a good buddy, creative energy, a benign grandfather, or even yourself. All these images grossly misshape God. Does that mean it is impossible to know the living and true God if I have spent my life believing such false images? The Bible everywhere rejects such an idea and offers instead to "open their eyes and turn them from darkness to light" (Acts 26:18). God is in the business of changing people's minds; he is not hindered by distortions. He can reveal himself, "[shining] in our hearts to give us the light of the knowledge of the glory of God in the face of Christ" (2 Corinthians 4:6). Life experience is not supreme; neither are the lies that people believe. God is, and he alone trumps what we bring to the table.

DAVID POWLISON

MARCH 29

GENESIS 19:1–24

You see a God of all grace. God sends two angels to urge Lot to leave doomed Sodom. God longs for Lot to heed their warnings, but he dallies. How can Lot be so clueless? Unfortunately, it's pretty easy. When you first get a warning, you take it seriously; you might even act on it initially. But if you need a warning, it means you're already partially blind, so it doesn't take much to completely close your eyes.

What do you see in this passage? You see sorry and pathetic people, but you also see a wonderful God, who does not mock, laugh, or use their failings to inflate his own sense of importance. You see a God of all grace. God tells stories about wretched people who can neither see nor do what is best for themselves or their families. In the telling, God tells you even more about himself. People make life hard on God. They doubt him, ignore him, disobey him, and are miserable to him. And in his response, God extends his sovereignty, power, and might on their behalf. He is kind to the undeserving.

Do you know yourself as undeserving? If so, take heart. We have a God who not only remains committed to his people despite their failings, but does so with compassion.

WILLIAM P. SMITH

MARCH 30

JUDGES 6

Gideon is hiding in a winepress when God addresses him: "The LORD is with you, mighty warrior." Gideon seems as surprised as we are. God chose that less-than-courageous circumstance to tell Gideon that he would save Israel. Gideon, unconvinced, asks for a sign to assure him that God is speaking to him. He asks if the angel of the Lord would stay for a meal as proof, and the Lord graciously stays. Later Gideon asks for more proof. He asks God to wet a fleece but not the ground around it. God complies. God shows us the weakness of his chosen vessel and, more importantly, his kind concern in the face of Gideon's doubt and unbelief.

God anticipates Gideon's faith battle and builds his confidence by infiltrating the minds of his enemies. Gideon can no longer doubt future victory when he hears the enemy prophesy their own defeat. God never berates Gideon for his lack of faith. Instead, he stoops ever lower to give him the faith to believe. Gideon's need for encouragement remains a constant, and God keeps intensifying his responses—from waiting for Gideon, to altering the physical world, to initiating the last sign. Gideon is not brave, but that doesn't keep God from using him. He takes the man he wants to use and delivers Israel from her enemies by his hand. He uses his chosen vessel despite that vessel's repeated struggle to trust God.

WILLIAM P. SMITH

MARCH 31

PSALM 119:65–72

"Give thanks in all circumstances, for this is God's will for you in Christ Jesus" (1 Thessalonians 5:18). The preposition "in" is important. In part, Paul is saying that even in life's hardest moments, God calls you to look for his grace, to search for his love, and to expect his mercy. Don't let grief rob you of worship or permit a complaining spirit to replace a thankful heart. God doesn't expect you to jump for joy when you suffer loss. But he has promised never to leave you. You will find blessings in the middle of your grief. Perhaps it will be someone's love and support. Perhaps it will be financial provision. Perhaps a confusing decision becomes clearer. Perhaps there will be precious family moments. Perhaps it will be a sense of God's presence in a moment of struggle. Maybe the wisdom of his Word will guide just when you need it most. Perhaps your relationship with the Lord will deepen. Suffering has a way of clarifying truth for us. We see how weak and needy we are and we gain a deeper understanding of God's powerful grace. We learn to seek him in ways we never have before and spiritual growth begins. Are you looking for the blessings that are hidden in your grief?

PAUL DAVID TRIPP

APRIL 1

PHILIPPIANS 2:1–11

This kingdom is a kingdom of the cross. For all of its joy and celebration and for all of its gifts of life and grace, the kingdom of God is a kingdom of sacrifice. The central event in the history of this kingdom is a shocking and unthinkable sacrifice. This moment of sacrifice confounded the followers who were there to see it and has interested theologians ever since. It is at once the most terrible and most beautiful event in the kingdom. It is a sacrifice that makes perfect sense and no sense at all. And this sacrifice forms the operating agenda of the kingdom from that time on.

Jesus, by his bleeding and broken body on the cross, not only gave the kingdom of God its life and hope, but its paradigm for living as well. That history-changing death on the cross is also the life-changing call of Christ to everyone who would follow him. And as it did on the cross, that willingness to die will always result in life. This kingdom is a kingdom of the cross, and everyone who celebrates that sacrifice is called to drag a cross along with them every day.

PAUL DAVID TRIPP

April 2

Psalm 22

I will express godly emotions. There is no scene more filled with emotion than the scene at Calvary. Christ cried out to his Father as he suffered and died. The Cross invites you to cry out to the Father as well. Christ cried to a Father who was silent as he let him die, so that you could cry to a Father who will hear you and give you what you need to live.

The more you understand who God is and who he has made you to be, the more you realize that the Christian life is not an emotionless, stoic existence. On earth, Christ expressed a whole range of emotions and, as you grow in Christ, you will too. Maturity expresses the right emotion in the right way at the right time. As Christians, we should be the saddest people on earth (because we understand the ravages of sin), and the most joyful people on earth (because we experience the grace of the crucified Christ).

There is a proper time for sorrow, joy, anger, fear, jealousy, happiness, gratitude, anticipation, remorse, grief, and excitement. The life of faith is a stained glass window, rich with the color of many different emotions, through which the light of Christ shines.

TIMOTHY S. LANE AND PAUL DAVID TRIPP

April 3

Romans 15:1–13

We can get tired pretty quickly of caring about someone more than we do ourselves. In Romans 15:5–6 Paul is talking about living in harmony with one another, and then he asks for help from "the God who gives endurance and encouragement." Notice how those two elements—endurance and encouragement—work together. When you'd like to stop trying to reach out to a difficult person, God enables you to endure, to keep on plugging even when things are rocky between you.

Your God is a God of encouragement. Your God brings light and joy to your soul as you strive to bring him glory through your relationships. The road of relational harmony is difficult (you will need this God of endurance!), but it's not bleak because he is an encouraging God. So when you are ready to quit, you need to ask him to encourage you. Let him remind you that because he is for you, no one can be against you (Romans 8:31). Hear from him again that Jesus gave up his life for you, and he fully intends to finish the work he began in you. He has not given up on you, although you know he has every reason to. It's his encouragement that will move you to repent of your self-focus and give you the desire to try again with others.

WILLIAM P. SMITH

APRIL 4

ROMANS 8:18–24

What is the kingdom of God all about? What new meaning and purpose is to become the focus of my life as a child of God? God has called us away from our autonomous, self-focused living to live transcendently once again—to live with restoration in view in every situation, location, and relationship in which God places me.

God's redemptive purpose is captured in Revelation 21:5, when God, seated on the throne says, "I am making everything new!" It is summarized in Romans 8:18–24, which pictures the whole of creation groaning, waiting for redemption. If the glory of God is reflected in all of creation, if the effects of sin reach to all of creation, and if the goal of redemption is to restore all of creation, then you and I should care about everything!

Your sadness with sin should be bigger than the fact that it complicates your life. Your sadness should extend as far as sin reaches. Your celebration of God's restoring grace should be bigger than the fact that it brings blessing to your private world. The goal of God's kingdom is the complete restoration of every last thing that was damaged by the fall. Grace calls you to shape your living to the contours of this amazing work of restoration. As the great old Christmas carol proclaims, "He comes to make his blessings known, far as the curse is found."

PAUL DAVID TRIPP

APRIL 5

1 CORINTHIANS 12:1–11

Paul grounds our unity in the unity of the Trinity, not in our ability to get along. We get along because Father, Son, and Spirit have allowed us to do so. We can give grace because we have been given grace. Jesus humbled himself. The Father gently and patiently works out our salvation. The Holy Spirit forbears and abides with us even in the face of our sin, convicting and correcting us, but never condemning. Father, Son, and Spirit were torn apart so that we might be united with them and with each other. This kind of relational integrity is a high calling, but the God who commands it provides us with everything we need to fulfill it.

Because it is grounded in the Trinity, our unity also allows us to celebrate our diversity in the body of Christ. There is one God, but three persons. God uses our diversity to accomplish his purpose—our growth in grace. Diversity is not an obstacle, but a very significant means to this end. Notice all the differences that exist among us. We have different gifts, serve in different capacities in the body of Christ, and are at various levels of spiritual maturity. All of these differences are there by God's sovereign apportionment. That is, God chooses to surround us with people who are different from us because he knows it will promote his purpose.

TIMOTHY S. LANE AND PAUL DAVID TRIPP

APRIL 6

1 Peter 1:3–12

God runs his universe in ways that are counterintuitive. There is a surprising door to joy—to face your suffering, to take hold of it instead of seeking to escape it. To stop what you are doing and honestly say to God, "I feel all alone right now. I'm tired. I'm bored. I'm hurt. I'm worried and stressed. But I know you are with me. I know you are my true refuge. Help me!"

Worship in the Bible expresses two things to God: our pain and our pleasure. For example, some psalms suffer honestly: "O God, I am in anguish. Deliver me from my sufferings and my sins." Other psalms delight honestly: "O my God, you are good. I thank you, worship you, and adore you."

In 1 Peter 1, suffering is the context in which you experience "joy inexpressible and full of glory" (1 Peter 1:8 NASB). In James 1, trial is the context of purpose, endurance, meaning, and joy. In Romans 5:3, we are told that "we rejoice in our suffering." In the midst of sorrows, anguish, misery, and pain we come to know that "the love of God has been poured out within our hearts through the Holy Spirit who was given to us" (Romans 5:5 NASB). Walking into suffering with eyes wide open opens the door to knowing the love of God.

DAVID POWLISON

COLOSSIANS 2:6–15

The cross has purchased daily power for you, because although the *power* of the little kingdom over your heart has been broken, the *presence* of little kingdom thoughts and desires still remains. Paul says, "And having disarmed the powers and authorities, he made a public spectacle of them, triumphing over them by the cross" (Colossians 2:15). You can stand and say, "No!" to the self-focused agenda of the little kingdom. In that moment at work, or in the family room, over the fence with the neighbor, at supper with friends, in the situation of parental discipline, or in a discussion with your spouse, you have not been left to your own strength. You have been given power beyond what you can imagine! Paul says: "Now to him who is able to do immeasurably more than all we ask or imagine, according to his power that is at work *within* us" (Ephesians 3:20, author's emphasis). One of the results of the cross of Jesus Christ is the gift of the Holy Spirit. Think about it. God in his awesome power and glory has come to live inside of you. Because of this you are able to be who he has called you to be and do what he has called you to do, even in the face of the powerful temptations you encounter in this fallen world. His presence in your heart guarantees your potential to endure.

PAUL DAVID TRIPP

APRIL 8

MARK 14

A deep sigh gives it away. Just one chapter of Scripture (Mark 14), chronicling only one day, reveals the extent to which Jesus shared our sufferings: the chief priests and teachers of the law were looking for a sly way to arrest Jesus and kill him; Judas agreed to betray Jesus for a fee; Jesus predicted that one of his followers would deny any knowledge of him; Jesus predicted that his other followers would abandon him; the leaders arrested him; he was spit on; he was struck with fists and beaten to the point where he could have died from the lashings alone.

He was called a "man of sorrows" (Isaiah 53:3). He was oppressed, afflicted, despised, and rejected, to the point where people would turn away to avoid seeing his face. You know these things about Jesus, but now that you, too, are familiar with suffering, it should shock you that anyone would voluntarily take such suffering on himself. Sufferers should be able to recognize other sufferers. As a sufferer, you should recognize Jesus' sufferings; he certainly recognizes yours. A deep sigh gives it away. When Jesus healed a deaf man, he let out a deep sigh as he looked up to heaven (Mark 7:34). He was moved by the suffering he saw around him, and as the risen Lord he continues to be moved by ours today.

EDWARD T. WELCH

APRIL 9

EXODUS 2:23–3:10

The word *grace* was initially associated with loveliness and favor. The apostle Paul added *gift* to its meaning, which could include both financial and spiritual gifts. This connected grace to our neediness and God's generous provision for our need. Since it implied that we are weak, grace also meant power. "My grace is sufficient for you, for my power is made perfect in weakness" (2 Corinthians 12:9). If there is any question that the words of God are good news, grace should resolve it, because the word has become the summary description of Christianity.

When you think about grace, your world is no longer one of fate, karma, or a deistic, passive god. The God of grace is very personal and active. He is especially attentive to those who are needy, and he delights in giving gifts and power to them. Call out in your need and you will be heard. As we saw with the early Hebrews, even if you *don't* call to God in your need, you will be heard, and when God hears, it means that he is already taking action.

EDWARD T. WELCH

APRIL 10

PSALM 66

Joy is not the opposite of suffering. If it were, a person practiced in joy could crowd out pain because one couldn't exist with the other. Instead, joy can actually be a companion to suffering. You can see this at Christian funerals. These are grievous events in the church because of the loss of someone beloved. But they are also some of the most joy-filled as worshippers contemplate the glories of heaven and remember that death is not the last word.

To simultaneously say that some things are bad and others are good seems like a precarious balance, but that is the nature of this time in history. The curse and sin persist; they are bad and we wait with hope for their eradication. But the original goodness of creation can still be detected, and the glories of the cross and everything it ushered in are evident through Jesus. These, of course, are great blessings that we enjoy and for which we praise God. We continue to suffer, but suffering cannot rob us of the eternal joy that has already begun.

Job spoke of his "joy in unrelenting pain—that I had not denied the words of the Holy One" (Job 6:10). He took joy in the fact that he had not denied God or questioned his faithfulness throughout his ordeal. He did not take pride in this; he found joy. He knew that God saw his faithfulness as a good thing and Job himself saw it was good as well.

EDWARD T. WELCH

April 11

Psalm 86

When my kingdom is at stake—my reputation, my quest for being loved—there is much to lose. Out of fear I commit myself to self-protection. When the things we value are threatened, we protect them. In this case it is the same as protecting ourselves. The alternative is to lose my kingdom and be a simple servant of the Most High God. His kingdom is never threatened because he is all-powerful and he doesn't need anything from us. He calls us to love and worship him, but he doesn't need it in the sense that we talk about needing love and affirmation.

This should sound liberating to those who are in bondage to the fear of other people. When we see ourselves as kings who need affection, we are highly vulnerable. But as children and servants, we owe a debt of love to others. We were loved by God more than we loved him; there will always be that imbalance in our relationship. The only appropriate and healthy response is to treat others the way God has treated us. The result? People's (perceived) opinions don't have the same power to crush us anymore. Instead, we are less concerned about how we are treated and more concerned with how we treat others. Rejection may still hurt, but it won't control us.

Edward T. Welch

MATTHEW 6:19–24

Christ warns against living for the physical treasures of the here and now. He warns against investing all of the gifts, talents, time, resources, and energy of your life on the impermanent and unsatisfying treasures of physical earth. But it is scary how magnetic and powerful these "treasures" are. I never wake up in the morning and say, "I want my job to be the single, life-organizing treasure of my life," but somehow it becomes that. I never say, "Today I will get my identity, meaning, and purpose from another human being," yet somehow the affection of a certain person becomes my treasure. I never say, "I have decided to find all of my personal happiness in the possession of material things," yet more and more I am living to acquire. Even though I have never made a conscious decision to make these things my treasure, the physical values of earth hook and enslave me. I never say, "I will make power and control the thing of highest value in my life," but somehow it is. I never say, "I will make the success of my children the central treasure of my life," yet somehow it happens.

We weren't created to find our satisfaction in the little, earthbound kingdom treasures of the here and now. We were created to seek a better treasure, and in so doing to be eternally grateful and satisfied.

PAUL DAVID TRIPP

APRIL 13

MATTHEW 18:21–35

When Peter asks Jesus how many times he should forgive someone, he thinks he is being rather noble by suggesting seven times. But Jesus rebukes Peter and says that forgiveness has no limits. There is no way around Jesus' words, and no use trying to soften the implications. The principle applies to countless offenses and even the same, endlessly repeated offense. We're tempted to think that once we have forgiven someone, we're done. But forgiving someone is not just a past event. It's something we must continue to practice, even when we are dealing with an offense we have already forgiven. Even if I have forgiven you for something you have done in the past, I need to be careful that I don't slip into bitterness some time in the future. I need to keep practicing forgiveness every time I see you or think of you.

Why is the process of forgiveness so important? Because even if you have forgiven someone for an offense, you will be tempted to think about it the next time you see her, or the next time she sins against you. Without realizing it, you will pile that sin on top of the old sins. This makes it harder and harder to forgive someone.

TIMOTHY S. LANE AND PAUL DAVID TRIPP

APRIL 14

HEBREWS 12:3–17

Persevere is something God does; it is not only something he says. It is one of the many aspects of his character. The reason it is of great worth is that it is one of the chief ways God has revealed himself to us. Scripture consistently points to God's perseverance and forbearance with his people. "The Lord is not slow in keeping his promise, as some understand slowness. He is *patient* with you, not wanting anyone to perish, but everyone to come to repentance" (2 Peter 3:9, author's emphasis). "May the Lord direct your hearts into God's love and Christ's *perseverance*" (2 Thessalonians 3:5, author's emphasis). "Let us fix our eyes on Jesus, the author and perfecter of our faith, who for the joy set before him *endured* the cross, scorning its shame, and sat down at the right hand of the throne of God" (Hebrews 12:2, author's emphasis).

Perseverance is only relevant in difficulties, and we are, in fact, very difficult people for God to deal with. Our Creator God has created us for himself and we respond too often with indifference or a quest for adolescent independence. Put even more personally, we are his beloved, but, in the face of God's unexplainable and lavish love, we pursue other lovers who ultimately abandon us. In this context, God reveals his perseverance with us.

EDWARD T. WELCH

APRIL 15

DEUTERONOMY 5:12–15; LEVITICUS 25:1–12

God intends for us to be free. Freedom from slavery is part of the Sabbath and the Jubilee. All of Israel, including servants, and even animals, are to observe this rest. "Remember that you were slaves in Egypt and that the LORD your God brought you out of there with a mighty hand and an outstretched arm. Therefore the LORD your God has commanded you to observe the Sabbath day" (Deuteronomy 5:15).

The focus and purpose of all of our labor, ultimately, is to serve him. No other person or institution may own our allegiance; any other allegiance is ultimately slavery. God has freed us and will continue to free us. These Sabbaths don't just point backward to the God of creation; they point to God as a deliverer as well. The year of Jubilee tells us that we can never lose our identity as God's freed children. He is the One who delivers the enslaved and those he sets free are freed forever. In addition, the Sabbath and Jubilee tell us that God has a home for us and will lead us there. God takes the enslaved and restores the created order of things by settling his people in his land. Who or what controls your world? Whom or what do you serve?

WINSTON T. SMITH

APRIL 16

1 Corinthians 15:1–11

He says it is "of first importance." When you page through Scripture with an eye to finding purpose statements, you can't miss the apostle Paul's summary, "For what I received I passed on to you as of first importance: that Christ died for our sins according to the Scriptures, that he was buried, that he was raised on the third day according to the Scriptures, and that he appeared to Peter, and then to the Twelve. After that he appeared to more than five hundred of the brothers at the same time" (1 Corinthians 15:3–6).

If you want an even more basic statement, Paul whittles it down to this: "Christ and him crucified" (1 Corinthians 2:2). When he personalizes it, he writes, "For to me, to live is Christ and to die is gain" (Philippians 1:21). Scripture is a story that climaxes in Christ. Our story, if it is to have enduring purpose, must stay focused on that same conclusion.

What's the use? Why bother? The answer is that Jesus Christ has been crucified and he has risen from the dead. You couldn't find a more complete answer. In it you find that you are called, forgiven, adopted into a new family, given gifts, given a mission, given a future. You are given love, and this love is so extreme it will take you all eternity to begin to understand it.

Edward T. Welch

APRIL 17

HEBREWS 10:1–14

Feel the futility of it. In the Old Testament, the priests of Israel were required to offer daily sacrifices to atone for sins. Hebrews points out that the fact these sacrifices had to be performed over and over for hundreds of years shows that they were ineffective in removing sin (Hebrews 10:1–2). Let the language of these tasks being "endless" and being required "year after year" make you tired.

But when Jesus comes, acting as our high priest, he makes a sacrifice of his own life and body that pays the debt once and for all. "But when Christ had offered for all time a single sacrifice for sins, he sat down at the right hand of God" (Hebrews 10:12). Jesus, unlike any other priest, completed his work and was able to sit down. Like his Father in Genesis 1, Jesus sits because his labor for us is perfect and complete. In other words, "It was very good." Because Jesus rests, you can rest.

Jesus' death and resurrection embody the promises of Sabbath. His work is perfect; complete. He has redeemed us from our sin. By trusting him and obeying his words and his Spirit within us, we are no longer slaves to our corrupted nature. We are free to be God's children. His resurrection is a picture and promise of the new life we have now and will have forever when Jesus returns and we are resurrected as well.

WINSTON T. SMITH

APRIL 18

ISAIAH 55

The call of Christ seems hard. "Deny yourself, take up your cross, and follow me." But this hard call is actually the call of grace. In calling you to your death, Christ is actually protecting you *from* death.

There is a rich and satisfying life to be found. If you are God's child, your life has transcendent meaning and purpose. But these things will never be found as long as you are holding tightly to your life. Isaiah would say to each of us, "Why are you working so hard for what will never satisfy? Why are you investing so much in what can never fulfill?" This amazing life of transcendent meaning, purpose, and joy is to be found on the other side of your death. It is only when you deny yourself, take up your cross, and follow your Lord that you begin to experience the transcendent humanity for which you were created.

Christ's call to you is a rescue. In asking you to deny yourself and follow, he is giving to you what you could never earn or achieve on your own. Christ offers you what you cannot earn and what the physical creation can never offer: the all-surpassing glory of knowing him. This is the world's best prize. This is the universe's best meal. This is the only thing that will give your life meaning and fill you with lasting joy.

PAUL DAVID TRIPP

APRIL 19

JOHN 19:16–30

"It is finished." Christ comes and satisfies God's wrath in a way that all former sacrifices and human intercessors could not. Jesus drains the cup of God's wrath against his people once for all. For those who hate and curse him, he pours out anger as punishment. When it is concluded, he declares, "It is done," though it takes an eternity for them to absorb it. Jesus also uttered, "It is finished" when he exhausted God's wrath on behalf of his people. Either people exhaust God's anger themselves or a substitute does.

In love, God finds a way to deal with the anger his people provoke, even though it means that he must bear the punishment his righteous wrath requires. He pays so that you do not. The consequences you suffer are not intended to pay God back. In that sense, they are not punishment, but rather training so that you might learn to live a holy life.

Anger that disciplines is different from anger that destroys. It's corrective, not destructive. More than that, being angry with family costs God, and he willingly pays the price. You don't need to be afraid of this awesome, powerful God, because he pays what you never could. That's a God you can have great confidence in, even when you've angered him.

WILLIAM P. SMITH

APRIL 20

JONAH 4:1–11

The character of God has infinite facets. "God is a Spirit, infinite, eternal, and unchangeable, in his being, wisdom, power, holiness, and truth" (Westminster Confession of Faith, Shorter Catechism, Question 4). Of these and many other attributes, Scripture often emphasizes that God is great and good, powerful and loving.

In Jonah's book, these qualities are on display. The crux of the book is Jonah's defense. "I knew that you are a gracious and compassionate God, slow to anger and abounding in love, a God who relents from sending calamity" (Jonah 4:2). The problem is that this knowledge didn't make a difference. If anything, it made things worse, at least from Jonah's perspective. Odd, given Jonah's confidence in God's love, that he would avoid trusting him. We might believe that God loves us, but we aren't so sure he will give us what we want. We want to be loved, and we also want to dictate the *way* and by whom we are loved. Jonah believed that God was gracious and compassionate, but he wanted love served up as judgment and destruction against his enemies.

Confession is once again the way out. With Jonah and ourselves, when our desires depart from God's, they become idolatrous. We don't want anything to get between us and our object of worship. Jonah didn't want to submit to God; he wanted to *be* a god.

EDWARD T. WELCH

APRIL 21

PSALM 133; MATTHEW 5:43–47

The Bible holds two pictures of relationship in tension. The leading theme, the richer theme, involves the people you truly enjoy—your beloved brother, sister, wife, the child you hold in your arms, and dear friends. In heaven you will see face-to-face the One you love, the supreme Person. But heaven is also a place full of other relationships you enjoy. These people love you without pretense, competition, or manipulation.

But side by side with that call to joyous intimacy is a call to get out of your comfort zone. The harder call of the Bible is to love enemies, strangers, people who are different from you, and those who are needy, sinful, and broken. This call comes for two reasons. First, it tests whether you are turning the innocent pleasures of intimacy into a stained pleasure. Are you and the people you enjoy turning into a clique? Second, the call tests whether we are willing to widen the circle of intimacy so that enemies become friends, strangers become like family, and someone you don't know becomes like a dear sister. The goal is always the simple, joyous relationship with others—the mutual affection and give-and-take. God calls you to widen the circle of your friendships, and to avoid making a god out of those who bring you the greatest pleasure. Doing these two things will fill your life with the pleasure of growing relationships with others.

DAVID POWLISON

APRIL 22

LUKE 9:18–27

It must have been a shock when Christ turned to his followers and announced that they must die. Christ was calling his listeners to something that is counterintuitive for us. We work to preserve both our physical lives and our own personal definition of life. We work hard to avoid danger, injury, suffering, difficulty, trial, and loss. This instinct to preserve and defend life is deep within all of us. Yet here the Creator of life is calling us to think positively about dying. It doesn't make sense until you begin to understand the profound logic in Christ's call: "If anyone would come after me, he must deny himself and take up his cross daily and follow me. For whoever wants to save his life will lose it, but whoever loses his life for me will save it. What good is it for a man to gain the whole world, and yet lose or forfeit his very self? If anyone is ashamed of me and my words, the Son of Man will be ashamed of him" (Luke 9:23–26).

Here is one of the most practical truths you will ever consider. It has everything to do with how you are investing your life, where you are placing your hope, and the transcendent life that you were created to enjoy. The little kingdom promises life, but brings you death; the big kingdom requires your death, but gives you life.

PAUL DAVID TRIPP

APRIL 23

PSALM 145

We were created to find our meaning, identity, and purpose in the existence, character, and plan of God. Our identity was meant to be rooted in his love. Our hope was designed to be tied to his grace. Our potential was meant to be connected to his power. Our purpose was meant to be structured by his will. Our joy was meant to be wed to his glory. In every way, our vision of what is necessary, true, worthy, and meaningful was meant to be rooted in a functional worship of him. We were created for the dignity of living large and meaningful lives—lives that literally are connected to things before the creation of the world and extending far into eternity.

This kind of big-God, big-picture living means that we care about things that do not immediately involve us, because God, who is the source and center of our lives, does. God's purposes become our functional life goals, the things God says are valuable become the real-life treasures we seek, and God's will provides the fences within which we live.

We start to understand that grace cuts a hole in sin's shrink-wrap. Grace reaches in, pulls us out, and locates us in a place that is more exciting and meaningful than anything we could have ever conceived of ourselves— the kingdom of God.

PAUL DAVID TRIPP

APRIL 24

PSALM 126

He knows our suffering. Have you noticed that sometimes, in the presence of someone whose suffering seems greater than our own, our suffering seems lighter, less intense? It is as if the suffering of another can temporarily take us out of ourselves. The sufferings of Jesus can, indeed, elevate us and take us out of ourselves.

The cross says that life will not be easy. If Jesus serves, we will serve. If Jesus suffers, we too will experience hardships. No servant is greater than the master. Yet things are not always the way they appear. Suffering is part of the path that leads to glory and beauty. "He who goes out weeping, carrying seed to sow, will return with songs of joy, carrying sheaves with him" (Psalm 126:6). Suffering has a purpose. It is changing us so that we look more and more like Jesus himself and even death is not the end of the story. When someone has suffered like you, they understand you before you speak. They can even supply words that describe your suffering. Jesus suffered; therefore, he knows our suffering.

EDWARD T. WELCH

APRIL 25

PSALM 32

The God who sees us clearly is full of mercy. He does not intend for you to spend the rest of your life wallowing in guilt. He wants you to face the gravity of what you have done so you will turn to him and find mercy. He wants this moment to be a turning point in your life—the moment where you turn and are met by God's love and mercy. James 4:6 explains it this way: "God opposes the proud" (those who won't admit their need), "but gives grace to the humble" (those who know their need). In fact, in that same verse James says that God "gives us more grace." No matter how bad the problem, grace goes deeper, higher, and wider.

God will meet you right where you are—in your silence, your humiliation, your guilt, and your shame. He came in the person of Jesus to redeem this world—to redeem you. He stepped into our brokenness, sin, disease, and pain and took it all on himself. He died on a cross for your sins. God's promise of mercy to you is backed up by the broken body of his Son. Jesus' death is your guarantee that when you come to God and confess your sins to him you will receive mercy. The gospel of Jesus Christ is for those who know and admit their sins (1 John 1:8–9).

DAVID POWLISON

APRIL 26

PSALM 73

Cry on your bed or cry to the Lord. Everything turns inward in depression. A beautiful flower momentarily catches your attention, but within seconds the focus bends back into your own misery. You see loved ones who are celebrating a recent blessing, but before you can synchronize your feelings with theirs, you have doubled back to your own personal emptiness. Like a boomerang that always returns, no matter how hard you try, you can't get away from yourself.

Pain is like that. If any part of your body is injured, you can't get away from the pain. You may have brief distractions, but then the throbbing breaks through your consciousness and dominates again. At its peak, there seems to be no way out. You feel trapped by it.

But there are choices. You are standing at a crossroads and you will take one path or another. There is no such thing as not choosing, because "not choosing" is one of the paths. It too is a choice. Your decision is between calling out to the Lord or not. This is the choice that has confronted those in misery throughout history. Listen to the prophet Hosea, who wrote these words on behalf of the Lord: "They do not cry out to me from their hearts but wail upon their beds" (Hosea 7:14).

EDWARD T. WELCH

APRIL 27

ROMANS 7:13–25

Our response to God's love is summarized as loving our neighbors. This simple expression of obedience is a profound treatment for failure and shame. At first it seems counterintuitive. After all, our problem was that we fell in love with what we could receive from others; it would make more sense to detach from them. This love, however, is different. It is the love of a person freed rather than enslaved. Having received the love of Christ, we are willing to say to other people, "My desire to love you will outweigh my desire to be loved [honored, appreciated, respected] by you." Can you imagine the freedom in this? No longer are we dominated by popular opinion. Perceived rejection doesn't control us as it once did. Instead, we keep coming back to the question, "What form will love take now?"

When you turn to Christ, you don't have to say, "I am special because God loves me," which is true but not the critical issue. And you don't have to say, "What a miserable, idolatrous wretch," which is also true but also not the critical issue. Instead, you simply think less often about yourself. Your successes and failures are still noticeable, but they don't encumber you the way they once did.

EDWARD T. WELCH

APRIL 28

1 CORINTHIANS 2:6–16

Scripture presents a tension in describing sinners. On the one hand, sinners are rebellious and disobedient. "There is no one righteous, not even one; there is no one who understands, no one who seeks God. All have turned away, they have together become worthless; there is no one who does good, not even one" (Romans 3:10–12). "Everyone who sins breaks the law; in fact, sin is lawlessness" (1 John 3:4).

Sinners are also deceived and enslaved. Jesus speaks plainly to the Pharisees: "Everyone who sins is a slave to sin" (John 8:34). The apostle Peter called false teachers "slaves of depravity," observing the more general truth that "a man is a slave to whatever has mastered him" (2 Peter 2:19). Proverbs 5:22 declares that "the evil deeds of a wicked man ensnare him; the cords of his sin hold him fast."

On the cross the Lord Jesus pleads, "Father, forgive them, for they do not know what they are doing" (Luke 23:34). Jesus views his crucifiers as self-deceived and ignorant, and he mercifully prays for their forgiveness. Similarly, Paul explains how unbelievers are blind to God's secret wisdom, the gospel: "None of the rulers of this age understood it, for if they had, they would not have crucified the Lord of glory" (1 Corinthians 2:8). Sin enslaves. It deceives. It blinds.

ROBERT D. JONES

APRIL 29

1 PETER 5:6–11

The King beseeches us to lay our burden on him. He is the God who comes to serve rather than be served (Matthew 20:28). There is nothing begrudging in his service. It is his choice, and he has sworn himself to it.

Peter is doing his best to persuade us to be a new people who call out to the Lord. He begins by exhorting us to know that our God is the Creator God. He holds history in his hand. He delivers with a mighty hand, the grandest display being the death and resurrection of Jesus Christ. That was the act that subdued enemy forces and conquered death itself. If he really did this, don't we see that his greatest act was a self-sacrificial act of service? In keeping with his character, he continues to serve; he invites us to cast our burdens on him as we would cast burdens on an ox. Granted, it isn't easy to say you need help. It is humbling—and that is the point. In one of the amazing paradoxes of the kingdom, when God takes our burdens and takes the position of a servant, he reveals our inability and his sufficiency. As such, he is exalted as the God of the mighty hand.

EDWARD T. WELCH

APRIL 30

GALATIANS 5:16–26

Good relationships demand character because our relationships are always lived out in the middle of some kind of difficulty. Remember, your relationships have not been designed by God as vehicles for human happiness, but as instruments of redemption. It isn't enough to ask for the character you need to survive the difficulties of life and the weaknesses of the other person. We have been called to minister to the people that God, in his wisdom, has placed in our lives. He wants to use us as instruments of grace in their lives. To live this way takes character.

It takes humility to live with a sinner in a world of difficulty. It takes gentleness to be part of what God is doing in someone's life and not get in the way. It takes patience to deal with the sin and weakness of those around you. It takes perseverance to be part of change in a relationship because that change is most often a process and rarely an event. It takes forgiveness to move beyond the times you have been mistreated by another. It takes forbearance to continue to love a person, even when you are being provoked. It is hard to respond in kindness when you are treated unkindly. It takes remarkable love to serve the good of the other person and not be distracted by daily needs.

TIMOTHY S. LANE AND PAUL DAVID TRIPP

MAY 1

GENESIS 3

Sin drives Adam and Eve into hiding. It produces fear in them. Adam and Eve don't pursue God, so he pursues them and asks a question: "Where are you?" God asks not for his own benefit, but for Adam and Eve's. They need the experience of answering the question and the responsibility of owning what they have done. God follows up the first question with another and, even though Adam and Eve attempt to shift the blame, God promises to send them someone who will deliver them from what they have done. God himself will take the punishment they deserve.

He is the same God today. He comes looking for you when you sin and fail. More than that, he is a God you want to come looking for you. You know that when he finds you he will make things better. True, he knows you're in trouble; you may have put yourself in danger. But he does not seek to ruin you. He seeks to rescue you. There will be consequences, but there will be goodness in those consequences. How could you be frightened when he comes looking for you? Instead, you are really glad he is seeking you out. It moves you to thankful worship.

WILLIAM P. SMITH

MAY 2

JAMES 1:1–18

Temptations grow in stages (James 1:13–15). The first stage is seduction (being "dragged away and enticed"). Temptation begins with desires. You believe you need something in addition to Christ in order to be happy. It could be anything—someone's approval, a possession, a pleasure, a job, a family, etc. A temptation might be obviously sinful, but often it can be a good thing. Your greatest opportunity to triumph over sin is at this beginning stage of temptation. Ask the Holy Spirit to help you see what you are drawn to besides Christ.

The second stage of temptation is conception ("after desire has conceived"). Now the initial desire is lodged deep in your heart and you start to plan how you can get it. What you want is becoming more important to you than God. You haven't committed the outward sin, yet your desires are sinful.

The final stage is birth ("birth to sin; and sin . . . gives birth to death"). The result of your desire for something besides Christ is being caught in full-blown sin. Notice that the birth is really a death—you are mastered by something other than Christ.

At any time during these different stages of temptation, you can run to Christ, repent of your sin, and learn from your failure how to withstand temptation. God can change your heart so that, instead of a particular sin dominating your life, bit by bit you will be tempted by it less and less. TIMOTHY S. LANE

MAY 3

EPHESIANS 4:15–29

Wise love is often both skillful and creative, but it cannot be reduced to a skill set or to creative imagination. I have seen wrecked lives changed simply because a friend cared and was willing to speak honestly like this: "I love and respect you as a person, and I want what is good for you. But you are destroying yourself with what you believe and how you are living." Those were precisely the words that changed my life. The cruise missile of wise love blew apart the bunker of self-will in which I lived. My friend's words were not a product of technique. But they had four things going for them. They were true, loving, personal, and appropriate.

The living God brought my friend's words home with power. Out of the collapse of core willfulness, I could hear for the first time the voice of another, even greater friend: "I will give you a new heart and put a new spirit within you; and I will remove the heart of stone from your flesh and give you a heart of flesh" (Ezekiel 36:26). This Wonderful Counselor's approach is best described as true, loving, personal, appropriate. Speaking the truth in love comes first. And those words of the Life-giver, the merciful Shepherd, my Father, were precisely the words that changed my life forever.

DAVID POWLISON

MAY 4

MARK 5:25–34

It was her faith that singled her out. Jesus was touched by thousands of people, but, up to this point, there was only one person singled out as having faith. This unnamed woman had spent everything she had on medical treatments and her bleeding only became worse. Yet when she heard Jesus was coming, she believed he could heal her. This indeed is great faith. After dozens of treatments, this woman had certainly given up hope. Sure, she might try the next treatment to come down the road, but she could have no confidence in it. She had learned by now that nothing was going to help. But when she heard Jesus was coming, she thought, "If I just touch his clothes, I will be healed" (Mark 5:28). Not "I might be healed." This woman was confident because she knew Jesus. This woman is a teacher of the fear of the Lord. She first listened to Jesus and saw what he did. Undoubtedly she was amazed by what she heard and saw. But her amazement led her to a confidence that Jesus was the Messiah, the Son of God.

What about you? When you read about these events, are you astonished, or are they just another Sunday school lesson? Allow this woman to let you see the Son of God in a new way, bigger than before. Then let her teach you further: "Don't just stand there with your mouth open. Believe!" Awe is good, but awe must lead us to faith, and faith must lead to action.

EDWARD T. WELCH

MAY 5

PSALM 119:97–112

The Scriptures are like good food—sweeter even than honey (Psalm 119:103). Do God's words delight and strengthen you every day?

To learn how to use the Bible to get to know your heavenly Father and his love for you, start by asking the Spirit to speak to you through the Bible—to use the Bible to connect you to God. In the midst of temptation, the Spirit then will be able to use God's own words to remind you who God is, how much he loves you, and how pleasing him is the best thing—better than whatever sin you are tempted to commit. Memorize Bible passages that will help you see Christ more clearly. A great passage to start memorizing is Philippians 2:1–11. Here Paul reminds us of who we are in Christ and calls us to treat others the same way Jesus has treated us. Instead of making others the place where you find acceptance, comfort, and love, this passage teaches that Christ came to deal with a deeper need than human approval. He came so you might receive and live in the reality of his forgiveness and comfort.

Meditating on Scripture also includes persistent prayer in light of the Scripture. God gave you the Bible to help you know him, and prayer is how that relationship becomes real and meaningful.

TIMOTHY S. LANE

MAY 6

PSALM 13

The Bible is honest about the sorrows of life. God welcomes you to be honest as well. The Psalms capture examples of such honesty. Psalms 13, 22, 38, 42, 55, 59, 61, 73, and 88 all record God's people bringing their honest grief, questions, and complaints to the Lord. Perhaps you are in a place where you are confused or even angry with God. You want to complain about his sovereignty. It is an act of faith to bring that complaint to him in the pattern of these psalms. Your faith in God should never silence you in the dark hours of grief. Rather, this is when we begin to understand how deep, rich, and sturdy God's love for us really is. He will not turn away from your questions or be surprised by your grief. He will not be repulsed by your anger or turn his back on your pain. He understands the darkest moments of human existence and enters them with boundless mercy, unending love, and amazing grace. The Psalms record the cries of God's people: "The LORD has heard my weeping" (Psalm 6:8). They invite us to bring our grief to the One who cares for us more than anyone else ever could. God never turns a deaf ear to the cries of his children. No cry is too anguished for his ears. He listens—and answers.

PAUL DAVID TRIPP

MAY 7

PROVERBS 4

The heart is the real or essential you. The average Christian defines sin by talking about behavior. For example, what is the goal of most Christian parents? Is it not to get their children to do the right things? We set up all kinds of relational, motivational, and corrective structures to constrain and direct our children's behavior. However, beneath the battle for behavior is another, more fundamental battle—the battle for the thoughts and motives of the heart.

All of the ways in which the Bible refers to the inner person (mind, emotions, spirit, soul, will, etc.) are summed up with this one term: *heart.* The heart is the steering wheel of every human being. Everything we do is shaped and controlled by what our hearts desire. That is why the Bible is very clear that God wants our hearts. Only when God has your heart does he have you (Proverbs 4:23). As much as we are affected by our broken world and the sins of others against us, our greatest problem is the sin that resides in our hearts. That is why the message of the gospel is that God transforms our lives by transforming our hearts. Lasting change always comes through the heart.

TIMOTHY S. LANE AND PAUL DAVID TRIPP

MAY 8

NUMBERS 20:1–5

Where are our greatest problems? In the wilderness the Israelites are tired of difficulty, and, as is so often the case with sinful human beings, they start looking for someone to blame. Moses is an easy target, but Moses was not responsible for the situation Israel was in. God (through the pillar of fire and the cloud) had led them to this exact location. He had done so because he had a specific purpose in mind. This would be another occasion for God to demonstrate his power to the doubting Israelites.

This passage shows how quickly pain morphs into anger. It calls us to humbly admit that, as sinners, we tend to respond sinfully to whatever difficulty we encounter. This passage makes one thing clear: the anger we reveal in the middle of a trial says more about us than it does about the trial. The Bible keeps the focus on us! It confronts the self-righteousness and spiritual blindness that make us think that our greatest problems are outside us, not inside. We maintain that changes in situation, location, and relationship would allow us to respond differently. We say that the difficulty causes us to respond in sinful ways. But the Bible teaches again and again that our circumstances don't cause us to act as we do. They only expose the true condition of our hearts, revealed in our words and actions.

TIMOTHY S. LANE AND PAUL DAVID TRIPP

MAY 9

MATTHEW 6:12–15

Because the people around you are (like you) still sinners, they will fail, they will sin against you, and they will disappoint you. That is when you can extend to them the same grace you have received. Our anger, irritation, impatience, condemnation, bitterness, and vengeance will never produce good things in their lives (or ours). But God can produce good things in them when we are willing to incarnate his grace. We become part of what he is doing in their lives, instead of standing in the way. So, what does it mean practically to let the cross shape your relationships?

It means being ready, willing and able to forgive. The decision to forgive is first a heart transaction between you and God. It is a willingness to give up your desire to hold onto (and in some way punish the person for) his offense against you. Instead, you entrust the person and the offense to God, believing that he is righteous and just. You make a decision to respond to this person with an attitude of grace and forgiveness. This vertical transaction (between you and God) prepares you for the horizontal transaction of forgiveness between you and the offending person, when you are given that opportunity.

TIMOTHY S. LANE AND PAUL DAVID TRIPP

MAY 10

1 TIMOTHY 6:11–19

The Father prefers to keep us on the edge. His plan is to liberate us from our defensive, hoarding, tight-fisted, miserly ways, and to teach us that when we have been given the kingdom—the kingdom!—stinginess is unnatural and unbecoming. We might prefer a different strategy, but if God is molding us to be chips off the old block, his strategy makes sense. It is exactly what we need, because our greatest need is to be what we were intended to be—to be like him.

So, the kingdom is God's and God targets the needs of those who have less than we do. In other words, not only is the kingdom about God, and not me, I don't even come in second! I am to consider others more important than myself in the kingdom. This seems like too much to ask until the King calls us his treasured possession (Exodus 19:5). He is seeking my allegiance with love, not with force and power. The reason we are called to lay up our treasures in heaven is because we are his treasure. When you are confident that you are the Father's treasured possession, you are also confident that his loving care will continue forever. Building warehouses is a waste of time and space. His gifts to you become things you want to give him back in gratitude. Then he gives you even more.

EDWARD T. WELCH

MAY 11

1 JOHN 4:7–21

You will always be looking in two directions when you purposefully make God's universal story your own. You will be looking backward to the cross and looking forward to the time when you see Jesus, the object of your hope. When we look back at the cross we see forgiveness of sin, the love and generosity of God to sinners, the fact that we now approach God without fear, the righteousness we receive rather than earn. We can live as people who have been given a great gift, so there is a persistence of thankfulness and joy. We have no reason to think we must repay God for our sins. We have no reason to fear. The cross means that we have freedom to make mistakes.

The resurrection of Jesus confirms that he truly was the Son of God with power; it redirects our attention to the future resurrection of all who believe. It points to heaven, and heaven is what brings meaning to the present. It means that your house will not be sold to a developer. Someday it will be a thing of great beauty, so you *do* change the carpets, work the garden, and paint the exterior. You know that your work will not be in vain; the master builder has determined that your less-than-professional attempts will contribute to the final masterpiece. Nothing we do because of Christ will be in vain. This brings purpose and diligence to the present.

EDWARD T. WELCH

MAY 12

Mark 11:20–25; Luke 17:1–4

The Bible is full of calls to forgive. There are two that almost seem contradictory: Mark 11:25 and Luke 17:3. Mark 11:25 seems to say that we are to forgive someone no matter what, while Luke 17:3 seems to say that you only forgive someone if he repents. Which one of these verses is right? They're both right!

These verses are talking about two different aspects of forgiveness. Mark 11:25 is talking about forgiveness as a heart attitude before God. The context is worship. When I consider someone's sin as I stand before the Lord, I am called to have an attitude of forgiveness toward the person who sinned against me. This is nonnegotiable. I do not have the right to withhold forgiveness and harbor bitterness in my heart. Luke 17:3, on the other hand, is talking about forgiveness as a horizontal transaction between me and the offender. This is often referred to as reconciliation. The point Luke 17:3 makes is that, while I am to have an attitude of forgiveness before the Lord, I can only grant forgiveness to the other person if he repents and admits he has sinned against me. Even if he never does this, I am called to maintain an attitude of forgiveness toward the offender. The vertical aspect of forgiveness is unconditional, but the horizontal aspect depends upon the offender admitting guilt and asking for forgiveness.

TIMOTHY S. LANE AND PAUL DAVID TRIPP

MAY 13

Matthew 18:1–14

There is a certain paradox in trusting God. When we trust him, we are saying that we are entirely inadequate, which is true though it doesn't do wonders for our self-image. But when we trust him, it is also as if we have arrived home. All is well. Yes, there may be many problems, but we are home, and the comfort and joy of home reduces the problems of life to the level of hassles.

As you turn back to the Lord, speak your confession to him. Tell him that your heart is prone to wander, your tendencies toward erecting idols incorrigible. Confession is speaking the truth about our hearts to the Lord. Although Scripture encourages us to make it a daily feature of our conversations with God (Matthew 6:9–13), it is a neglected discipline. A rule of thumb in confession is to keep at it until you have inklings of hope or joy. Confession is not a time to grovel. It is a time to trust in the God who delights in forgiving because it brings him glory. Don't forget the story of the joy the shepherd takes in the one lost sheep that is found. Yes, you wander off, but focus on the happiness of the shepherd. It isn't what you expected.

EDWARD T. WELCH

MAY 14

PSALM 21

The real object of joy, of course, is God. He is what all earthly joys reflect. Throughout history people have found great joy because the Lord is present (Psalm 21:6). God is the joy and delight of his people (Psalm 43:4).

This was Jonathan Edwards's test of true religion. Do you find joy in God? "Joy . . . consists in the sweet entertainment their minds have in the view or contemplation of the divine and holy beauty of these things [the character of God], as they are in themselves. And this is the main difference between the joy of the hypocrite and the joy of the true saint. The former rejoices in himself . . . the latter rejoices in God" [Jonathan Edwards, *Religious Affections* (New Haven: Yale Univ., 1959), p. 240].

Some find the thought of heaven boring. But once you start finding joy in the Lord, you will find an inexhaustible delight. God is the God of joy and gladness, he freely and liberally gives joy to his people, and he actually commands us to search for it in him (Psalm 106:4–5; 1 Thessalonians 5:18). Therefore, the psalmist truly understands God's thoughts when he prays, "Let me hear joy and gladness; let the bones you have crushed rejoice" (Psalm 51:8). This is not a selfish prayer; it is purposeful. The psalmist wants to be what he was intended to be, the person every follower of Christ will one day be—a joyful worshiper.

EDWARD T. WELCH

PSALM 119:129–136

A timely passage orients a person to his life. It lays out to the person the moral landscape within which he lives: "The unfolding of your words gives light" (Psalm 119:130). If someone gets lost in dark woods, a good map and the light of dawn are extremely helpful! They don't actually get him anywhere, but they help him to see where he's gotten and where he needs to get. It must be simple and concrete—something riveted to real life. Theological generalities and intricacies don't do the job. General truths about your tendencies, patterns, and themes in your personal history don't change you either. You must be able to identify where your particular current struggle lies, what it means, what exactly is at stake, and where to go. Where is the firefight between good and evil today? You must be able to trace the difference between truth and lies, hope and illusion, insight and self-deception, true need and wild desires, living faith and functional godlessness. Where do you need God's redemption and help? When you are disoriented in your current struggle, you don't know even your choices. When your way is deep darkness, you don't know what makes you stumble. The right bit of Scripture reorients you.

DAVID POWLISON

MAY 16

REVELATION 5

Many years ago in *Time* magazine there was an article about people who were facing death. Hundreds of terminally ill people were interviewed and photographed. Most of the people looked dreary and sad. But an elderly man's picture almost jumped off the page. His face was full of life and vitality. In his interview, he said he couldn't wait to see Jesus. He was joyful in the face of death because he was looking forward to seeing his Savior.

You cannot face death with true, honest courage unless you are looking forward to meeting Jesus—the one who faced death for you and is now alive and with you. Are you looking forward to meeting the Lamb of God who took away your sins? Do you long to hear your Good Shepherd call you by name? Are you looking forward to going to your heavenly Father's home? It's a home of glory, filled with the radiance of the Holy Spirit. In God's home all wrongs are made right, all darkness becomes bright, all losses are restored, and all tears are wiped away.

When you pass through death, you will pass through to the moment when faith becomes sight, when you will actually see the one whom you love sight unseen. To die in the hope that God is with you is to pass through the loss of all things into the gain of all things, into the gain of Christ.

DAVID POWLISON

MAY 17

ROMANS 5:1–11

God's holiness is summed up in the holy gospel. As the fear of the Lord surfaces in your heart, notice how mercy and justice hold each other in a system of checks and balances. Love and mercy never become sentimental; justice and sternness don't veer off into wrath that abandons all offenders. "Righteousness and peace kiss each other" (Psalm 85:10) in the death and resurrection of Jesus Christ. That is the gospel.

The holiness of God, expressed in both his love and justice, finds its zenith in the gospel of Jesus Christ. The gospel announces the liberation found in the death and resurrection of Jesus Christ. In that death we find the seriousness of sin: The Son of Man was crushed instead of us; Jesus himself drank the cup of God's wrath in our place. God's anger and righteousness are truly holy. Yet in the gospel we also find unprecedented mercy, love, and forgiveness. The penalty our sins deserve is redirected so that all we receive is grace.

EDWARD T. WELCH

MAY 18

PSALM 55

God might feel far away, but our feelings mislead us on this one. Scripture is filled with promises of God's presence with his people. Do you want evidence? God speaks to us, and desires to be spoken to. Only someone close can do such things. He speaks to us, especially through Scripture, and he calls us to speak with him. When we are tongue-tied, he actually gives us words to say. Yet it is not a script that he gives us. When we speak from a script, we are pretending. We wear the mask of another. We become actors. Instead, God gives us poetry that, somehow, gives voice to the silences in our hearts. If we had the skill and the words, we would write many of those same words. The Psalms are where you find many of these poems. They are God's liturgy, prepared for you in advance.

"My heart is in anguish within me; the terrors of death assail me. Fear and trembling have beset me; horror has overwhelmed me. I said, 'Oh, that I had the wings of a dove! I would fly away and be at rest—I would flee far away and stay in the desert'" (Psalm 55:4–7).

Don't forget that, although these psalms are expressing very raw emotions, they are words that God himself is giving you. He is the minister who has arranged the order of service. He is the father who is teaching you how to speak.

EDWARD T. WELCH

MAY 19

1 CORINTHIANS 10:6–22

Hopelessness is lethal whether you have killed it or never nurtured it. You have heard the question, "Do you want to change?" Now you understand why such a question is important. There are logical reasons to resist change. For example, what if hope creeps in? You might want to feel less miserable but not at the expense of awakening hope. Most likely, you want to change less than you realize. So don't be deceived. We do hopelessness. We choose it. But there is a way out.

Part of the answer goes back to what God says to people who fear. The connection is that fear, like hopelessness, is reluctant to trust God for the future. God says that he will give you grace to handle the disappointments that lie ahead; your task is to live for him in the present. At first, this feels reckless, as if you were enjoying the thrill of a speeding car when you are courting devastation at the next turn. But it isn't reckless to trust in God rather than yourself. Therefore, to fight against hopelessness is to take action in the present. You think that checking off a to-do list is unspiritual? When done by faith, it is heroic.

EDWARD T. WELCH

MAY 20

I PETER 1:3–12

The child is in us all. If you farm or do gardening, you know something about perseverance. When you plant seeds, the ground will not yield corn quickly. When you plant fruit trees and grapevines, it could be a few years before you actually eat their fruit. When you decide to take up the violin, the instrument produces squeaks and scratchings long before it reluctantly yields Beethoven etudes. If you have skill in anything at all, it has come through persevering.

Children are notoriously poor at waiting and persevering. "When will we get to Grandmom's house?" "Soon," is the typical though unsatisfying reply. "Mommy, when you are going to play with me?" "Not yet. Not until I finish this report." Fifteen seconds later the child asks the same question, this time with a tone of voice that can drive you mad.

But the child is in us all. We too look forward to the day when we have learned perseverance before the Lord. It is the older wise man or woman who can take the many hassles of life in stride, without grumbling and complaining, with contentment rather than resignation. God has chosen to inject his character of perseverance and patient waiting into everyday, earthly life. We are patiently waiting for the Lord's coming. Creation itself is patiently waiting for the time when it will be liberated from bondage (Romans 8:22).

EDWARD T. WELCH

MAY 21

DEUTERONOMY 10:12–22

Fear of the Lord means that I carry around with me such a deep awareness, awe, and reverence for the power, holiness, wisdom, and grace of God that I would not think of doing anything other than living for his glory. Fearing the Lord means that this worshipful awe is the single and unchallenged motivator of everything I think, desire, say, and do. What does it mean to live a Christ-centered existence? It means that the fear of the Lord, more than fear of anything else, sets the agenda for our actions, reactions, and responses.

The kingdom of self is driven by all kinds of other fears: fear of man, fear of discomfort or difficulty, fear of failure, fear of not getting my own way, etc. The principle here is that if God doesn't own the fear of our hearts, he will not own our lives. You and I are always living to avoid what we dread. If we dread displeasing God more than anything else, because our hearts have been captured by a deep, worshipful and loving awe of him, we will live in new ways.

PAUL DAVID TRIPP

MAY 22

EPHESIANS 5:1–21

This is our purpose. Fear God and keep his commandments, love God and others, glorify God, "for me to live is Christ"—these are all purpose statements. They are all different ways of reminding us who we really are. Human beings were created as God's royal offspring, intended to bear the distinct character of the Father. Our purpose is to bear a family resemblance. What God's law does is describe the character of the King so we can imitate him.

But there are prodigal yearnings within each of us. We want to find our own way. Even though we get hopelessly lost, there is something in us that prefers aimless wandering to childlike imitation and obedience. The cross is God's pursuit of wayward children. It is the invitation back to the family.

"Be holy, because I am holy" (Leviticus 11:44), "be imitators of God" (Ephesians 5:1), "live as children of light" (Ephesians 5:8), "your attitude should be the same as that of Christ Jesus" (Philippians 2:5)—these are familial exhortations. Study Jesus, your older brother and your God, and imitate him by faith.

EDWARD T. WELCH

MAY 23

Exodus 16:1–12

When God's mighty acts are on display, it means he is near. Kings can do their bidding from a distance through intermediaries, but God chooses to come close. He sits on the throne of the universe, but he also dwells with commoners. This is music to the ears of worriers. "Then Moses told Aaron, 'Say to the entire Israelite community, "Come before the LORD, for he has heard your grumbling."' While Aaron was speaking to the whole Israelite community, they looked toward the desert, and *there was the glory of the LORD appearing in the cloud*" (Exodus 16:9–10, author's emphasis). The glory of the Lord means the presence of the Lord.

Nearness and presence will be recurring themes in God's words of comfort to fearful people. Of course, the earth belongs to the Lord and, as Spirit, God is not bound by the limitations of space. He is everywhere at all times. When he underscores his presence, as he does here, it means that he is working on behalf of his people. It means that he is for them. He is an active, protecting, comforting presence. When he says he is near, watch for his mighty acts. When he is near, he is *really* near.

EDWARD T. WELCH

MAY 24

GENESIS 2:4–25

Transcendence Is a part of humanity. Adam and Eve weren't placed in the garden for self-survival and self-satisfaction. They were immediately given a vision and commission that would take them far beyond the borders of their own needs and concerns. They were given amazing capacities to do what no other creature could do.

Think about what this means for all of us who are the sons and daughters of Adam and Eve. You and I were created for more than filling up our schedules with the self-satisfying pursuits of personal pleasure. We were meant to do more than make sure that all of our needs are fulfilled and all our desires are satisfied. We were never meant to be self-focused little kings ruling miniscule little kingdoms with a population of one.

God's grace invites you to be part of something that is far greater than your boldest and most expansive dream. His grace cuts a hole in your self-built prison and invites you to step into something so huge, so significant that only one word in the Bible can adequately capture it. That word is *glory*.

PAUL DAVID TRIPP

MAY 25

HEBREWS 10:19–25

We hold on to one hope: Christ. The Christian hope is more than a redemptive system with practical principles that can change your life. The hope of every Christian is a person, the Redeemer, Jesus Christ. He is the wisdom behind every biblical principle and the power we need to live them out. Because Christ lives inside us today, because he rules all things for our sakes (Ephesians 1:22–23), and because he is presently putting all his enemies under his feet (see 1 Corinthians 15:25–28), we can live with courage and hope.

Our hope is not in our theological knowledge or our experience within the body of Christ. We are thankful for these things, yet we hold on to one hope: Christ. In him we find everything we need to live a godly life in the here and now. Paul captures it so well: "I have been crucified with Christ and I no longer live, but Christ lives in me. The life I live in the body, I live by faith in the Son of God, who loved me and gave himself for me" (Galatians 2:20).

TIMOTHY S. LANE AND PAUL DAVID TRIPP

JEREMIAH 31:31–34

Is the evidence of having forgiven someone forgetting what he has done to you? Jeremiah 31:34 is often quoted, where God says, "I will forgive their wickedness and will remember their sins no more."

There are at least two problems with this understanding of forgiveness. First, it is not realistic. Trying to forget a sin someone has committed against you will only encourage you to remember it. Completely erasing an offense from your memory is not realistic. Second, it is not biblical. Our omniscient God does not forget anything! The word "remember" in Jeremiah 31:34 is not a memory word, but a promise word, a covenant word. God is promising that when we confess our sins, "I will not treat you as your sins deserve. Instead, I will forgive you." Forgiveness is a past promise you keep in the future. It is very important to understand these two dimensions of forgiveness. If you don't, you will veer off in one of two equally wrong directions: (1) You will be plagued with doubts about whether you have forgiven someone because you think that forgiving equals forgetting. Or (2) you will give in to bitterness because you think that, since you have forgiven someone in the past, you are allowed to hold onto the vestiges of hurt in the present. Neither reflects the way God has forgiven us.

TIMOTHY S. LANE AND PAUL DAVID TRIPP

MAY 27

JOHN 3:1–21

Death doesn't have the last say for those who know Jesus, it has the next-to-last say. The last word for the Christian is the resurrection. The last word is life. The last word is mercy. The last word is that God will take us to be with him forever. God's free gift of eternal life stands in stark contrast to "the wages of sin is death" (Romans 6:23). Jesus stands in contrast to the killer, the murderer, the slayer. He, the only innocent person who ever lived, faced death not for his own sins, but for the sins of his people (John 3:16). Jesus faced death for you.

On the cross he faced death in all of its dimensions. He was killed by asphyxiation and torture, but this was only the physical cause of his death. As he died he bore the wages of sin, suffered the malice of the evil one, and experienced the holy wrath of God. He, the innocent one, willingly died for the guilty.

When he freely gave up his life, death was slain by God and Jesus rose to new life. God's grace destroyed the destroyer and death was thrown into hell. Because of Jesus, life has the last say. Because of Jesus, you don't have to experience death as he did. He has already paid for your sins. You will die physically, but rise to life eternal.

DAVID POWLISON

MAY 28

PHILIPPIANS 4:4–7

When you worry and obsess, you are living as if just you and your struggles are going one-on-one. If you remember, in even the worst circumstances, that the Lord is near, then you will have a rock on which your heart can rest. You have a hope that is bigger than any threat, even death. You draw near to the Lord who is close. After all, this Lord created the whole universe and controls every moment of your life. He counts the hairs on your head and notices each one that falls. You are living in his world. And this Lord is not only the all-powerful Creator of the world, but he has also experienced first-hand the anxiety-producing fragility of life. This Lord anguished honestly. He became human and, although he didn't want to experience devastating suffering, he chose to commit himself to his Father. He trusted his Father with his life because he knew his Father's love. He is raised from the dead. He will raise you with him.

When you know this is true, then you have a hope bigger than any loss. What you have been given in this Lord weighs more and has more lasting power than anything you might lose here on earth. When you know that Jesus is near, the worried, obsessed, sinful anxiety dissipates. The caring, concerned, trusting sort of anxiety grows, and you grow in faith and love.

DAVID POWLISON

MAY 29

PSALM 130

Here's a new kind of waiting. The psalmist holds loosely onto his personal dreams and tightly onto his God who, if he forgives sins, must be good. How do we wait? In our grief we rest in the promise of renewal that is packaged with the resurrection. Along the way we ask for prayer and search out companions from Scripture, such as the psalmists, who have learned the secrets of waiting on the Lord. Bad things certainly can and will happen, but there is a resurrection ending. So your task is not to transform into a superficial, sunny optimist. It is to grow to be an optimist by faith. The kingdom is advancing; God's reign is spreading; there will be justice; and when we belong to Christ, it will end with joy.

As for me, I want to watch and endure, not worry. I want to be like the night watchmen who are waiting to see first light. God is the God of suspense, but it is a suspense that teaches us peace. He is the God of surprises, but the surprises are always better than we could have dreamed. I can't put him in a box and assume that he should act according to my time schedule and according to my less sophisticated version of what is good. I need the mind of Christ. I can do with nothing less.

EDWARD T. WELCH

MAY 30

PSALM 16

Who or what owns your love: this is what big kingdom and little kingdom living are all about. The fundamental difference between big kingdom and little kingdom living is what has captured the love of our hearts. Remember, as Christ said during his earthly ministry, the kingdom of God is not a location. You couldn't say, "Honey, let's get up tomorrow morning and go visit the kingdom of God for the day." No, Jesus said, "The kingdom of God is within you." Both the big and little kingdoms are kingdoms of the heart. The big kingdom is shaped by a deeply thankful love for God, and the little kingdom is shaped by a love of self. When my true spiritual condition reveals that I, in fact, love me more than anything else, I will always shrink the size of my care and concern, sacrifice and discipline, and hopes and dreams to the size of my own life. If I love God more than anything else, I will be pulled way beyond the borders of my own wants and needs to the spaciousness of God's kingdom, where redemption and restoration of all things is the order of the day, every day.

PAUL DAVID TRIPP

MAY 31

PSALM 26

Park your mind on what is true (Philippians 4:8). Anxiety is full of lies. What are some of them? First, you believe the world needs to be under your control. Second, you think it is out of control. And third, you imagine that your worry will get it under control. But the truth is that this is God's world. He controls it, and your worry will not change a thing. So when you are tempted to worry, reject the lie that it is up to you to keep yourself and those you love safe. Especially reject all lies that contain the word *more*. For example: "I would be safe if I had more friends, more money, more time, and more respect." Also reject all the lies containing the word *different*: "I would be safe if I had a different spouse, different family, different friends, different job, different house, and different church." These statements are all fundamentally false. Ask God to help you anchor your mind on what is true, and then you will be able to tackle your real problems in the right way.

DAVID POWLISON

JUNE 1

PSALM 86

Share God's steadfast love and faithfulness. In the Old Testament two Hebrew words are often used to describe God: *chesed* and *emet*. *Chesed* is translated in the Old Testament as "lovingkindness," or "steadfast love." It means committed kindness, a chosen generosity, a resolution to do good to another person no matter what. *Emet* is translated as "faithfulness" or "truth." When we say of someone, "She was a true friend," we're using the word *true* in the sense that the Bible uses the word *emet*. It's someone who's looking out for your well-being, who is genuinely concerned for your welfare (Philippians 2:20). God is full of *chesed* and *emet*—steadfast love and faithfulness—toward you. *Chesed* and *emet* are also used in the Bible to describe human relationships. Most people seek their own interests, and instinctively do things that create distance and destroy intimacy in their close relationships. But when you are committed to treat someone with kindness, when you are genuinely concerned for someone else's welfare, you will start to be and do the kinds of things that actually build trust, intimacy, and companionship. *Chesed* and *emet* are what God is fundamentally like toward us. He is a God who keeps his promises, a God of kindness, a God who forgives. And *chesed* and *emet* are also the attributes you need to make your closest relationships deeply joyous and intimate.

DAVID POWLISON

JUNE 2

ROMANS 8:15–32

God's love is effective, and he wants you to know and experience his love for you. His Word is full of reminders that he personally and powerfully loves his children: "This is love: not that we loved God, but that he loved us and sent his Son as an atoning sacrifice for our sins" (1 John 4:10), "If God is for us, who can be against us? He who did not spare his own Son, but gave him up for us all—how will he not also, along with him, graciously give us all things?" (Romans 8:31–32). "God has poured out his love into our hearts by the Holy Spirit, whom he has given us" (Romans 5:5). "You received the Spirit of sonship. And by him we cry, 'Abba! Father.' The Spirit himself testifies with our spirit that we are God's children" (Romans 8:15–16). These aren't just words. God does what he says. They aren't just good intentions. He initiates a living relationship.

These passages speak of two central ways that God shows his love to us. First, the historical fact: Jesus Christ went to an agonizing death out of love for his children. Second, the powerful dynamic within our hearts: the Holy Spirit pours out God's love in us to create the child's trusting response. Did God act in love in history? Does God act now in love within our hearts? Yes! God's love is effective, both then and now.

DAVID POWLISON

1 CORINTHIANS 13

We know specific things about love. In 1 John 4:9–10, we learn that love became a human being named Jesus who lived among us. Ultimately, love is a person, not an experience. When you need help loving someone, you can look to Jesus and learn from him. Jesus, as love, took action. He spoke and acted in ways that made a difference, ways that made love visible among us. As we trust him and learn from him we can *do* love too.

There are two critical ingredients to loving in a Christlike way. The first ingredient is connecting with and depending on Christ, not as a religious man who lived two thousand years ago, but as God's own Son who is with you and able to help you. The second ingredient is knowing what love looks like in the details of the moment. Jesus does not just motivate us to love; he teaches *how* to love in the moment—what it looks like and how to do it. Remember that faith is only a prelude to action. You need faith that Jesus will help you every step of the way, but you also need to take concrete action.

WINSTON T. SMITH

1 Peter 5:6–11

"Cast all your anxiety on him because he cares for you." Some people have scribbled their various worries on pieces of paper and then thrown them in the trash as a way to dramatize Peter's teaching. But don't miss the holiness that infuses Peter's words about God. Peter is writing to people who are in real trouble. They have made a stand for Christ on the front lines of the battle against the kingdom of earth, and the war is raging. They have many reasons to worry. They have lost friends, jobs, and social status. They have seen brothers and sisters tortured and even martyred because of their faith in Christ. And then, of course, they have their own internal troubles within the church.

Through all these difficulties Peter exhorts Christians to be submissive and humble. Do good to those who are bad to you. Don't retaliate. Follow the example of Christ, who subverted the world order through his humble obedience in life and death. Such humility before other people is possible only as we walk humbly before God. This is where we pick up the passage about casting our anxieties on the Lord: "Humble yourselves, therefore, under God's mighty hand, that he may lift you up in due time. Cast all your anxiety on him because he cares for you" (1 Peter 5:6–7).

Edward T. Welch

JUNE 5

2 CORINTHIANS 12:7–10

Paul had a weakness that he called a "thorn in my flesh." He begged God to take his weakness away. He said, "Three times I pleaded with the Lord to take it away from me" (2 Corinthians 12:7–8). Paul received from God this response: "My grace is sufficient for you, for my power is made perfect in weakness." God's power is perfectly revealed in our weakness. God will use your weakness to show you that what drives your life is not you, but the power and mercy of Another. Paul responded to God by saying, "I will boast all the more gladly about my weaknesses, so that Christ's power may rest on me" (2 Corinthians 12:9). The very things that the world despises become the occasions for the power of Christ to be displayed in Paul's life. Then Paul said, "For Christ's sake, I delight in weaknesses, in insults, in hardships, in persecutions, in difficulties" (2 Corinthians 12:10). Such troubles are no fun to experience. But he's content in them for Christ's sake, and he concludes, "For when I am weak, then I am strong."

People value being strong and independent. But the dynamic of weakness and dependency makes Christ matter in your life. When Christ matters in your life, he shines through your life. People see the evidence of something wonderful—the hand of Another at work in you.

DAVID POWLISON

JUNE 6

DEUTERONOMY 8

"What hope do we have?" Israel asked. On the eve of entering the Promised Land, Moses preached a sermon series that became Deuteronomy. Israel desperately needed to hear what he had to say. The desert years were behind them, but the conquest of Canaan lay ahead. They still had to deal with the "giants" who lived in the land, and taking the land from them was still a frightening prospect. Can you hear them asking, "What hope do we have? Our parents blew it when they got here. If they couldn't trust God, what chance do we have?" Worst of all, Moses was staying behind. He was the one who had shepherded and led them all those years and interceded for them with God. How could they consider entering the land without him?

Often God reminds his people of what he has done for them and what he will do. Apparently he thinks this is pretty important. If that is so, we need to be reminded also. By linking his past actions for you with his present commands to you, he doesn't let you think that you can obey apart from believing what he has said. If Israel is going to take the land, it is because they believe his promise to give it to them. If they don't go, it is because they do not believe him. Their actions and ours—our obedience or disobedience—express our faith.

WILLIAM P. SMITH

JUNE 7

GALATIANS 3:26–4:7

"You are all sons of God through faith in Christ Jesus, for all of you who were baptized into Christ have clothed yourselves with Christ. There is neither Jew nor Greek, slave nor free, male nor female, for you are all one in Christ Jesus. If you belong to Christ, then you are Abraham's seed, and heirs according to the promise" (Galatians 3:26–29).

Paul highlights three common categories used to differentiate people in his day—Jew versus Greek, slave versus freeman, male versus female—and tells us that in Jesus Christ these divisions no longer exist. Paul is not blind to ethnicity or racial heritage, oblivious to master-slave workplace dynamics, or ignorant of the birds and the bees. On the contrary, elsewhere in his letters he directly addresses Jews, Greeks, masters, slaves, men, and women—people marked by the distinctions he claims no longer exist.

What is Paul's point? Simply this: Jesus Christ defines us not by our social standing, but by our connection to him. The gospel does not obliterate our social class or neuter our gender; it relativizes them. It subordinates them so that they no longer define and control us. At the end of the day, the bottom line is that we are Christians, sons and daughters of God, heirs of Abraham's promised blessing through Jesus.

ROBERT D. JONES

JUNE 8

ISAIAH 49:8–18

People change when the Holy Spirit brings the love of God to their hearts through the gospel. Whoever receives the Spirit of adoption as God's child learns to cry out, "Abba, Father." People change when they see that they are responsible for what they believe about God. Life experience is no excuse for believing lies; the world and the devil don't excuse the flesh. People change when truth becomes clearer and brighter than previous life experience. We change when our ears hear and our eyes see what God tells us about himself: "For the LORD comforts his people and will have compassion on his afflicted ones. But Zion said, 'The LORD has forsaken me, the Lord has forgotten me.' 'Can a mother forget the baby at her breast and have no compassion on the child she has borne? Though she may forget, I will not forget you! See, I have engraved you on the palms of my hands'" (Isaiah 49:13–16).

Also, "He does not treat us as our sins deserve or repay us according to our iniquities. For as high as the heavens are above the earth, so great is his love for those who fear him; as far as the east is from the west, so far has he removed our transgressions from us. As a father has compassion on his children, so the LORD has compassion on those who fear him" (Psalm 103:13).

DAVID POWLISON

JUNE 9

JOHN 1:1–14

God "pitched his tent." In his desire to restore the relationship between himself and his images, God came to us in a human body. John tells us that Jesus "tabernacled" among us—literally, he "pitched his tent" (John 1:14). God was no longer hidden. If you saw Christ, you saw the Father. There was now direct contact between God and humanity again. You could touch him and talk with him, though he could only be in one place at a time. After atoning for our unholiness and returning to heaven, Jesus broke all geographical and temporal boundaries by pouring out his Holy Spirit. Through the Spirit he was no longer shrouded or restricted to one location. We can enjoy direct communication with God anywhere, all the time. As if that were not enough, we look forward to a future we barely understand; a time when we will be interconnected with each other, creating a place where God will choose to live among us. In short, as his plan unfolds, God comes nearer and nearer to his people. His relational presence becomes more personally intense even while it expands geographically to cover the globe. He restores relationships that have been twisted and destroyed, spreading his image across the earth so that it shines more and more brightly with his glory, as he originally intended.

WILLIAM P. SMITH

JUNE 10

LUKE 19:1-10

Being with Jesus changes you. We know absolutely nothing about the conversation between Jesus and Zacchaeus during dinner. Luke records no sermon on sin, grace, and God's free gift. We're not told that Zacchaeus prayed a "sinner's prayer" ending with "in Jesus' name, amen." Not one key witnessing tool of the last century is in evidence, yet Zacchaeus suddenly confesses ways in which he had wronged people. Zacchaeus was a new man, and what made him new was his encounter with Jesus. The critical factor in Zacchaeus's renewal was not what he learned or had been taught, but whom he'd been with.

In the presence of God, Zacchaeus experienced personal, specific conviction. Yet it was not a conviction that produced despair. In his case, conviction produced salvation that changed his life. Because his heart was touched by God, caring for the people God cares for became far more precious to him than the wealth he had amassed. It's not enough to analyze your life, to reflect on what you've done wrong, or to meditate on how great God is. All those things are worthwhile, but they never substitute for actually meeting Jesus. They can pave the way to such an encounter by helping you see your need for Christ. But renewal and change grow out of being with Jesus. To put it more strongly: being with Jesus irresistibly changes you.

WILLIAM P. SMITH

JUNE 11

MATTHEW 18:21–35

When you forgive someone, you absorb the cost of the offense committed against you. You cancel the debt, and when you do, you make a three-fold promise: (1) "I will not bring up this offense again or use it against you"; (2) "I will not bring it up to others in gossip, or malign you because of it"; and (3) "I will not bring it up to myself and dwell on this offense."

Bitterness destroys the hearts and relationships of those who refuse to forgive. Jesus focuses our attention on the eternal, vertical dimension. The failure to forgive reveals an unforgiving heart and an unforgiven heart.

Peter asks, "How many times shall I forgive my brother when he sins against me? Up to seven times?" Jesus answers, "Not seven times, but seventy-seven times." When you forgive someone that is not the end of the matter. Every time you remember the offense, you must continue to forgive. When you do not understand forgiveness as both an event and a process, discouragement and guilt can set in because your decision to forgive may not immediately eradicate the hurt, lack of trust, and anger you have towards the person. But if you see forgiveness both as an event and a process, the discouragement and guilt are minimized. This awareness keeps you vigilant against the sin in your own heart. It leads you to God for his cleansing and strength when you struggle with your attitude toward the person.

TIMOTHY S. LANE

JUNE 12

PROVERBS 4

The heart oversees the "whys." Why work? Why play? Why love? Your story, your interpretations, your motivations, and your beliefs come out of your heart. This is the center of your life. It is the defining feature of humanness.

When you get to the farthest reaches of the human heart, you will find that it has everything to do with God. All life is lived *coram deo* (before the face of God). This doesn't mean that we are always *conscious* of God. Teens who violate parental commands rarely perceive their infractions as personal attacks against their parents. They are thinking, *I want to go my own way. I want independence. My disobedience is "nothing personal."*

All of life, however, is personal. At some level, all people know God (Romans 1:21). We don't just have a fuzzy idea that there is a god, gods or "higher power" out there somewhere. Within the human heart, there is a personal knowledge of the God who is, and we are either trusting him or something else. To use more religious language, we are either worshiping him, or we are worshiping idols such as pleasure, money, success, and love. Ultimately, the heart is either/or.

EDWARD T. WELCH

JUNE 13

PSALM 23

When it comes to human shepherds, few are like Philip Keller's winsome portrayal of the care and wisdom of the shepherd's craft (*A Shepherd Looks at Psalm 23*). What if any real-life shepherds you knew were ignorant laborers or drunken drifters? Or what if all you've known are storybook scenes of lambs and fair youths gamboling in green meadows? Is either picture helpful in understanding God? Does that mean that Psalm 23 is powerless to strengthen you until you know a Philip Keller-type shepherd? Of course not. Think also about the shepherds of God's flock you've known. Some people can point with joy to a "godly pastor who made such an impact on my life." But other people grew up under false teachers—greedy, willful, and arrogant men like those in Ezekiel 34. Does this mean that you can't be comforted that the Lord is a shepherd until you know a godly pastor? Ezekiel 34 and John 10 argue the opposite. God assumes we can hear comfort straight from him even if people have betrayed our trust: "I am against these evil shepherds, and I, the good shepherd, will myself come and take care of you, my flock." The existence of perversity does not make us blind to purity. Get first things first. The Holy Spirit often uses godly shepherds but he does not require them. He is powerful enough to reveal the Chief Shepherd even without noble human models.

DAVID POWLISON

JUNE 14

PSALM 28

If the Lord is near, if he is someone who knows what's on your heart, who knows what weighs heavily on you and preoccupies you, then he is a hearer of his beloved children. Many psalms start out by pleading with God—*Lord, listen to me, bend your ear, you must hear me, I need you to listen and act on my behalf.* These are not calm psalms; they are intense and pointed. In Psalm 28, David tells God that if God doesn't hear him, he will die. This is faith talking, and David talks this way because God is listening. God's listening does not guarantee that what is making you anxious will go away— that your financial problems will be solved, that you will be cured of cancer, or that whatever else is worrying you will disappear. You may not be healed, people you love may die, and you may struggle with financial stress. But God comforts, strengthens, and gives hope in the midst of the most difficult circumstances. Jesus did not want to drink the cup of God's wrath. But God strengthened him, and he was fully willing. There's help from him for whatever worries you. So when you are anxious pour your heart out to God. He is listening.

DAVID POWLISON

JUNE 15

ROMANS 13:8–14

A fall into sin develops over time, so don't downplay the daily battle that is a part of the Christian life. Every day a war is raging for your heart and affections. In any given hour of your day, there are many things that can take your gaze off of Christ. Be vigilant in the little moments of your life. This is where the battle will be won or lost. Your goal should be to cultivate a normal, regular, moment-by-moment awareness of your relationship with God and your need for his grace and power. So live wide awake. It is easy for daily life with all of its seemingly unimportant details and decisions to lull you to sleep. You start living casually because you only see the big tragedies or big decisions as the places where you need to be spiritually alert. But if you aren't vigilant moment by moment, then, when the big things come your way, you will be caught by surprise. Think of it this way: You can't be a couch potato for years, and then run a marathon. Since your heart, muscles, and lungs weren't conditioned daily, you will collapse a few blocks into the run! The same principle applies to temptation. It's important to see every moment of life as an arena for keeping in spiritual shape as you deal with little irritations and small successes. Then, when the big things come your way, you will be ready.

TIMOTHY S. LANE

JUNE 16

ROMANS 8:18–30

"Lord, I am willing." Timothy Richard in his book, *Forty-Five Years in China* (1916), wrote about a Chinese cult leader trying to accuse Christians. As evidence against them, he held up a surgical text used by some of the missionary doctors. "Ignorant of the humane objective of surgery, he regarded operations as proof of the cruelty of Christians." Suffering is God's surgery that leads to health when responded to by faith.

Do you want to see evidence of the Holy Spirit in your life? When you say, "Why bother?" answer, "Because of Jesus." Many times our lives intersect nicely with God's laws because his laws make sense. Life tends to go better when we speak the truth, forgive, love, and don't murder. But sometimes we want to go one way and God calls us to another. Or we feel paralyzed when God calls us to act. It is at those times that faith and the work of the Holy Spirit will be apparent. What will imitation or obedience look like? Since Jesus became a man, thereby giving great dignity to the ordinary activities of human life, we should expect that purpose-driven faith will look fairly ordinary. It will look like serving God and others by greeting them, asking about them, praying for them. It will be saying, "Lord, I am willing, what would you have me do today?"

EDWARD T. WELCH

June 17

How does anxiety misfire? Anxiety can serve a useful function when it alerts us to trouble and drives us to bring those troubles to God. But usually anxiety is also part of the trouble. First, we overreact to real trouble. Second, we become upset about things that ought not to trouble us. In both cases, our bad anxiety reaction reveals what is really going on in our hearts. In every situation where you feel sinfully anxious, you believe something is threatening your world. Your world feels out of control; you are afraid something bad might happen; and you are trying to control your world to keep that bad thing from taking place. How do you respond when you don't get what you want? Or when you get what you don't want? Are you full of fear, anxiety, and worry? Do you have trouble sleeping? Do you become obsessed with your problem? Does your mind go over your troubles again and again? All of these responses give you a window into your heart. They help you see which of your hopes, dreams, and wishes you have organized your life around. They tell you what it is that you believe you can't do without. They let you know which of your desires has become your master. The Bible has a very graphic phrase for those desires. It calls them the "lusts of our flesh" (Ephesians 2:3; 1 Peter 2:11 NASB).

David Powlison

JUNE 18

LUKE 15:1–7

Focus on following Christ and living in the kingdom *today*. When tomorrow comes, trust him to give you the grace you need. Such trust pleases him. Even the most doubt-ridden believer must acknowledge that God has chosen to reveal his sacrificial love as the fullest expression of his being. All Scripture is fulfilled in the gospel, the death and resurrection of Jesus Christ. Everything points to this event. It was the moment when kingdoms were realigned and human life changed. In the gospel God revealed himself as the Servant of humanity. The Father did what Abraham didn't; he sacrificed his only Son. That sacrifice effectively put an end to the entire sacrificial system.

You can't doubt that God loves at the cross. And, as God himself argues, if he demonstrated sacrificial love then, how could you think he would leave you on your own now? God argues that he did not deliver us so that we could be left to ourselves. He delivered us so that we would belong to him and receive all the benefits of being brought into God's family.

EDWARD T. WELCH

JUNE 19

1 CORINTHIANS 2

Real encouragement is more about sightedness than it is about explanation. When I talk about sightedness, I am not talking about physical eyes, but the eyes of the heart. God has given us the capacity to "see" unseen spiritual realities that are as real and vital as any physical thing we can see or touch. Spiritual sightedness is a precious gift. We get overwhelmed and discouraged in relationships not because we don't understand what is going on, but because we don't see Christ. We see the husband who barely communicates. We see the friend who has been disloyal. We see the child who rebels. We see the boss who is unrelentingly critical. We see the wife who is bitter and angry. We see the small group frozen in casual relationships. We see neighbors more concerned about boundaries than community. Our relationship problems can loom so large that they obstruct our view of the one thing that can give us the hope and courage to go on—*Christ.*

Encouragement is about giving struggling people the eyes to see an unseen Christ. He is the only hope when the call of relationship has taken me way beyond my own wisdom, strength, and character. As we live with each other in the middle of the already and the not yet, we need eyes to see this one amazing reality: we are Christ's and he is ours.

TIMOTHY S. LANE AND PAUL DAVID TRIPP

JUNE 20

COLOSSIANS 1:3–23

What God has begun, he will complete. Perhaps you are thinking, *I'm glad there is a final destination for me, but I just don't think I'm going to make it.* God never expected you to make the journey by yourself! He provides the best possible help all along the way. In Paul's words, "For in Christ all the fullness of the Deity lives in bodily form, and you have been given fullness in Christ, who is the head over every power and authority" (Colossians 2:9–10).

This fullness refers to the moment in Christ's life when the Holy Spirit descended on him like a dove. The fullness we have been given by Christ is that same Holy Spirit. God himself comes to live within us and we have everything we need to be transformed into Christ's own image. This fullness is not something we have to earn or achieve. It is already within us as a gift of his grace!

This means that spiritually, you are never empty; you are never on your own; you are never left to your own strength, resources, or wisdom. Why? You have been given the "fullness" of the Holy Spirit! What God has begun in you, he will complete. Your destiny has already been decided. The One who decided it will give you all you need to get there.

TIMOTHY S. LANE AND PAUL DAVID TRIPP

JUNE 21

EPHESIANS 2:1–10

God commands and helps us to love each other. The Bible teaches us that love is about a person—God—who is love, and we only know what real love is because he first loved us (1 John 4:16, 19). God pours his love into us, and then calls us to imitate him by loving others as he does (Romans 5:5; Ephesians 5:1–2). As those who are dearly loved by the God of the universe, it's our privilege to love others with the love we have been given.

God's love can't be earned. We are loved because of God's amazing grace that comes to us through Jesus. God saw that we were helpless to love him or others. He knew that without his love and grace we were doomed to die and be separated from him forever. So as an act of love and grace, God sent his only Son to this earth to live the perfect life we couldn't live and to die in our place for our failure to love others. All who put their trust in Jesus' life, death, and resurrection are accepted into God's family.

No one in God's family deserves to be there (Romans 3:23). We regularly violate his love and deserve his rejection. God includes us in his family only because of his grace. God calls us to love others in the same way that he loves us.

WINSTON T. SMITH

JUNE 22

GALATIANS 2:15–21

The cross changes you. From birth, each of us was under the control and dominion of sin. In his physical death, Christ broke the spiritual power and authority sin had over us. In Galatians 2:20, look at the words, "I have been crucified." The verb tense points to a definitive action in the past, with a continuing and permanent result. What Christ did then on the cross permanently alters who you are now and who you will continue to be. But Paul goes even further. He says, "I no longer live." Paul is saying that the changes inside him are so basic to who he is as a human being that it is as if he no longer lives! Yes, he is still Paul, but because of his death in Christ, he is a Paul who is utterly different at his core.

When you grasp the fundamental nature of this change within you as a believer, you will begin to grasp your true potential. You are not the same as you once were. You have been forever changed. You no longer live under the weight of the law or the domination of sin. Christ's death fulfilled the law's requirements and broke the power of sin. You do not have to give in to sin. You can live in new ways amid the same old situations, because when Christ died physically, you died spiritually. This constitutional change is permanent!

TIMOTHY S. LANE AND PAUL DAVID TRIPP

JUNE 23

GALATIANS 5:16–26

How does God respond when something important in his world is wrong? He responds redemptively. Is God angry when people act like their own god? Yes. But how did he express that anger? By sending his own Son to this broken world to be broken on the cross. He sacrificed his Son so his people can be forgiven, transformed, and restored to a right relationship with him and others. Your anger can also result in redemption. When you come to God and find forgiveness for Jesus' sake, you will be filled with God's Spirit. Because you are filled with his Spirit, it will be possible for you also to respond redemptively when you are angry.

Being filled with the Spirit means everything about you will start to resemble God. Instead of responding with sinful anger to unimportant things, you will start to see your life from God's perspective. You will begin to care about things that truly matter, instead of overreacting to relatively unimportant things. When Jesus was on earth, he was not a stoic. No one cared more than he did about the things that were wrong in this world. He cared so much that he gave his life to right those wrongs. But his upset was driven by faith and love, not by pettiness, hostility, and aggression. Becoming like God means that you will care about the things Jesus cares about—the things that truly matter in God's world.

DAVID POWLISON

JUNE 24

GENESIS 15

How strong was Abraham's faith? Genesis 15 tells us that Abraham believed that God would give him a son—he had faith—and God credited his faith as the kind of righteousness he desired. God promised to give him the land he was standing on and Abraham responded, "O Sovereign LORD, how can I know that I will gain possession of it?" This is a statement of faith in that he is talking to God. It's not outright unbelief. But it's not complete confidence either, seeing that he is asking for something to back up God's words.

God responds by making his covenant with Abraham. He didn't merely make a verbal promise; his presence passed between two rows of cut-up animals. In this vivid picture, God swore to carry out his promise or be sliced in two, just like the sacrifices. He answered Abraham's fears and faith struggles by basing his promise on his own faithfulness.

Abraham's faith was not perfect—far from it. But the covenant was never based on his perfection. It was based on God and God's perfection. Abraham believed that God would do what he said, despite his own human failings. This is our hope too. It's the confidence Paul expresses when he quotes, "If we are faithless, he will remain faithful, for he cannot disown himself."

WILLIAM P. SMITH

JUNE 25

GENESIS 3

Adam and Eve know they have ruined everything. When they rebelled against God, they attempted to hide. Notice how quickly these people, who had never experienced a negative moment with their Creator, expected an unpleasant encounter. Sin strikes quickly and dramatically at relationships!

There is almost no end to the crushing ways we handle each other's failings. Some believe it's their right to pour out their anger when another sins against them. Others run out of breath listing all the ways the person has hurt them. Others resort to ridicule, aiming to humiliate the person. We provide powerful incentives for others to run and hide rather than confess what they have done wrong.

But God is different. He doesn't swoop down on Adam and Eve and start demanding, "What were you thinking?!" He doesn't berate, badger, and interrogate them. Nor does he hold himself aloof, waiting for them to make the first move. Instead, he comes to them. They have no idea how to make things right. They're not even sure they can. God knows they're afraid, and so he comes to them.

WILLIAM P. SMITH

JUNE 26

ISAIAH 30:12–18

Seeking forgiveness is always the result of having another kingdom in view. You are owning the fact that you were not made for you. When you live for you, you forget God and his kingdom and travel outside the boundaries of his will. Not only that, but every time you ask for forgiveness from God or people, you are admitting that you are part of the massive problem that the big kingdom addresses. The golden offer of the kingdom of God is forgiveness. This is why Jesus told his disciples to preach a message of repentance as they announced the kingdom. God establishes his kingdom so that all that sin has broken can be fully and completely restored. In the center of the kingdom of God, you do not find a gargantuan palace inhabited by an unapproachable king. No, in the center of the kingdom of God is a bloody cross, on which hung a broken King, who welcomes us as we are. This King did not demand righteousness from us, for if he did, none of us would ever be qualified to live in his kingdom. No, he was righteous for us, and although he was King, he willingly took our criminal's death so that we might be forgiven. What this King demands is confession, and in the moment when we confess, we are liberated from our bondage to ourselves and freed to live for another.

PAUL DAVID TRIPP

JUNE 27

Isaiah 55

God's Word changes people dramatically. The rain that soaks the parched land always has an effect. It bathes soil, which feeds roots, which nourish plants, which produce flowers. So it is with the Word of God. It changes what it touches, producing beauty and fruitfulness in people's lives. These changes point to two wonderful realities. First, we are in fact, God's covenant children. He has promised to be our God, to be with us and to bless us. Second, these changes point us to his glory. The flowers and fruit that the rain produces give glory to the One who sent it. As we bring God's Word to one another, we re all signs pointing to his glory.

What is the hope here? It is the hope of the kingdom. The King has come and has sent his children to one another with his life-changing Word. People who were lost find their way; people once paralyzed with discouragement walk in hope; alienated people live in community as broken relationships are restored; confused minds think in ways that are true, pure, and right; and the person who once lived for his own power now rests in God's. God's rain waters the roots of the heart, and the person's life bursts forth with new fruitfulness. This is the way of the Lord, the hope and work of his kingdom.

Paul David Tripp

JUNE 28

JAMES 4:1–10

When two people have conflict, it's easy to see the war on the outside. But James points out that this war is an outgrowth of a war inside each person's heart. Desires are not being met, so people lash out in an attempt to satisfy those desires. In verse 4, James goes even further. He says that people engaging in ungodly conflict have already begun to worship someone or something other than God. They are guilty of spiritual adultery, which is another way to describe idolatry. The person is giving himself to a false lover.

This simple yet profound explanation of why we do what we do can have a radical impact on a person's life. It is radical because understanding our heart's idolatry opens the door for us to appropriate and apply the gospel. We have finally gotten to the root of things; we are no longer floating on the surface. We know that God is committed to reclaiming our hearts through the work of Christ and the Holy Spirit.

"Purify your hearts," says James. Look at what you've allowed to become more attractive to you than the Lord. "Wash your hands," he continues. Exchange your sinful responses for godly ones. It is all by grace, but that does not mean we are passive! Christian growth is warfare.

TIMOTHY S. LANE AND PAUL DAVID TRIPP

JUNE 29

MATTHEW 13:1–23

It's easy to think that our faith is strong when things are going well. But it's the troubles of life that expose what's really in our hearts. Jesus explained this in the parable of the sower. When the seed (the Word of God) lands on rocky ground (our hearts) it grows quickly, but its roots are not deep. The shallow root of faith is exposed when "trouble or persecution comes because of the word" (Matthew 13:21). Then the plant of faith quickly withers and dies. Suffering teaches us to depend on Jesus. Jesus, when tempted by Satan in the same way as the Israelites (in the desert, famished after fasting forty days, and urged to provide food for himself), responded by quoting Deuteronomy 8:3: "Man does not live on bread alone but on every word that comes from the mouth of the Lord" (Matthew 4:4). When Jesus responded with perfect faith and perfect trust even as he suffered, he passed the test of faith not just for himself, but for all who put their faith in him. So don't be discouraged when suffering in your life exposes your unbelieving heart. Instead, confess your lack of faith to Jesus and ask him to fill you with himself. He promises to forgive you and to pour his Spirit into you so you can respond faithfully in the middle of suffering and temptation (John 14:26; Acts 2:38; 1 John 1:9).

WILLIAM P. SMITH

JUNE 30

MATTHEW 5:1–12

Keep going to Jesus. As you grow in wisdom and self-control, you will become part of a constructive solution instead of a destructive force that makes things worse. Jesus said, "Blessed are the peacemakers" [not the peace lovers or peacekeepers who always avoid conflicts] (Matthew 5:9). God uses his sense of justice and fairness to make peace with us, and then teaches us to make peace with each other.

Every time you are angry, ask: What was happening when I got angry? How did I act? What were my expectations? Then remind yourself of God's love and mercy to you. As you keep going to Jesus, you will notice that real change is happening. Your willingness to be mastered by Jesus and to make following him your first priority will allow you to imitate him in expressing your anger in a redemptive way. Then your conflicts won't end with slammed doors, hurt silences, and sharing others' sins. Instead, there will be a constructive back-and-forth that is colored by mercy and a desire for each of you to grow in God's image. Your real, living relationship with the God who loves you to the uttermost will allow you to grow in having real human relationships, where the conflicts you have will become an opportunity for growth, understanding, and expressing the fruit of the Spirit.

DAVID POWLISON

JULY 1

PROVERBS 18

Autonomy is closely linked to arrogance. They are both expressions of human pride, but autonomy suggests that we want to be *separate from* more than *over*. We want to establish the rules rather than submit to the lordship of the living God. This was the essence of Adam's original sin. We want to interpret the world according to *our* system of thought. We want to establish our own parallel universe, separate from God's. One popular expression of autonomy is American deism. Deism acknowledges God, but it believes that he is far off, too preoccupied to be involved in daily affairs. Its mottoes are "God helps those who help themselves" and similar principles that avoid trust or faith as the primary human response to God. In deism we can settle the frontier without anyone meddling in our business. God says you are forgiven in Christ, yet you create new rules that mandate contrition, penance, and self-loathing. If God says he loves you, you insist it is impossible. There it is: your system is higher than God's.

The way out of autonomy begins with a simple prayer. "Lord, teach me. I want to think like you." Just think what it would be like to be certain that the God of the universe loved you.

EDWARD T. WELCH

JULY 2

PSALM 25

You must turn to God for help if your wrong anger patterns are going to change. Turn to the God who loves you and tell him all about what is making you angry. Name your suffering, your expectations, your desires, your sins, and all the evil you see and do, and bring yourself to the one who suffered and died for you. In your honest conversation with God, use the Psalms. God has given us the Psalms so we have many different ways of talking with God about the things that really matter to us. Some psalms speak to God about our sins: e.g., Psalms 32 and 51. Other psalms speak about suffering injustice at the hands of others: e.g., Psalms 10 and 31. And many psalms speak of both: e.g., Psalms 25 and 119. All the psalms speak of God and reveal what he is like, what we need from him, and how we express love for him. The Psalms are poetic, but they are not poetry; they are living examples given to teach us how to talk honestly with God about things that matter. Your relationship with a living person is what sets the Bible's approach to anger apart from self-help books, medications, and mind control. Being in relationship with the living God is what will gradually change your anger from destructive to constructive.

DAVID POWLISON

JULY 3

PSALM 55

God wants to hear *you*. He wants you to direct your cries and fears to him. Does that seem impossible? If so, he will help you to find the words. Psalm 55 can get you started: "My heart is in anguish within me; the terrors of death assail me. Fear and trembling have beset me; horror has overwhelmed me. I said, 'Oh, that I had the wings of a dove! I would fly away and be at rest—I would flee far away and stay in the desert; I would hurry to my place of shelter, far from the tempest and storm.'" (Psalm 55:4–8)

Psalm 55 has given a voice to human betrayal for centuries. If the words fit your experience, then you are now part of a much larger body of people who have sung this psalm and made it their own. One person in particular leads the singing. Yes, King David wrote this psalm, but he wrote it on behalf of the perfect King who was to come after him. It is Jesus' psalm, and they are his words you're sharing in. He was the innocent victim of evil people. He was betrayed, tortured, and suffered a terrible death at their hands. To be part of his chorus, all you have to do is follow him. Indeed, you are not alone.

EDWARD T. WELCH

JULY 4

PSALM 71

How can you deal with a painful experience? God, in the Bible, doesn't offer you platitudes and pat answers. He gives you something much better—in response to your sorrow, your emotions, and your unanswered questions, he gives you himself. Edith Schaeffer once used a tapestry metaphor to talk about the difficult things in life. She pointed out that the front of the tapestry was a beautiful pattern, but the back was a mass of knots and tangled threads. Your painful experience is one of the tangled and knotted areas on the back of your tapestry. No matter how long you look at it, you won't be able to make sense out of it. This is one of life's broken, dark experiences in which you must find that the promises and presence of your God and Savior are real. In the midst of this grave darkness, God calls you to live a life where faith and love still shine. One day, you will see the front side of the tapestry, instead of just the tangled back. One part of the beauty of the tapestry will be the way you learn to know God and love others by going through difficult experiences.

DAVID POWLISON

JULY 5

PSALM 88

Psalm 88 is a song. Why would God ever want his people to sing such a discouraging dirge? What would be the point of putting, "The darkness is my closest friend" to music? This is where the psalm becomes most encouraging!

Psalm 88 is a song of the sons of Korah. The Korahites were the doorkeepers of the tabernacle, those who led Israel in procession to the tent of worship and sacrifice. This mournful song was one of the songs they would sing! Do you see what this means? God intended the darkest human laments to be brought together with the brightest human hopes. Honest expressions of fear, pain, and doubt were welcome in the place of worship, atonement, and forgiveness. The mess of human misery was welcomed into the place of mysterious, glorious grace. No psalm more powerfully communicates, "Come to me as you are, with all your doubt and fear, pain and discouragement. Hold before me your shattered hopes and dreams, and find redemption and rest when it seems there is none to be found. Don't hesitate because your heart is weak and your mind confused. Don't hesitate because you have questioned my goodness and love. Come as you are, for my sacrifice is for you, just as you are."

TIMOTHY S. LANE AND PAUL DAVID TRIPP

JULY 6

REVELATION 3:14–22

Honest self-examination and repentance enable you to see your neighbor better. If ungodly ruling desires blind you to your neighbor (James 4:2), a pure heart will bring that same neighbor back to your mind's eye. Whenever God enables us to reorient ourselves vertically toward him, according to the first great commandment (love your God with all your heart), we are then more likely to obey the second great commandment (love your neighbor) as well.

For example, in 1 Peter 3:7–8 Peter is encouraging husbands to love their wives. The application is specific to husbands, but he then applies the principle to all believers. Peter calls husbands to live with their wives with consideration. The best way to translate this powerful word is to use the metaphor of living in the other person's shoes or skin. Peter is urging husbands to live with their wives in such a way that they know what it must feel like for their wives to be married to them!

In light of this passage, it is clear that a key ingredient to godly conflict is to understand the other person.

TIMOTHY S. LANE

JULY 7

ROMANS 6:15–23

God's holiness should startle us. All disobedience is personal. Our sin is not just against God's law; it is against God. Any time we stray away from the kingdom of God, whether by following our own desires, following other gods, or imitating the Father of Lies, we provoke the jealous God to anger. His anger will accept only death as the appropriate penalty for treason (Deuteronomy 6:14–15).

When we complain, we hold him in contempt. The white lies we tell are against the God of truth. The anger we display is murderous toward others and stands in judgment of God himself. And it is not just what we do that is so serious; it is also what we don't do. We don't love God and neighbor with our whole heart. In our spiritual indifference we can go for days thinking that our personal interests are paramount; that is, we forget God. When there is persistent sin, there is no fear of God (Romans 3:18).

For all this, the wrath of God is poured out. It will fall on us, if we insist on living in the anti-God kingdom and trust in ourselves, or it falls on Jesus. Either way, the wages of sin is death.

EDWARD T. WELCH

JULY 8

1 Corinthians 2:6–16

God spoke to Adam and Eve immediately upon creating them. This mundane moment was a moment of transcendence! The Lord, King, and Creator of the universe was speaking the secrets of his divine wisdom into the ears of the people he had made. In this act God was calling Adam and Eve to transcend the boundaries of their own thoughts, interpretations, and experiences. They were to form their lives by the origin-to-destiny perspective that only the Creator could have. God had hardwired Adam and Eve with the communicative abilities that they would need in order to receive his revelation, because the glorious truths that God would progressively unfold to them were meant to shape everything they thought, desired, decided, and did. By themselves they never could have discovered the things he told them. These treasures of wisdom would only be known by Adam and Eve because God decided to reveal them. God's words contained knowledge of him, the meaning and purpose of life, a moral structure for living, the nature of human identity, a fundamental human job description, a call to human community, and a call to divine worship. Never were Adam and Eve built to exist on conclusions drawn from their experience, or concepts resulting from autonomous interpretations. Every thought was meant to be shaped by the truth glory that he would patiently and progressively impart to them.

PAUL DAVID TRIPP

JULY 9

1 JOHN 5:1–12

At the center of the kingdom is the King; and therefore the center of kingdom living is a deep, abiding,
life-shaping affection for the King. This one central love
fuels everything else we are meant to pursue as we exit
the narrow confines of our self-defined kingdoms and
begin to enjoy life in the kingdom of God. We are simply meant to be madly in love with Christ. He is meant
to be the thing that occupies our minds and fills our
hearts. He is meant to be what excites us and brings us
joy. He is to be the One whom we are living to please.
You really will expand your life to the size of the kingdom of God when you heart is absolutely captured by
this one central romance.

At its core, life in the big kingdom is not so much
about pursuing a thing; it is about pursuing a person. It
is about having the eyes of my heart focused on Christ.
It is about a soul that is filled with appreciation and
brimming with affection. It is walking around astound-
ed that he would place his affection on me and even
receive my flawed love. It is living with the hope that
someday we will no longer be separated; someday I will
be united to him and live with him forever.

PAUL DAVID TRIPP

JULY 10

2 CORINTHIANS 5:11–21

Jesus lived and died so that "those who live should no longer live for themselves but for him who died for them and was raised again" (2 Corinthians 5:15). God's love comes into your life to change what you live for.

Peter puts it this way: "That . . . you may participate in the divine nature and escape the corruption in the world caused by evil desires" (2 Peter 1:4). We all want the wrong things, but God is in the business of changing what we want. Everything you ever say or do is the result of some kind of desire. The change Peter talks about is change at the most fundamental level. Peter says that God works to replace my sinful, selfish nature with his divine nature! God reshapes me into his own image. Amid all of life's confusion, he transforms my heart so that I can think, desire, speak, and act in ways consistent with who he is and what he is doing on earth. Positive personal change takes place when my dreams of change line up with God's purposes for change. As I leave behind goals of personal comfort and self-fulfillment, I reach out for Christ. I want to be more like him each day. As I do, I become more prepared for my ultimate destination, eternity with him.

TIMOTHY S. LANE AND PAUL DAVID TRIPP

JULY 11

COLOSSIANS 3:1–17

"Be humble, gentle, patient, bearing with one another in love" (Ephesians 4:2). Note that these are character qualities before they are actions toward others. Humility enables us to see our own sin before we focus on the sin and weaknesses of another. A gentle person is not weak, but someone who uses his strength to empower others. A patient person is someone who places the needs of others higher than, or at the same level as, his own. He doesn't come with a self-centered agenda. A forbearing person is someone who does all this even when provoked. In other words, people who are patient and forbearing are humble and gentle even when they are provoked or when the investment they have made in a relationship turns sour. Do you love people with limits that are driven by your own perceived needs or interests? Do others feel as if they must always return a favor to keep you happy with them?

These character qualities create a climate of grace for relationships. Usually, relationships are governed by a structure of law, offense, and punishment. I have a set of rules you must abide by. I am watching to make sure you follow these rules. If you don't, I feel justified in meting out some form of punishment. This is a contradiction of the gospel, and it prevents the glory and worth of God's grace from showing itself in your relationships.

TIMOTHY S. LANE AND PAUL DAVID TRIPP

JULY 12

EPHESIANS 4:1–16

Our purpose is to get what we want, but God's purpose is to give us what we really need. Paul argues that our relationships are valuable because God has a purpose for them. Whenever we try to give our relationships purpose, we become impatient, frustrated, and exploitative. And since we are all sinners, we will always thwart each other's purposes. This dynamic begins to reveal why God has put us in relationships. God ultimately wants us to mature, to be built up, and to stop acting like infants. He wants the things that ruled Christ's heart to rule ours as well.

We think things are going well only if we are getting along with others. But God says that it is also when we are not getting along with others that he is accomplishing his purposes! For example, if you quit at the first sign of fatigue when you exercise, you miss the chance to become more fit. Exercise after exhaustion is the most efficient and productive time for physical fitness. This is true of relationships as well. God has designed our relationships to function as both a diagnosis and a cure. When we are frustrated and ready to give up, God is at work, revealing the places where we have given in to a selfish agenda (the diagnosis). He then uses that new awareness to help us grow precisely where we have struggled (the cure).

TIMOTHY S. LANE AND PAUL DAVID TRIPP

JULY 13

EXODUS 31:13–16

Slow down and rest: God commands it. In fact, resting is so important that it is the fourth of the Ten Commandments (Exodus 20:8–10). The word *Sabbath* comes from the Hebrew word for "ceasing" or "stopping." Have you ever wondered why God thinks that having a day of "stopping" is so important? The first instance of Sabbath features God himself resting. In the opening chapter of Genesis, God creates everything that exists in six days. And "God blessed the seventh day and made it holy, because on it he rested from all the work of creating that he had done" (Genesis 2:3). In some ways this seems natural enough; after all, God had just created everything! But every act of creation required nothing more of God than a spoken word. God isn't toiling in sweat and anguish—just the opposite. Every creative act began with a word and ended with the pronouncement, "And God saw that it was good." God effortlessly creates and orders all things to be beautiful reflections of his glory and power. His day of rest is a demonstration of his absolute mastery and the happy obedience of his creation. God's rest isn't a picture of tiredness, but a display of his absolute sovereignty.

WINSTON T. SMITH

JULY 14

LUKE 6:27–36

God delights in showing mercy even to those who offend him deeply. His forgiving mercies extend from east to west (Psalm 103:12). He mercifully saves us despite our unrighteous deeds. His mercies are new every morning (Lamentations 3:23).

At the final judgment we will all want God's mercy. We don't want to stand before him on our own merits. James says, "Judgment without mercy will be shown to anyone who has not been merciful. Mercy triumphs over judgment!" (James 2:13). Mercy always marks the godly person. "He has showed you, O man, what is good. And what does the LORD require of you? To act justly and to love mercy and to walk humbly with your God" (Micah 6:8). The godly person loves mercy. He is a merciful person, like God, his Father: "Be merciful, just as your Father is merciful" (Luke 6:36).

Shakespeare's heroine Portia understands this as she entreats the evil Shylock to spare the life of Antonio: "The quality of mercy is not strained. It droppeth as the gentle rain from heaven. . . . It is twice blest: It blesseth him that gives and him that takes. . . . It is an attribute of God himself " (*The Merchant of Venice,* Act IV, Scene 1). Extending mercy toward our enemies brings blessing both to those we forgive and to us who extend it. As our Lord Jesus said, "Blessed are the merciful, for they will be shown mercy" (Matthew 5:7).

ROBERT D. JONES

JULY 15

MATTHEW 16:21–28

Our love of self shapes everything we do and say from the earliest age. If we were really honest, many of us would say that we would be completely satisfied living our own lives for the sake of our own selves. But Christ asks us to do something unthinkable. He asks us to be willing to say "no" to the one person we have the most trouble saying no to—us!

Essentially Christ is saying, "If you want to live, if you want to experience the transcendent joys of my eternal kingdom, then you must let go of your hold on your life. You must loosen your grip and with open hands give your life back to me." Ask yourself: "Am I following Christ's call where I live and work?" Well, think of your life as an investment. Every day each of us invests our time, money, gifts, talents, energies, re- lationships, and resources in the pursuit of something. Is your life invested in pursuing your life? Does it have a higher goal than your personal wants and needs? Do you find it hard to say "no" to you? Do you find yourself struggling with irritation, impatience, and anger when others unwittingly get in the way of what you want? Are you still holding tightly onto your life as if it really did belong to you?

PAUL DAVID TRIPP

JULY 16

MATTHEW 6:25–34

Christ says something radical here: you cannot reduce your life down to simply making sure all of your needs are met. Then he says, "Your life is more important than that!" You see, I was not created to shrink the size of my life to the size of my felt needs. If true humanity is bound up in community with God and godly community with others, I will never experience it when all my eyes ever see is my own need.

This way of living is always riddled with anxiety and fear. I will never be able to control all the things that need to be controlled in order for me to guarantee that all of my needs will be met. When I carry the meeting of my own needs as the most dominant focus of my living, I will always struggle with the anxiety that comes from the realization of how small the circle of my control actually is.

But there is another thing that happens here. The more I focus on my needs, the more things in life get loaded into that category. The more I live with the meeting of my needs as my central focus of concern, the more things in my life get defined as needs.

PAUL DAVID TRIPP

JULY 17

PSALM 119:49–56

Suffering is used by God to make us more like him (Romans 8:28ff). God uses suffering to expose our hearts, to teach us to depend only on him, and to train us in faith. How does that happen? Suffering shows us what is in our hearts. Consider what happened long ago when Moses led the people of Israel out of Egypt. They were at the edge of Canaan, the land God had promised them, but they didn't believe God was going to help them conquer the land. Because they doubted God, he allowed them to spend the next forty years wandering in the wilderness. When the Israelites were on the verge of entering Canaan for a second time, Moses explained their wilderness suffering by telling them that God brought them into the wilderness to humble them and to reveal what was in their hearts (Deuteronomy 8:2–3). When they were hungry, would they grumble and complain? Or would they rely on God to care for them and supply their needs? Suffering exposes our hearts in just the same way. Do we trust God, or is our hope in the good things he has given us? Suffering burns away self-deception by making us aware of what we turn to apart from Jesus to make our lives work the way we want. As we suffer, we find out if our faith in God is genuine.

WILLIAM P. SMITH

JULY 18

PSALM 121

Christ's grace and truth comes through God's word. Something that God is, says, and does must invade your struggles to teach and master you. What about God in Christ do you need today? The map-giver personally guides you through the dark woods. You need help, and the Lord is a very present help in trouble. You can't make it without grace to help in your time of need.

The first beatitude on essential poverty, need, and weakness comes first for a reason: We need what God gives. We need our Father to give the Holy Spirit to us, so that Christ dwells in our hearts by faith, and so that the love of God is poured out within us right when the heat is on. Augustine summarized the immediacy of grace this way: "Give what you command and command what you will." Some part of the good news of the Lord's redemptive purposes, will, and promise is absolutely necessary—right now. A good theology book rightly asks, Who is God? and goes on to fill 400 pages with truths. But Psalm 121 cries out, "Where does my help come from?", and seizes on one necessary thing: "The LORD keeps me."

DAVID POWLISON

JULY 19

PSALM 22

How did Jesus face death? Was he calm and unaffected? No, he experienced death as a terrible enemy. On the cross he cried out words from Psalm 22: "My God, my God, why have you forsaken me?" (Psalm 22:1; Matthew 27:46). Jesus lived out this psalm of death and torture on the cross. But this is also a psalm of hope: "For he has not despised or disdained the suffering of the afflicted one; he has not hidden his face from him but has listened to his cry for help" (Psalm 22:24). Jesus' cry of desolation and forsakenness was in the light of his certain hope that God does not finally forsake those who are afflicted.

Jesus was not a stoic as he died. He looked death right in the eye, felt keenly its pain, degradation, horror, and loss, and then trusted his heavenly Father as he said, "Into your hands I commit my spirit" (Psalm 31:5; Luke 23:46). These words are not calm, cool, and collected. They are the words of a man who is fully engaged with his troubles, fully engaged with his God, and bringing the two together in honest neediness and honest gratitude. The two sides of faith—the need and the joy—are both present in Jesus' experience.

DAVID POWLISON

JULY 20

PSALM 27

Light is a good thing in Scripture. Bad things lurk in shadows, but the light exposes them and they flee. God's first creative act was to command light to come into the world. When we are fearful or worried, we feel like we are walking in a dark place that is known to be dangerous. Into this vulnerable place comes the God who is light, and the light penetrates everything. Light means life, truth, the banishment of evil.

"My salvation" could also be translated "my victory" or "my deliverance." It summarizes all of God's victories. With Egypt, it was the strongest army on earth on one side and unarmed slaves on the other. With Midian, it was an army "thick as locusts" with innumerable camels against 300 unarmed men (Judges 7:12). God likes his people to be outnumbered because then there is no mistaking that he alone is the Deliverer.

"My stronghold" evokes images of a safe place. While David was on the run from Saul, he had a particular stronghold in the wilderness that was impregnable. There he was safe. Here he confesses his deeper insight into the nature of strongholds: any safe place is a sign pointing to The Stronghold. His wilderness lair was safe only because God was there. Armed with this knowledge of God, David could look back and remember times of God-wrought deliverance. He could look forward with confidence to the battles he would inevitably face.

EDWARD T. WELCH

JULY 21

PSALM 37:1–11

Anxiety is like a red warning light on the car dashboard that tells you there is a problem, but doesn't tell you exactly what the problem is. Anxiety points to a real problem. Ask God to show you the problem underlying your anxiety. Then bring that problem to him and ask him to help you trust him with all the big and small things that are troubling you. Ask him to show you what you are trusting in instead of him, and ask for his forgiveness. Dare to believe in the forgiveness of sins and that God's good care of you is constant through all of your very real troubles. Then decide what small act of love God is calling you to do today, and take a step of faith and do that one small thing. Your goal is not a bland, "no-worries" way of handling life. When you read a passage like Philippians 4:6 that says, "Do not be anxious about anything," you might think that God is telling you to never become agitated or emotional. But in that same letter, Paul talks about being intensely anxious for the welfare of those he loves (Philippians 2:25–28). So there is a right kind of anxiety that's actually an expression of love and faith. You are not looking for an anxiety-free life, but for a life where you, minute-by-minute, cast all your cares on him who cares for you (1 Peter 5:7).

DAVID POWLISON

JULY 22

PSALM 42

Suffering advances the purposes of God in the lives of his people and his kingdom. Take Joseph for example. His brothers sold him into slavery and he was taken to Egypt where he suffered terribly. Yet years later he was able to feed his family during a famine. When he met his brothers after many years, they worried that he would pay them back for what they did. But Joseph told his brothers not to be afraid. He said, "You intended to harm me, but God intended it for good" (Genesis 50:20).

All the things Joseph suffered weren't just about making him a better man. He suffered so his family could survive, so they could find shelter in Egypt, so that years later they could become a nation and eventually have their own land. He suffered so that even later the Messiah could come to fulfill God's promise of a Redeemer (Genesis 3:15). In a very real way, what Joseph endured, he endured for you.

Suffering is also a strong reminder that God's kingdom is not of this world, and this earth is not our home. Suffering helps us to consider ourselves as strangers and aliens on this earth waiting for a better home. Why does God let bad things happen to you? That you might know him, be like him, and be a part of his kingdom going forward. That's not a completely satisfying answer, but it's not a bad start either.

WILLIAM P. SMITH

PSALM 71

His refuge, his hope, his confidence, and the object of his delight and praise are some of the words the psalmist uses to describe God. Now ask yourself: Where do you take refuge? Who is *your* rescuer and deliverer? Into whose ear do *you* speak when you need help? A best friend? A neighbor? Your spouse? Do any of these substitute for seeking help from God himself? Maybe your refuge is not a who, but a what. Do you look for refuge in "harmless" distractions—books, TV shows, work? These things are not bad in themselves, but they become bad when they function as gods in your life, preventing you from knowing and loving God.

Where do you place your hope and confidence? What fills you with excitement and joy so that you burn to tell others about it? Where do you go for wisdom and knowledge? If you honestly examine yourself can you say that God fills all of those roles? Are you loving him with your entire being?

This understanding of worship exposes us all as worshipers who have gone astray. Even the atheist places faith in something. Everyone has answers to the questions that Psalm 71 raises. The question is not whether or not you will worship; the question is who or what you will worship.

WINSTON T. SMITH

July 24

Psalm 88

God doesn't prescribe a happy life. Depression is a form of suffering that can't be reduced to one universal cause. This means that family and friends can't rush in armed with THE answer. Instead, they must be willing to postpone swearing allegiance to a particular theory, and take time to know the depressed person and work together with him or her. What we do know is that depression is painful and, if you have never experienced it, hard to understand. Like most forms of suffering, it feels private and isolating.

It is common for spiritually mature men and women who feel depressed to think that they are doing something wrong. After all, Scripture is filled with words of joy and happy hearts. When they aren't feeling happy, they feel that they must be missing something or that God is punishing them until they learn some hidden lesson. On earth, however, God doesn't prescribe a happy life. He doesn't legislate emotions. Look at some of the Psalms. They are written by people of great faith, yet they run the emotional gamut. This one even ends with "darkness is my closest friend" (Psalm 88:18). When your emotions feel muted or always low, when you are unable to experience the highs and lows you once did, the important question is, "Where do you turn—or, to whom do you turn?"

EDWARD T. WELCH

REVELATION 4

It's not just about being thankful for his provision, for fellowship, sound teaching, and worthwhile causes to give my energies to. No, central to big kingdom living is being thankful for *him*; for *his* presence, *his* forgiveness, *his* patience, *his* mercy, *his* gentleness, *his* wisdom, *his* compassion, *his* companionship, *his* kindness, and *his* love. Big kingdom living is about feeling incredibly blessed, not just because of the physical things, the beneficial circumstances, and the many people who have been placed in my life, but feeling blessed because of him. I cannot believe that he would love me! I cannot believe that the King of kings, the Creator, the Savior, and the Ruler of the universe would ever desire to be my friend. And I live with grateful amazement at the lengths to which he went to have this love relationship with me. It is this one central romance that gives motivation and direction to every other good thing that defines what it means to live for God's kingdom and glory. And when your heart is not captured by this love, no matter how many external Christian pursuits you are giving yourself to, you are still actually living in the little kingdom.

PAUL DAVID TRIPP

JULY 26

ROMANS 5:12–6:7

A Hebrew was always part of a larger group. What happened to the patriarch of the clan happened to you. You were united with him. If he suffered shame, so did you. If he won a victory, it was on your behalf. It would be as if you yourself had won.

In a similar but even more profound way, Christ is our new Patriarch or King. Our previous head was Adam (Romans 5:12–21). His death was our own. All the good things we could possibly do were not enough to loose us from his legacy of condemnation. Only a new head, who demonstrated a new obedience and who died but could not be held down by death, could give us a death that leads to life.

What Jesus experienced, we too experience. If he is honored, we are honored. If he dies, we die. Therefore, the apostle Paul can say that we died. We died to our old master. We died to the reign of sin. We died to the way of life of the old kingdom. "I have been crucified with Christ and I no longer live, but Christ lives in me. The life I live in the body, I live by faith in the Son of God, who loved me and gave himself for me" (Galatians 2:20).

EDWARD T. WELCH

JULY 27

1 JOHN 3:11–24

Eternity will be better than the present, most people believe. This, of course, is true for those who hope for Jesus' return. When we see Jesus, "there will be no more death or mourning or crying or pain" (Revelation 21:4). But there is something that is arguably even better. Therefore, if you are going to look forward to the gifts God gives us when we see him face to face, hope for this: when we see Jesus, we will no longer be people who sin (1 John 3:3).

Yes, that is what is better. Think of it. We will love God perfectly. We will love others without reservation. We will think less often of ourselves and delight in the fact that eternity is about God and not us. We will be thrilled by the fact that God's glory is on display for all his people to see. Being pain-free will be no more than a pleasant realization that occasionally sneaks into our awareness. Given a choice, a sinless eternity with the loving God is much preferred over a pain-free one where sin still bedevils. Be certain to incorporate this into your story. You are becoming what you were intended to be—a sinless child of the Most High God.

EDWARD T. WELCH

JULY 28

1 PETER 4

God understands suffering. When your life falls apart—your husband dies, your wife cheats on you, you lose your job, your children reject you, your parents disown you, you become ill, or any other hard thing happens—you want someone in the universe to hear how difficult your struggle is and affirm that you are not crazy or wrong to feel so much anguish. God does see and hear your suffering. His eyes and ears are peculiarly tuned into it (Genesis 16:7–14; Exodus 2:23–25). We see this most clearly when we consider Jesus. While he lived among us he experienced undeserved deprivation, ridicule, cruelty, and then suffered unimaginable physical and emotional pain as he died on the cross for us. Because God knows suffering firsthand, we can't say to him, "You don't know what this feels like!" The Bible tells us that Jesus is a man of sorrows, who is well acquainted with grief (Isaiah 53). He knows more about suffering than anyone else ever has or ever will. And he cares enough to do something about it, though it's often not what you might first expect or want. He comes near to us, and in his presence we are revived to withstand what we're enduring.

WILLIAM P. SMITH

JULY 29

1 TIMOTHY 2:1–6

All intercessors needed an intercessor. In the Old Testament, God-appointed intercessors all had their own shortcomings. They, too, needed someone to intercede for them. Nothing captures God's combined desire and disappointment better than Ezekiel 22:30: "I looked for a man . . . who would . . . stand before me in the gap on behalf of the land so I would not have to destroy it, but I found none." God did not delight in destroying his people. He longed for someone to intercede for them. But he did not find the person who could satisfy that longing until Jesus. In him, God supplies all we need.

This is far more than a well-meaning counselor sending up a quick prayer. This is not a friend who asked for your help last week with his own sins. This is Jesus, the Father's own Son. This is the Chosen One who functions now in his ordained role before the Father. Do you think his intercession will be fruitless? Do you think that somehow his prayers for you to turn from sin to holiness and fellowship with him will not be answered? That won't happen. It cannot! You will rise again from the ruin you make of your life and one day you will see Jesus. He intercedes for you so that you are not destroyed. You will be brought into the Promised Land.

WILLIAM P. SMITH

JULY 30

2 CORINTHIANS 1:3–11

We too will find ourselves in situations that seem far beyond our ability to endure. Maybe problems in our church have left us overwhelmed. Perhaps finances are a trial. Maybe parenting has left you feeling exhausted and inadequate. Maybe living a godly life in a godless workplace seems like an impossible calling. Or maybe you feel defeated by soured family relationships. Where do you feel like you are beyond your ability to endure? The Bible speaks into just that kind of experience. God enters our stories with the hope of Christ and shows us where we are and where we need to go.

You and I do not have to be lost in the middle of our own stories. We do not have to wonder how we got where we are and how we will get where we need to be. You can know exactly what Christ has provided so that you can live as he has called you to live. As he did with Paul, God meets us and changes us in the middle of life's challenges. The heat may not go away. In fact, it may get hotter! Yet we are never alone. God is with us to provide the grace we need to face what he calls us to face.

TIMOTHY S. LANE AND PAUL DAVID TRIPP

JULY 31

2 PETER 1:3–9

Our acceptance into the family of God is not the end of God's work in us, but the beginning. God has not called us to a life of "I have spiritually arrived" or "I am just waiting for heaven." Rather, he calls us to a life of constant work, constant growth, and constant confession and repentance. Making us holy is God's unwavering agenda until we are taken home to be with him. He will do whatever he needs to produce holiness in us. He wants us to be a community of joy, but he is willing to compromise our temporal happiness in order to increase our Christlikeness.

Any time we find ourselves in difficulty or trial, it is easy to think we have been forgotten or rejected by God. This is because we do not understand the present process. God is not working for our comfort and ease; he is working on our growth. At the very moment we are tempted to question his faithfulness, he is fulfilling his redemptive promises to us. After all, it's not like there are only some people who really need to change. Change is the norm for everyone, and God is always at work to complete this process in us.

TIMOTHY S. LANE AND PAUL DAVID TRIPP

AUGUST 1

GALATIANS 6:12–18

Never a day goes by when we do not fail to do what Christ has enabled us to do. Despite all of the gifts flowing from our union with Christ, sin still remains in us. That's the reason you need to know that Jesus has broken the power of sin—because its presence still remains! We should not be shocked that the war still rages inside us. We have been changed, we have been empowered, but we have not yet been perfected.

What do you do when you sin and fail? Do you excuse and rationalize? Do you wallow in self-defeating guilt and regret? The cross calls you away from both responses. It gives you the freedom to admit your sin and repent. It is impossible for your sin to shock the One who died because of it. The cross also gives you the freedom to seek and receive forgiveness each time you fall. We do not have to carry the sins Christ took on himself. He paid the price we could not pay so that we would never have to pay it again. When you fail, keep Jesus and his work in view. Run to your Lord, not away from him. Receive his forgiveness and follow him once more, knowing that each time you fail, you can experience your identity as one for whom Christ died.

TIMOTHY S. LANE AND PAUL DAVID TRIPP

August 2

What did the Serpent hold out to Adam and Eve that was attractive enough for them to consider stepping away from the one central thing for which they were made? He offered them an *independent* glory—autonomy. If they would just step out on their own, they could be transcendent beings like God.

The quest for autonomy will always crush transcendence. Rather than the huge glories of living for the glory of God, I end up with little shadow glories filling the dim cubicle of my own glory. As 2 Corinthians 5:15 makes clear, human beings were never meant to "live for themselves." So, when Jesus touches me with his rescuing grace, he is freeing me from my bondage to me!

Since that horrible moment in the garden, every human being has tended to confuse autonomy with transcendence. The inertia of sin is always away from the Creator and toward ourselves. As long as sin still dwells in our hearts, autonomy will war with transcendence. We are quite able to shrink the transcendent promises, glories, and hopes of the gospel to the size of our own lives, forgetting that, by God's grace, we have been rescued from our self-constructed cubicle and welcomed to the vast expansiveness of the kingdom of God. One day the war between independence and transcendence will end, and we will live in glory, with glory, forever.

PAUL DAVID TRIPP

August 3

If we learn to cry out to God for help and depend on him for everything when we suffer, then God will use our suffering to train our faith. God did this for the Israelites as they wandered in the wilderness. When the next generation stood poised to enter Canaan, they had even more reason to doubt God's promises than their parents: Canaan was full of cities and armies that were bigger and stronger than they were forty years before, and Moses, the only leader they had ever known, wasn't going with them. Yet the Israelites responded faithfully. They had allowed their hardships to train them in godliness (Deuteronomy 8:5; Hebrews 12:4–11). Instead of doubting God, they lived with confidence in his promises. Through many hard experiences they had found that it was true that "man does not live on bread alone but on every word that comes from the mouth of the Lord" (Deuteronomy 8:3). How has God used suffering in your life to train you in faith? Are you learning to live by "every word that comes from the mouth of the Lord?"

William P. Smith

AUGUST 4

ISAIAH 43:14–25

All of Scripture points to the forgiveness of sins through Jesus Christ. "All the prophets testify about him that everyone who believes in him receives forgiveness of sins through his name" (Acts 10:43). God is never silent. He always speaks to you with words of invitation.

God does not forgive you based on the quality of your confession or your resolve to be a better person. But you keep thinking otherwise. Your standard is what *you* would do to someone like yourself, and chances are that you would not let the incident pass quickly. God, however, forgives for his own name's sake. "I, even I, am he who blots out your transgressions, for my own sake, and remembers your sins no more" (Isaiah 43:25). There may be no finer words in Scripture. God bases his forgiveness on himself and his forgiving character, not on the quality of your confession.

So confess your sin to God in faith. By that I mean you confess sin, believing that God is exactly who he says he is. You confess while you give God all authority to interpret reality, instead of giving your personal feelings authority. Your feelings will say condemnation, but God says he doesn't treat you as your sins deserve. God must win in this interpretive battle.

EDWARD T. WELCH

August 5

Isaiah 59

The problem with relationships is that they all take place right in the middle of the story of redemption—God's plan to turn everything in our lives into instruments of Christlike change and growth. Our relationships are lived between the *already* and the *not yet*.

Already Jesus has come to save us, but his saving work is not yet complete. Already the power of sin has been broken, but the presence of sin has not yet been eradicated. Already we have changed in many ways, but we are not yet all we will be in Christ. Already we have learned many lessons of faith, but we don't yet trust God fully. Already God has established his kingdom in our hearts, but that kingdom has not yet fully come.

Our life with others is always life in the middle. We are always building community in the tension between God's already-and-not-yet grace. And we have no more control over the not-yet than we have had over the already. The timetable is in the hands of the sovereign Lord of grace. Our job is to learn how to live in the middle. We live as broken people who are being repaired, among neighbors in the same condition—always thankful for what has already been done, but ever aware of our need for what we have not yet been given.

Timothy S. Lane and Paul David Tripp

August 6

Psalm 24

Idolatry is always rooted in self. In one sense, idolatry is the way sinners look *outside* of themselves to find salvation, salvation being rescue from hardship and a path to fulfillment. We hope that acceptance, comfort, control, power, success, or something else will make our lives okay. Our idols may seem to focus and depend upon others. Though our idols may require the participation of others, idolatry is a strategy to benefit self. So, for example, I want to please others so that I will feel better about myself. Making others happy is only a means to an end, not an end in itself. As a strategy for gratifying myself, it is inherently *self*-ish.

But more than selfishness, at its root, idolatry is the way we play God. When we refuse to worship the true God and choose to build our lives around something or someone else, we are exalting ourselves above God. As idolaters we, in effect, survey the universe, including God, and decide what is best for us. God created all things to worship and serve him, but as idolaters we play God by devising strategies to make the world serve us. But even our efforts to rid ourselves of God take on the expression of worship. This is because we were made for worship, and even in our rebellion against God we cannot stop worshiping; we just find a "worshipful" way to serve ourselves.

Winston T. Smith

August 7

Psalm 23

Praying through a psalm is one way to experience the pleasure of a growing relationship with God. In Psalm 23 notice how the psalmist takes hold of suffering. He looks the shadow of death right in the eye: "I will fear no evil." He knows the Lord is with him. Notice how he switches from talking about God in the third person ("he") to the second person ("you") in an amazing expression of intimacy with God. The last two lines say, "I am being pursued by your goodness and mercy all my life, and then I will live with you forever." This is the supreme pleasure.

Now rewrite this psalm to reflect your life. How has Jesus been your Good Shepherd? What places of beauty, peace, and safety has he led you to? Thank him for the ways he has guided you. What hard times has he walked with you through? Can you say with faith that "goodness and love will follow me all the days of my life"? When these things are hard for you to pray, ask Jesus to teach you about himself. Go to John 10 and read about Jesus, the Good Shepherd. Ask him to give you the joy of hearing him call you by name, of knowing that he is walking with you. These are prayers that God delights to answer.

David Powlison

AUGUST 8

Psalm 51

One piece of evidence of kingdom life is that you will see *more* sin, not less. Outside the kingdom of heaven, there is no concern about sin. Unbelievers are indifferent to the fact that their sin is against God. When you are brought into the kingdom of light, you both see sin and get in a battle with it. The battle means you are alive.

The rules of engagement are simple. When you see sin, confess it as ultimately being against God. Respond in gratitude for the forgiveness he already gave you because of Jesus' death, which was the payment for sins. Knowing that you have been given the Spirit so you can do battle with sin, you attack. Ask for the power to love. Ask others to pray for you and counsel you. Adopt a zero-tolerance policy with sin. When you fall in defeat, learn from it and get right back into the battle.

You will see more and more sin, but you will also notice that the Spirit is changing you. There have been times when you responded in humility rather than arrogance, love rather than indifference or even hatred. The change will be gradual but noticeable. Keep your eyes open. How are you different because of what Jesus has done? When you see it, the apostle John says that you can allow that evidence to assure you that you truly belong to God.

Edward T. Welch

AUGUST 9

PSALM 88

The Bible doesn't offer a sanitized version of life or our reactions to it. Dark, shocking, and painful stories abound. Scripture shows us people who think, act, plan, decide, and speak just like we do. If the Bible left out these real-life stories of murder, rape, famine, disease, judgment, depression, war, adultery, theft, corruption, and overwhelming fear, how likely would we be to believe that God's Word could help us?

It is incredibly encouraging to realize that the Bible addresses the world as we know it. God makes it very clear that he understands the Heat we face every day. It isn't always pleasant to read the honest stories of Scripture, but it is comforting. We realize that we will never face an experience, no matter how dark or difficult, that would be a shock to our God. The hope and help God offers his children reflect his knowledge of the full range of human experience. That's why some of the most comforting passages of Scripture may not even have the word *comfort* in them. They may not be neatly tied together with a happy ending or say much about God's promises, love, and grace. Yet they give hope in their accurate depiction of the things we face.

TIMOTHY S. LANE AND PAUL DAVID TRIPP

AUGUST 10

REVELATION 7:9–17

Your destination is secure. All of the things that are truly worth living for cannot be taken away from you! Yes, you can lose your job, your health, your house, your car, or your friend. The loss of any of these things would be hard. But you cannot lose your identity in Christ. You cannot lose his love and grace. You cannot lose his gift of forgiveness or the place reserved for you in heaven. When you keep your eyes on this destination and pursue the things that move you there, you can live securely in a world where it seems as if nothing is guaranteed. You will not escape the difficulties of life, but you can rest assured that your Savior will use each one to prepare you for the place he is taking you. Think about it for a moment. You can be at peace even though you do not know how today's drama will end or what tomorrow will bring. You can live with joy even when things make you sad. Christian joy is not about avoiding life while dreaming about heaven. It is about taking an utterly honest look at all earthly life through heaven's lens. There we find real hope.

TIMOTHY S. LANE AND PAUL DAVID TRIPP

AUGUST 11

ROMANS 8:1–17

The problem of being morally corrupt and sinful can't be solved by working harder. Who can do the work that won't just cover up the symptoms but really fix who we are? Jesus has done the work required to clean up the filth in our hearts, to purify us and make us acceptable before God. It can be hard for us to accept and trust that Jesus has done our labor for us in a way we never could. There are few experiences in which the good efforts of another can make up for our own. Jesus really did do our work for us in living a life perfect in every regard, keeping the whole of God's law, and paying the penalty for our countless violations. God has truly credited us with Jesus' perfection and success. It's not fair, but that's the whole point: It is what the Bible calls "grace." Grace means we don't get what's fair or what we deserve; we get God's forgiveness and love instead. And not only are we credited with Jesus' perfection, we also, in time, gain the ability to do what is right. We aren't simply being let off the hook, but truly redeemed, or fixed, on the inside. By trusting in Jesus we are spiritually joined to him so that not only his credit, but also his very nature begins to take over ours.

WINSTON T. SMITH

AUGUST 12

2 CORINTHIANS 12:7–10

God wants to use your suffering. Paul sees that his suffering—his thorn in the flesh—serves a good purpose. God is using it to keep him humble, to protect him from exalting himself. When you turn to God in your weakness, things start to happen that you would have once thought were impossible—things such as learning deep contentment and living with a profound sense of purpose. You will speak of your weakness as the place God most richly reveals himself to you. For example, fatigue forces you to wrestle with how your life still counts even when what you do, how much you do, and how often you can do it are greatly reduced. God is more interested in who you are in Christ than in what you do for him. God wants you to grow to be like him. He wants your character to resemble his character. Your "thorn" is the context he is using to make his character shine through your life. God wants to use your suffering to teach you his patience, endurance, perseverance, and longsuffering (Romans 12:12; 1 Corinthians 13:4; Ephesians 4:2).

DAVID POWLISON

AUGUST 13

2 Thessalonians 3

It *is* God's will for us to work hard to provide ourselves and our families with life's necessities, but Paul doesn't stop there. He also says that the fundamental goal for our work is to have something to share with others. Instead of working hard to enhance our own lifestyles, Paul's revolutionary idea is that God's ultimate purpose for our work is to enable us to give to others. He explains this in his farewell to the Ephesians in Acts 20:34–35 (see also Ephesians 4:28 and 2 Thessalonians 3:10). Paul is saying that the big picture of God's will for us financially is both profound and quite simple. The money God grants as a fruit of our labor is given that we might love our "neighbor" as we love ourselves. We work hard not only to provide for ourselves and our dependents, but also to help the weak, the lost, and the needy. This makes our work truly a labor of love.

Focusing only on providing for our families is like being a baseball player who is satisfied with getting to second base in a baseball game. It's great to get on base, but the goal is to score a run, not end the inning stranded on base. So it's great to provide for our families, but God has given us a greater goal for our money: loving our neighbors as ourselves.

JAMES C. PETTY

AUGUST 14

EPHESIANS 2:1–10

What's behind all of your wrong anger? Whether you are angry about something trivial or something serious, your wrong reaction reveals that you are living as if you are in charge of the world. You believe you have the right to judge the people around you and the way God is running the world. Think about when you get angry. Aren't you insisting, "My will be done; my kingdom come"?

Anger is merciless. Anger sees, punishes, and gets rid of all offenders. But God has chosen to be merciful to wrongdoers, including someone like you, who struggles with taking God's place in the world (Ephesians 2:1–5). God's mercy brings life to you. If you struggle with bitterness, if you grumble, if you yell and argue, then you need God's mercy. You will receive mercy and help when you confess to God your struggle with trying to control everything, with wanting to be God, and with judging those around you. God's just anger toward sinners like you was poured out on his Son on the cross. Because Jesus died, you can be forgiven and have a whole new life. When you honestly confess your sins to God and ask him to forgive you for Jesus' sake, you will receive forgiveness and the gift of God's Spirit. The Spirit will give you the power to express your anger not your way, but God's way.

DAVID POWLISON

AUGUST 15

DEUTERONOMY 7:6–9

If God is to be our treasured possession, we can expect that he has first made us *his* treasured possession. You don't have to be concerned that you somehow misled him with a one-time display of grace and beauty. If he ever saw you at your worst, you don't have to worry that he would renege on his declaration of "treasured possession." His commitment and love go deeper than his response to anything in you. Instead, he loves you because that is the way *he* is: He is a lover, a faithful, extravagant lover. He was not initially drawn to your greatness, and he won't run away when your less attractive side is revealed.

And there is more. He is the King, and when he brings you to himself he offers you everything that is his. He doesn't say, "Up to one-half of my kingdom." He says he is pleased to give us the kingdom. Why worry about a stolen bike when, by faith, you have received the kingdom of heaven, and you can never lose it?

"In his great mercy [God] has given us new birth into a living hope through the resurrection of Jesus Christ . . . and into an inheritance that can never perish, spoil or fade—kept in heaven for you, who through faith are shielded by God's power until the coming of the salvation that is ready to be revealed in the last time" (1 Peter 1:3–5).

EDWARD T. WELCH

COLOSSIANS 3:1–17

The hardship of relationships includes what God calls us to be and do in the middle of their difficulty. God calls us to be humble, patient, kind, persevering, and forgiving. God calls us to speak with grace and to act with love, even when the relationship lacks grace and we have not been treated with love. Because of this, your relationships will take you beyond the boundaries of your normal strength. They will take you beyond the range of your natural abilities and beyond the borders of your natural and acquired wisdom. Relationships will push you beyond the limits of your ability to love, serve, and forgive. At times they will beat at the borders of your faith. At times they will exhaust you. In certain situations, your relationships will leave you disappointed and discouraged. They will require what you do not seem to have, but that is exactly as God intended it. That is precisely why he placed these demanding relationships in the middle of the process of sanctification, where God progressively molds us into the likeness of Jesus. When you give up on yourself, you begin to rely on him. When you are willing to abandon your own little dreams, you begin to get excited about his plan. When your way has blown up in your face again, you are ready to see the wisdom of God's way.

TIMOTHY S. LANE AND PAUL DAVID TRIPP

AUGUST 17

GALATIANS 5:1–6

Does your world have no room for God? The apostle Paul, in the book of Galatians, tells how we are always trying to construct our own religion. When Galatians was written, people were trying to use circumcision as a way to make themselves acceptable to God. Now we use different rituals, but it all comes down to the same thing: We believe we can be made right by something we do. You might not be thinking about God at all, but deep inside you there is a desire to be "right" and "acceptable." It's easy to substitute yourself or other people as the final judge of what it means to be right. If you are thinking about God at all, you probably believe that you have to become a better person before you can have a relationship with him. You're hoping that your own laws will show you the way. Meanwhile, you are constructing a world that has no room for God. The apostle Paul explains how this works in Galatians 5:1–6. There is a way out: "by faith," "through the Spirit," and "faith expressing itself through love." It is not rule-keeping that saves you; it is your faith in Jesus that makes you clean, holy, and right (Romans 1:17; 8:1).

EDWARD T. WELCH

August 18

We all desire something more. This is woven inside each of us. We crave to be part of something bigger, greater, and more profound than our relatively meaningless day-by-day existence. We simply weren't constructed to live only for ourselves. We were placed on earth to be part of something bigger than the narrow borders of our own survival and our own little definition of happiness. The desire resides in each of us, and it is called *transcendence*. To transcend is to be part of something greater. We were created to be part of something so big, so glorious, so far beyond the ordinary that it would totally change the way we approach every ordinary thing in our lives. And in all of sin's blindness, brokenness, and rebellion, that desire to transcend has now been crushed.

This desire for transcendence is in all of us because God placed it there. He constructed us to live for more than ourselves. He designed us to want meaning, purpose, and consequence. We were not wired to be fully satisfied with self-survival and self-pleasure. God purposed that the borders of our vision would be much, much larger than the boundaries of our lives. We were meant to see more than our physical eyes can see, and it is that greater vision that was meant to engage, excite, connect, and satisfy us.

Paul David Tripp

AUGUST 19

GENESIS 21:1–21

The invisible God of the universe is with you—but how do you know it? Look at the evidence from the past. The Bible is full of stories about God hearing the cries of his people and coming to their rescue. In Genesis, Hagar and her young son were unfairly sent from their home and left in the wilderness to die. She turned her back on her son so she wouldn't have to watch him die, and they both wept. They thought they were utterly alone, but God heard them. "God heard the boy crying, and the angel of God called to Hagar from heaven and said to her, 'What is the matter, Hagar? Do not be afraid; God has heard the boy crying as he lies there. Lift the boy up and take him by the hand, for I will make him into a great nation'" (Genesis 21:17–18).

Some people can hear and do nothing, but when the God of heaven and earth hears, he acts. He gave Hagar and her son water and made her son the father of a great nation. So don't think that God merely listens. His listening always includes action. We may not see all of what he is doing, but make no mistake, he is acting.

EDWARD T. WELCH

AUGUST 20

JAMES 1:1–18

James is savvy about real life. If you think that Scripture is not up to speed on real life—that saints spend their time thinking about the next life rather than dealing with the present—then read the book of James. James is highly practical; he is familiar with suffering and persecution. His counsel is given not to mystics who shun the world but to ordinary people who have to face it. Notice why he is excited about trials: trials, he writes, have a purpose. They test our faith. They reveal what we worship, what we trust, what we love. His desire is that we become "mature and complete, not lacking anything."

James does not naïvely assume that our hardships will be over this side of heaven. He assumes that they will continue. But James presents an emotional experience that is difficult to describe: joy, he writes, can be present during any wilderness experience. The cross can wipe out any doubt; on this end of history we can actually sing songs with joy when we are in the wilderness. Does all this seem unattainable? If so, treat these verses like the Psalms; let them be a vision for what lies ahead. Pray that God would receive glory by giving you joy in the midst of your trials.

EDWARD T. WELCH

AUGUST 21

JAMES 4:1–10

Wrong anger creates a big problem between you and God. Because your wrong anger has to do with your relationship with God, you can't deal with it by learning a few strategies or techniques. He doesn't like upstarts who try to take over his universe. Your anger is not just about you and all the frustrating things that happen to you. It's not just about you and your cranky, oppositional personality. And it's not just about you and all the unreasonable people in your life. It's about you, those frustrating circumstances, all those unreasonable people . . . and the living God. It's about you acting like you are in charge of God's world and other people. But God is in charge. Acting as if you are God—pride—is the beating heart of what it means to be a sinner. This insight into anger is hugely freeing and very sobering. Anger going wrong testifies to our pride. When you see yourself as a sinner, instead of focusing on how everyone around you is wrong, then God's grace and mercy is available to you. God's mercy is for those who honestly confess their sins to him and ask for the grace to change. James also says, "God opposes the proud but gives grace to the humble."

DAVID POWLISON

AUGUST 22

JOHN 17:1–19

What does this have to do with the heart? Many people have been hurt and rejected by others. They feel as though basic relational needs have not been met, and they will be stuck until they are. Rejection from parents, spouses, or friends has left a profound emptiness that feels like an emotional handicap.

Consider first the example of Jesus. He is God, but he was truly human. If anything is clear from his life, he didn't get love from people, he never prayed that he would know the love of other people, and he didn't seem emotionally undone by rejection and misunderstanding. Rather, his deepest needs, as noted in his prayers, were for the glory of his Father to be revealed and for his spiritual children to be protected from the evil one and united in love.

The desire to be loved is natural. If you don't have that desire, something is wrong. Yet there is something deeper still. This unmet desire does not quite go to the core of our being. We can go a step further and ask, *Why do I feel this need for love? What is it really saying?* The desire for love is good. The problem is that, left unchecked, it never stops growing. Keep in mind that our hearts keep repeating the chorus, "I want." We want more love, and more again. It is here that you observe the spiritual roots.

EDWARD T. WELCH

AUGUST 23

LEVITICUS 25:1–24

Do you really trust God? God's command to rest goes far beyond setting aside one day a week. In addition to a Sabbath day, every seventh year was to be a Sabbath year in which no crops were to be planted or harvested. Food could be taken directly from the fields, but not planted or harvested (Leviticus 25:1–7). The Sabbath year is a time for the land to rest. No doubt it benefits the soil to lie fallow, but if that were all God had in mind, he could have explained it that way. The fact that this is considered a Sabbath "to the LORD" (Leviticus 25:4) alerts us to its deeper significance, which becomes clearer when God anticipates Israel's reaction: "You may ask, 'What will we eat in the seventh year if we do not plant or harvest?'" (Leviticus 25:20). It's easy to understand Israel's concern. Is God asking us to starve? Again, the Sabbath reveals hearts. You have enough faith to rest for one day a week, now rest for an entire year. Do you really trust God? God graciously answers our questions before they come to our lips. "I will send you such a blessing in the sixth year that the land will yield enough for three years" (Leviticus 25:21). "Yes, I will care for you. Trust me." God doesn't respond, "How dare you doubt me you faithless people!" Familiar with our frailty and doubts, God speaks reassuring words while he asks us to take up the challenges of faith.

WINSTON T. SMITH

AUGUST 24

JOSHUA 1:1–9

We want what we want more than we want what God wants. Since the cross and resurrection, we recognize that the greatest enemies to godliness are not outside us but within. We want comfortable lives more than we want to depend on Christ for his daily provisions. Obeying God's call did not make the Israelites' lives nicer. They escaped Egypt to walk in the harsh desert. They evicted the Canaanites only to face ungodliness among their own tribes.

If you are controlled by an agenda other than growth in godliness and a Christlike love for others, you will be overwhelmed by your inabilities and the situation's impossibilities. You will decide in advance to cut yourself out of the action because you don't expect to make a difference anyway. With that perspective, God's promise to be with you can seem weak. But if you want his will to be done and realize that he will not fail to bring it about in your life, his presence is more than comforting.

WILLIAM P. SMITH

AUGUST 25

LUKE 15:11–32

We sometimes put our trust in a person (something created) and what we can get from that person *rather than* putting our trust in Christ and loving others. Once again, it comes down to spiritual allegiances. Like the ancient idolaters, we have said that God is not enough.

The feeling of emptiness is usually a sign that we have put our trust in something that can't sustain us. It reminds us that we were created to trust in our heavenly Father and nothing else. We were created to enjoy the many things God gives without making them the center of our lives. When we confuse the two, our lives feel out of kilter. To feel better, we try again and search for love apart from God, but when we finally realize that it is elusive, we forsake the quest and quietly despair.

Keep probing. Life is ultimately about God. When you get to God, don't stop until he surprises you with his beauty and love, which shouldn't take too long. After all, if you can find mixed allegiances, dual allegiances, spiritual unfaithfulness, or a wandering heart in your life, you are essentially guilty of spiritual adultery, and, contrary to your expectations, your God delights in your return.

EDWARD T. WELCH

AUGUST 26

LUKE 19:1–10

Jesus was on a mission. He singled Zacchaeus out and chose to go to his home. What did Jesus see in the man that drew him? Jesus explains his choice by saying that he came to seek and to save the lost (Luke 19:10). The quality that drew Jesus to Zacchaeus was the fact that he was a lost man.

In seeking out Zacchaeus, God shows you his heart. So often we talk about what Jesus did or said but ignore his attitude toward us and what drives him. Your God is passionate. Jesus came to look for those who wander through life dazed and confused. He searched them out intently, looking beyond those who clamored for his attention to locate those who had no hope. Jesus was not put off by Zacchaeus's despicable sins. He did not recoil from him. Rather, Jesus saw his lostness and found him.

Jesus is the same today. The same grace that moved him to leave heaven and cross time and space to find one pathetic conniver half-hidden in a tree is the same grace that moves him to look for you. He looked for you when you first came to know him and he looks for you even now. Desperate people—lost, confused, frightened—need to know that God searches for them.

WILLIAM P. SMITH

AUGUST 27

MARK 12:28–34

"Why do you fight?" James's answer is the opposite of what we often say. He says the problem is on the inside of each person! He does not talk about each person's circumstances, but rather what is going on in each person's heart: "Don't they come from your desires that battle within you?" There is war on the outside because there is war on the inside. How many times have you said, "I would be more patient if you would do what I say"? James says the real problem is that a desire for something has grown from a simple desire into a self-centered, sinful demand. This is how sin blinds and enslaves us.

Before you can begin a cure, you must diagnose the disease. The difference between ungodly and godly conflict starts with the ability to see the log in your own eye. This includes both heart and behavior. Why is this so important? James 4:3 says that these ungodly ruling desires eclipse your love for God, so that either you don't pray or you pray with selfish motives. Verse 2 says that you fail to love your neighbor. When ungodly desires rule, you break the first and second great commandments. This serious sin lies at the heart of your conflict. Ask, What do I want right now more than Christ and how am I acting to get it?

TIMOTHY S. LANE

1 JOHN 2:1–14

You are free to love the people in your life when you love God more than anything. Because their love and acceptance is not your ultimate goal, you won't be enslaved by your expectations for them and the disappointments that inevitably follow. Jesus is calling you to turn from love of self to love for him. Think about how Jesus has loved you—he lived the perfect life you should have lived, and he died the death you deserved. When you wake up every morning and interact personally with the one who has done all this for you, your family's slights and insults won't plague you in the same way. This won't be automatic or easy. Jesus said that each of us must take up our cross every day (Luke 9:23). You must daily die to your self-centeredness by finding your identity in what Jesus has done for you in his life, death, and resurrection. As you do this every day, you will turn from making anything else in creation more important to you than the God who has rescued you from your self-centeredness. Growing as a disciple is gradual, in the same way that the crucifixion was slow and agonizing. As we die to self and embrace our new identity in Christ, God is slowly and patiently bringing us to the end of ourselves, so that he might fill us with the life of Christ.

TIMOTHY S. LANE

AUGUST 29

MATTHEW 23

The ultra-religious Pharisees, diligently following every detail of the law. One of the requirements of the law was that a tenth, or *tithe*, of one's possessions be given to God. Jesus points out that the Pharisees are scrupulous in keeping this demand. In fact, they are so careful to uphold their religious duty that they even tithe their "mint, dill, and cummin" (Matthew 23:23–24)—the herbs and spices that grow in their gardens! They seem to love God with all their hearts and with all their souls and with all their minds. They seem not to hold anything back from God.

But Jesus calls them hypocrites: they claim to be one thing, but, in reality, are something different. The Pharisees claim to love God, but have, in fact, neglected the heart of God's commands—justice, mercy, and faithfulness.

The Pharisees show the same disconnect that many of us suffer from. They only know worship as religious ritual. Their definition of worship does not include relationships, and Jesus can see that their relationships are not shaped by the God they claim to worship, the God who says that he is love.

WINSTON T. SMITH

AUGUST 30

PHILIPPIANS 1:3–11

God is at work in you. Paul prays that the Philippian believers' love for God would result in acts of love for others. This is where God wants to take them, and where God wants to take us as well. No matter what you face today, you can be encouraged that God's good work continues in your life, even when you don't see it. God continues his work right in the middle of that tough situation at work, or with your teenager, or that battle with your weight, or your struggle with discouragement. God moves you forward as you submit yourself to him. His presence and faithful work give us confidence. As you have that tough conversation with a friend, you can say to yourself, Christ is working right now to complete what he started in me. As you struggle with your finances, you can say to your spouse, "We can get through this because Christ is working right now to complete what he has begun in us." When it seems that you are in a losing battle with sin, you can say, "I have hope for victory because Christ is working in me right now to complete what he has begun."

TIMOTHY S. LANE AND PAUL DAVID TRIPP

AUGUST 31

PHILIPPIANS 4:4–13

God wants you to be content. True contentment is usually learned on the down cycle—in loss, deprivation, and financial need. As your own dreams of financial security are shaken by your circumstances, you have the opportunity to turn from trusting and hoping in material things to trusting and hoping in God. This might not seem so great right now, but think about it: if your contentment is based on what you have or own, it can be easily lost. But contentment based on your relationship with God is on the unshakeable ground of God's unfailing love.

In Philippians 4:11–13 Paul is saying that true contentment (or lack of it) doesn't come from our circumstances; true contentment comes from "him who gives me strength." Because he trusted Jesus, he was at peace in all kinds of material circumstances. He knew that even in times of financial stress he was not missing out on anything essential to life. His identity, hope, and wellbeing did not come from what he owned or what goal he achieved. Rather, it rested on his relationship with his heavenly Father, who loved him and gave his Son for him.

JAMES C. PETTY

September 1

Psalm 115:1–8

You become like the treasure you seek. This principle is one of the most important things Psalm 115 teaches. It is an eloquent and accurate principle. When I live for material things, I increasingly become a materialistic person. I start to care about things more than people, thus becoming like the things I crave. Similarly, the person who lives for the little kingdom treasure of control will inevitably become a power-obsessed, controlling person. Someone who gets his identity and meaning from relationships will become driven by what people think of him, living in unending fear of man.

Rather than developing the traits of Christian character, which are the result of pursuing and treasuring Christ, I will take on the qualities of my Christ-replacement. This is why so many people in our churches are not growing in Christlikeness. To the degree that Jesus is not the treasure I seek, I will not be progressively taking on his likeness. Instead, I will begin to look more and more like the treasure of the kingdom of self that I am actually living for.

PAUL DAVID TRIPP

SEPTEMBER 2

PSALM 119:17–24

"Open our eyes, LORD, and we will behold wonderful things in all that you have spoken to us!" Where do you need Psalm 119 to help you? Is it sleepless nights? Does some form of lovelessness repeatedly puncture your life—worry, fears, sexual lust, bitterness, lying, temper, despair, procrastination? Where do you need real help, not good intentions or quick fixes? "I am yours. Save me. Teach me."

Is it the sharp-edged pain of some suffering? Have you been betrayed? Is there a rift in a relationship? Is your body failing? Is your child straying? "I would have perished in my affliction."

Do your joy and delight simply need to become more vocal? Does your confession of faith simply need to become more head on? "You are my Father. You established the earth. All things are your servants." Psalm 119 teaches us that way of talking.

Go through Psalm 119. Listen for affirmations about God. Listen for struggles and cries of honest need. Listen for expressions of conviction and delight. Find one affirmation about God that you need to voice. Identify one struggle with inner evil or outer pain that maps onto your own struggles. Choose one request that captures what you need God to do. Select one joyous assertion that expresses what you long to become in full.

DAVID POWLISON

SEPTEMBER 3

PSALM 31

God will use what you suffer as the door into a deeper knowledge of his love. As you read the Psalms, you see that those who know God well know themselves to be afflicted, weak, oppressed, broken, humble, and needy. Psalm 31:5—"Into your hands I commit my spirit"— was on Jesus' lips as he hung on the cross, powerless and in great pain. He became this for us. Hebrews 4:15 says, "We do not have a high priest who is unable to sympathize with our weaknesses, but we have one who has been tempted in every way, just as we are—yet was without sin." Jesus lived in weakness. He knows what it's like to depend on the mercies of God for every breath. Jesus' experience of weakness is the door to one of the most marvelous promises of God in the next verse: "Let us then approach the throne of grace with confidence, so that we may receive mercy and find grace to help us in our time of need" (Hebrews 4:16). You are struggling. Life is hard. You are living through a dark time. You need. Your Lord sympathizes with your need. He promises you grace and mercy—immediate help in the context of your need.

DAVID POWLISON

SEPTEMBER 4

PSALM 46

Fearful? Worried? There are two things you should know about fear or worry. First, like any strong emotion, it wants to be the boss. It wants authority. It claims to tell us how life really is, and it won't be easily persuaded otherwise. If my experience of fear says that there is danger and you say there isn't, my fear wins. If my experience of fear says that there is danger and God himself says he is with me, my fear wins. Fear doesn't trust easily. It tenaciously holds onto its self-protecting agenda. Think about it. When was the last time God's comforting words made a difference to you?

Second, when fear escalates, it wants relief and it wants it now. Fear is impatient. Of course, we are all impatient, and whenever we experience something uncomfortable we want to get rid of it as quickly as we can. Fear is no different. It will alight on a promising treatment, give it a few seconds, then flit to something else without ever returning. Fear has tried God and God didn't work. To reconsider God goes against fear's manic style. Why highlight this? Because one of the first steps in combating fear and worry is to slow down. "Be still" (Psalm 46:10) is another of God's exhortations to fearful people. *Quiet!* is the way some have translated it, and you can understand why.

EDWARD T. WELCH

SEPTEMBER 5

PSALM 62

Too often we live on little scraps of meaning. It is amazing how we can survive on so little: a three-percent raise, a new pair of shoes, a one-night stand, an Internet relationship. We manage to eke out meaning and purpose from fumes.

Depression feels like a state of not-thinking, but it is also a place of insight because you see that what seemed meaningful and real has turned out to be a façade. Pleasures were fleeting. Nothing lasted. Such insight, of course, is painful, and it feels like it could cost you your life. But if you are willing, the next step begins a significant stretch on the path of wisdom. Many sages have traveled this way. "Meaningless! Meaningless!" says the Teacher. "Utterly meaningless! Everything is meaningless." What does man gain from all his labor at which he toils under the sun? (Ecclesiastes 1:1–2).

This, however, is the way he starts, not the way he finishes. Depression says, "You will not find meaning in what you are doing," and depression is right. What it doesn't tell you is, "Keep looking, you will find it. You are a creature with a royal purpose." For this, you need to listen to others who have gone this way before. They urge you to continue and point the way.

EDWARD T. WELCH

SEPTEMBER 6

ROMANS 6:8–14

It is so easy to coast! We have been accepted into God's family, and someday will be with him in eternity. But what goes on in between? From the time we come to Christ until the time we go home to be with him, God calls us to change. We have been changed by his grace, are being changed by his grace, and will be changed by his grace.

What is the goal of this change? It is more than a better marriage, well-adjusted children, professional success, or freedom from a few nagging sins. God's goal is that we would actually become like him. He doesn't just want you to escape the fires of hell—though we praise God that through Christ you can! His goal is to free us from our slavery to sin, our bondage to self, and our functional idolatry, so that we actually take on his character! Peter summarizes the change this way: "Through these he has given us his very great and precious promises, so that through them may participate in the divine nature and escape the corruption in the world caused by evil desires" (2 Peter 1:4).

TIMOTHY S. LANE AND PAUL DAVID TRIPP

SEPTEMBER 7

2 CORINTHIANS 3:7–18

Our expectations and desires do play an enormous role in determining our actions and responses to life, and the Bible does call us to change the way we think about things. But this approach omits the person and work of Christ as Savior. Instead, it reduces our relationship to Christ to "think his thoughts" and "act the way Jesus would act." If you have a problem with anger, you are told to memorize certain verses so that you can recite them in moments of anger. If you struggle with fear, you should read Scripture passages that focus on trusting God when you are afraid.

This emphasis on thinking as the solution to our problems fails to introduce the Person who has come not only to change the way we think about life, but to change us as well. We are more than thinkers. We are worshipers who enter into relationship with the person or thing we think will give us life. Jesus comes to transform our entire being, not just our mind. He comes as a person, not as a cognitive concept we insert into a new formula for life.

TIMOTHY S. LANE AND PAUL DAVID TRIPP

SEPTEMBER 8

COLOSSIANS 1:3–23

There is no place for Christ in many people's Christianity. Their faith is not actually in *Christ*; it is in *Christianity* and their own ability to live it out. This kind of "Christianity" is about the shadow glories of human knowledge and performance. It does not require the death of self that must always happen if love for Christ is going to reign in our hearts.

When Christ isn't central in the life of a Christian, his Christianity will always get reduced to *theology* and *rules*. It will cease to be the central organizing principle of his life. It will give way to other powerful motivations and move to the fringes of his life. I think this is the experience of many Christians. Their Christianity is missing Christ! It then becomes little more than an ideology with an accompanying set of ethics. What is incredibly dangerous about this is that if Christ isn't central in our hearts, something else will be. Christianity as theology and rules will allow self to be at the center. It is only Christ who can free you and me from bondage to the little kingdom. Christianity gutted of Christ is devoid of both its beauty and its power. Only love for Christ has the power to incapacitate the sturdy love for self that is the bane of every sinner, and only the grace of Christ has the power to produce that love.

PAUL DAVID TRIPP

September 9

Colossians 2:6–15

The fullness of Christ gives us two things: it cleanses us from sin, and it raises us to new life! Paul is stressing that the forgiveness of sins brings us freedom over the powers of evil. We have a new record. Jesus' payment for sin and his righteous life becomes ours. We also have new power. The Holy Spirit that raised Jesus from the dead now lives in us, bringing new life and power to grow in Christlikeness.

Notice that the Bible does not separate our new record and new power. One without the other is not true fullness. What if you were given a new record but no new power to live the Christian life? That would be hollow and empty because you would soon fall. What if you were given a new power but no new record? You could change but you would still stand condemned because your past could not be erased. But in Christ, you get it all. You are regenerated, forgiven, and treated as if you had perfectly obeyed the law. The Holy Spirit gives you the power to grow in your sanctification. And you are promised that one day you will be made perfect and live with God forever. No wonder Paul argues that you are full to overflowing! You lack nothing. You don't need Christ plus something else. He is enough. All that he is, we are.

Timothy S. Lane and Paul David Tripp

SEPTEMBER 10

EPHESIANS 6:10–20

He invites us to join him in battle. There is a way to do conflict that is pleasing to God. One theme that runs from Genesis to Revelation is the theme of conflict and war—and God is the Warrior! He battles against the darkness and chaos of sin and suffering. Ultimately, Jesus joins the fight and gets bloody and dies. But he emerges as Victor over the forces of darkness through his death and resurrection. He opens the way for enemies like us to be forgiven and reconciled to him, and then invites us to join him. Christians are called to take up arms against sin and darkness in the same way Jesus did: through humility, love, and self-sacrifice.

Most of us think of conflict as something to avoid, but conflict is a trial that gives us an opportunity to grow in tremendous ways. In fact, James says that without such trials, we will remain immature, incomplete, and lacking many godly character qualities (James 1:2–4). While conflict will rarely be fun, it should be seen as an opportunity to grow in grace. When a conflict is severe, this idea can be hard to swallow. But the truth remains: God, who is sovereign, loving, and wise, sends people into our lives so that he might work in us in ways that can only happen in conflict.

TIMOTHY S. LANE

SEPTEMBER 11

JEREMIAH 9:12–24

When we put our trust in others, we are saying something to God. We are saying, "I don't trust you." "You are not enough." You believe that God offers you heaven, but can he satisfy your ever-growing psychological desires? Can he make you an "A," at least in some areas, when you feel like a "C-minus"? But that's missing the point. Our purpose is not about us, it is about God. For this reason, God seems to prefer the average and below average. Otherwise it would be about our talents and abilities. "But God chose the foolish things of the world to shame the wise; God chose the weak things of the world to shame the strong. He chose the lowly things of this world and the despised things. . . . 'Let him who boasts boast in the Lord'" (1 Corinthians 1:27–28, 31).

Life is not about my résumé; it is about ways to extend the fame of Jesus. And one way to do this is to say that God is more than enough. After all, he *is* love. It has been proven at the cross. All other loves are, at best, imitations that point back to the original rather than usurp it. To trust is to say that we need Jesus. Our search for self-satisfaction has been a failure, and we now turn to the One who, all along, has been our true destination.

EDWARD T. WELCH

SEPTEMBER 12

JOB 1:13–22

Come and be surprised. At its very roots, life is about God. Whether you shake your fist at him, consider him so distant that his existence is irrelevant, or tremble before him because you feel that you are under his judgment, the basic questions of life and the fundamental issues of the human heart are about God. Whom will you trust in the midst of pain? Whom will you worship?

Consider Job: now that suffering was a resident in his home, would he still trust and worship God? His answer was unambiguous. When he lost all his children, "he fell to the ground in worship," and made a shocking declaration. "The LORD gave and the LORD has taken away; may the name of the LORD be praised" (Job 1:21).

At this moment you may not feel like falling to the ground in worship. But at least consider who God is, and as you consider God, expect to find fallacies in your thinking. In other words, although you may think that you know all you need to know about God—or all you want to know—you don't. If you resist such an offer, you are probably angry with God, in which case it is all the more reason to consider who he is. He invites angry people to come and be surprised.

EDWARD T. WELCH

JOHN 6:60–69

All or nothing: this is the rule of kingdom investment. All hedged bets are deposited in the earthly kingdom—the one with "mine" written all over it. Everything must go into one account or the other. This doesn't mean that every penny must go into the offering basket. You might be a world-class giver, at least on your 1040 form, but you still fret about finances. You are not confessing what percentage you give and keep; you are confessing how money has been your hope, security, and confidence. The problems, at root, are relational, and the way to deal with relational problems is to confess them to the Lord.

Have you ever known that you had wronged another person and, instead of confessing it, you just tried to be extra nice? It doesn't work. For one thing, you never know for how long you must be overly nice. For another, you are always wondering if the other person noticed the offense and if he is thinking about it. Confession is the only way to deal with relational wrongs. Confession changes everything. When we confess to God that our worry is a sin against him, we turn away from the kingdom of earth. We burn our bridges and say with Peter, "Lord, to whom shall we go? You have the words of eternal life" (John 6:68).

EDWARD T. WELCH

SEPTEMBER 14

LUKE 12:22–34

God will give us what we need for today alone. "Take as much as you want, but don't keep even a crumb for tomorrow." In various forms, this will become God's plan for human life. You will encounter it again when Jesus trains his disciples and sends them out on a missionary journey with no extra supplies (Mark 6:7–9). The plan, of course, is genius. Dump a year's supply of manna into cold storage and, guaranteed, you will forget God until the supply disappears (Deuteronomy 8:10–14). Such prosperity would be a curse. God's strategy is to give us enough for today and then, when tomorrow comes, to give us enough for that day too.

Do you see how this is exactly what we need? Fears and worries live in the future, trying to assure a good outcome in a potentially hard situation. The last thing they want to do is trust anyone, God included. To thwart this tendency toward independence, God only gives us what we need when we need it. The emerging idea is that he wants us to trust him in the future rather than our self-protective plans.

EDWARD T. WELCH

SEPTEMBER 15

LUKE 14:25–35

Think of all the anger, anxiety, irritation, impatience, envy, fear, discouragement, obsession, vengeance, bitterness, and violence that result from lesser treasures controlling our hearts. Think how a person's life gets distorted when his job is what he lives for. Think of the bad things that happen when a person becomes the central value in my life. Think of what results when my life is controlled by the quest for a certain position or possession. Why do I get so angry at you? Why do I struggle with impatience? Why am I ever eaten by envy or bitterness? Why would I ever plot vengeance? What would cause me to speak or act unkindly toward you?

It is only when my heart is owned by Christ that I will be free from the driven and anxious pursuit of things that I cannot properly hold, cannot control, and that will quickly evaporate. Jesus calls you to die to all that you treasure so that he can be the central treasure of your heart. When you value him more than anything else in your life, you are no longer shrinking your life down to what you can hold in your hands and control with your plans. You are beginning to live for something bigger than yourself. When you hold everything in your life with open hands for his taking, you expand everything you touch to the size of his kingdom.

PAUL DAVID TRIPP

SEPTEMBER 16

MARK 4:13–20

What are killers of spiritual life and growth? "Satan." We knew that. "The deceitfulness of wealth." There are plenty of warnings about this in Scripture. Most notable is the case of the rich young man who, although a fine, moral person, walked away from the kingdom of God (Matthew 19:23–24). No surprise here. "The desires for other things." This is another phrase for lust. We are all familiar with it and there are many warnings about it. Covetous desires are caused by sin (Romans 7:8). Left unchecked, they will master us.

"Worries." What? No way. Worries feel so bland and harmless. This is the last thing we would expect to make the list. Everyone has worries, and they seem so . . . ordinary. Worries are our "legitimate concerns." But Jesus is saying that when you see worry—and you will see it—be careful. It makes sense when you think about it. Worry is focused inward. It prefers self-protection over trust. It can hear many encouraging words—even God's words—and stay unmoved. It can be life-dominating. It is connected to your money and desires in that it reveals the things that are valuable to you. It can reveal that you love something more than Jesus. It crowds Jesus out of your life.

EDWARD T. WELCH

SEPTEMBER 17

MATTHEW 19:16–22

"Which commandments should I obey?" the young man asks. Jesus' answer can be summarized as "love people." His answer provides a clue to the kinds of commands the young man wants to avoid thinking about or just does not understand: "'All these I have kept,' the young man said. 'What do I still lack?'" Jesus tells the young man to sell all his possessions, give to the poor, and follow him. Because the young man will not do it, Jesus makes the point that if he wants eternal life he will have to learn to love as God has commanded, even with his wealth. Jesus asks the young man to love in a way he has never considered.

Jesus has put his finger on a major area of the young man's life in which he is blind to the needs of others—an area in which he is unwilling to love. This is a *rich* man surrounded by *poor* people. For all of his concern about how to please God and achieve eternal life, the rich man is blind to God's most clearly stated concerns and to the need of those right in front of him. Jesus clarifies, for this particular man, what loving should look like, "sell your possessions and give to the poor." No doubt the young man never expected the conversation to take the turn that it does.

WINSTON T. SMITH

SEPTEMBER 18

MATTHEW 6:19–34

"Seek first his kingdom and his righteousness, and all these things will be given to you as well" (Matthew 6:33). The word *but* is a welcome to a new way of living. What is the old way fueled by? The old way is driven by earth-bound treasures and anxiety-bound needs. The old way is driven by forgetting the Father and his unshakable commitment to provide all that his children need to do his kingdom work. Not much good ever comes out of functionally focusing on self, while consistently forgetting the Father.

The new way is driven by a focus on the transcendent glories of God's big kingdom purposes. Those purposes span all of history and spread to all of creation. They can never be squeezed into the constricted quarters of my little kingdom. The new way is also driven by a daily and heartfelt admission of my weakness, along with a joyful rest in the faithful provision of my Father. You and I can get up in the morning with a calm joy in the loving provision of our heavenly Father, while being enthralled by the fact that we have been included in the transcendent joys of his kingdom. There are glories to be enjoyed that you will never experience in the confines of your kingdom of one.

PAUL DAVID TRIPP

SEPTEMBER 19

PROVERBS 16:1–21

Our hearts are out of kilter. There is a specific way our hearts are misaligned. They were intended to be devoted to God, but they aren't. Instead, they are devoted to a strange brew of God, ourselves, and the objects of our affections, a.k.a., our idols. Why this misplaced and compromised devotion?

We are proud—our hearts are proud. Since ancient times, people have bowed down to idols in the appearance of humility and contrition. But their goal wasn't to be mastered by the idol. People worship to *get* things. We choose idols in part because we believe that they will give us what we want. The god of drugs brings fearlessness; the god of sex promises pleasure and intimacy; the god of wealth holds out power and influence. We can feel miserable about ourselves because we want to be great, at least at *some*thing, and we are not feeling very great. Like the prophets of Baal, we are arrogant enough to believe that we can manipulate the idol—whether by cutting (1 Kings 18:28) or some other form of works righteousness—so it will relent and give us what we want.

EDWARD T. WELCH

SEPTEMBER 20

PSALM 86

Are your sins too bad? One common feature of all world religions, except for the religion revealed in the Old and New Testaments, is that the gods demand some kind of human penance when they are wronged. Human beings must pay the gods back by giving more money, adhering to proper rituals, going through some form of self-punishment, or practicing some means of works righteousness. When religions are shaped by the way people treat one another, such a system is unavoidable. The psalmist knows this. He knows that all other gods keep records of who has been naughty and who has been nice. But God is holy, and his forgiveness is holy. Nothing can compare to it. As a result the psalmist says, "If you, O LORD, kept a record of sins, O LORD, who could stand? But with you there is forgiveness; therefore you are feared" (Psalm 130:3–4).

Do you ever think that your sins are too bad, and that forgiveness for those sins requires you to get your act together first? If so, you don't fear God. You are minimizing his forgiveness. You are acting as though his forgiveness is ordinary, just like that of any person or make-believe god. If you think like that, you don't believe he is holy. In contrast, the fear of the Lord leads us to believe that when God makes promises too good to be true, they are indeed true.

EDWARD T. WELCH

SEPTEMBER 21

ROMANS 15:1–13

Relationships are not easy. Paul knows this is true even among people who have the Spirit. "Make every effort to keep the unity of the Spirit through the bond of peace" (Ephesians 4:3). Paul says that our relationships with other Christians are not something we should take for granted. He says that we are to maintain—not create—these relationships. If you are a Christian, you automatically are in relationship with other Christians. You are united to one another because you are united to Christ. Because of the indwelling of the Holy Spirit, you already share a deep bond that has been given to you by grace. Therefore, these relationships are gifts to be managed with great care. I am either being a good or a bad steward of these gifts. If I hinder my relationships with other believers in any way, I am devaluing these relationships. But if I am willing to pursue, forgive, and serve, I demonstrate care for these gifts.

Have you ever noticed how distasteful, unsatisfying, and uninteresting relationships suddenly become when they require work? Paul says that we find excitement and satisfaction within the context of hard work. But most of us give up when we decide that the dividend yield is not worth the investment. Sadly, we frequently do the accounting with our personal interests at the center instead of God's call.

TIMOTHY S. LANE AND PAUL DAVID TRIPP

SEPTEMBER 22

JOHN 5:16–27

Come to Jesus, ask for forgiveness for your many sins, and believe that his death paid the price for your sins and his resurrection is your guarantee that you also will live forever. This is Jesus' promise to you: "I tell you the truth, whoever hears my word and believes him who sent me has eternal life and will not be condemned; he has crossed over from death to life" (John 5:24). Because of Jesus you don't have to fear that when you die you will experience God's judgment. Jesus has already experienced that for you. What is waiting for you after death is real life—eternal life. You don't have to earn this life. It is God's gift to those who put their trust in Jesus. This is how the apostle Paul explains it: "For the wages of sin is death, but the gift of God is eternal life in Christ Jesus our Lord" (Romans 6:23). We all deserve death, but Jesus died in our place. When you trust in him, you no longer have to fear death, because now you share in Jesus' life.

The eternal life Jesus gives is life the way it was meant to be—free from evil, sorrow, and sadness, and rich in everlasting joy, peace, and purity. The natural, well-earned wages of human life bring death and grief, but God's mercy and grace bring the delights that are at his right hand forever.

DAVID POWLISON

JOHN 13:1–17

As Jesus came to wash his feet, Peter could not bear to see Jesus in this place of abject submission. He doesn't allow him to proceed. Jesus explains what he is doing and what it means. In verse 7, Jesus says, "You do not realize now what I am doing, but later you will understand." He then says, as Peter protests, "Unless I wash you, you have no part with me." What do these cryptic words mean? Jesus is saying that what he is doing symbolizes something even greater. His humble service of washing their feet points to what he will do for them on the cross in just a few days. But instead of water, his blood will be poured out as he gives his life for them. The sacrifice of his blood will be the cleansing agent to wash away their sins and make them living temples in which the Holy Spirit dwells. Jesus tells Peter that if he will not humble himself and receive what he is about to do for him on the cross, Peter will have no part with him. Jesus knows that proud sinners who can't receive grace as a gift from God will not be likely to offer it. You can't serve other sinners if you don't receive Jesus' service for you. There is no way you will be up for the task.

TIMOTHY S. LANE AND PAUL DAVID TRIPP

SEPTEMBER 24

JOB 38:3–11

If you are looking for answers, Job is one of many places you can turn. Another is to God's promises. "No temptation has seized you except what is common to man. And God is faithful; he will not let you be tempted beyond what you can bear. But when you are tempted, he will also provide a way out so that you can stand up under it" (1 Corinthians 10:13). This is one of the better known promises, and it is one where God appears to have reneged, because suffering often feels like more than you can bear. Therefore, it is important to consider for two reasons. First, it is a great promise. Second, if you are starting to believe that it isn't always true, then you may start asking where else God's promises might have exceptions. Such doubts erode faith.

This passage is saying that you too will go through a desert, and when you do, the Spirit will strengthen you in such a way that you can avoid grumbling and idolatry. God's promise is that he will never put us in a situation where we have no choice but to sin. He either will relieve the intensity of the temptation or he will give us grace to trust and obey in the hardship.

EDWARD T. WELCH

September 25

When you take refuge in God, he not only delivers you from shame and guilt, he also rebuilds your broken life. It's easy to think that you have missed God's best for your life. It is true that your sin has consequences. But remember what Holocaust survivor Corrie ten Boom said, "There is no pit so deep that God's love is not deeper still."

Thousands of years ago, God sent his people into exile because of their sins. But they didn't stay in exile forever. Despite their sins God said to his people, "'For I know the plans I have for you,' declares the LORD, 'plans to prosper you and not to harm you, plans to give you hope and a future'" (Jeremiah 29:11). These words are also meant for you. God does have a future for you. Jesus' death and resurrection are your guarantee that you will live forever with him in heaven. And God does have plans for you—plans for the rest of your life, to bless you and to make you a blessing to others. This is always God's way. He takes broken things, redeems them, and makes them useful in his kingdom. You can look with hope to see how God wants to use you to love others right now.

David Powlison

SEPTEMBER 26

GENESIS 16

How many people do we see every day? Shop clerks, bank tellers, trash collectors, neighbors, people we pass on the street—all these people blend into the background of our busy lives. We give them a nod, but that's it. Have we looked at them and seen them as people God has put in our paths to love, even in the simplest ways? God sees us and watches over us. Remember Hagar in Genesis? Sarah could not conceive Abraham's child, so she decided that Hagar her maidservant should bear Abraham a son. When Hagar conceived Ishmael, she treated Sarah with contempt. Sarah reacted by driving Hagar into the desert. The angel of the Lord followed Hagar and spoke with her. Hagar was amazed! She said, "You are the God who sees me" (Genesis 16:13). Hagar, a slave woman, was not invisible to God. Should anyone now be "invisible" to us?

In Luke 7 Jesus was on his way to Nain. A large crowd followed. Amid all the activity, Jesus saw a grieving mother and his heart went out to her. He stopped to comfort her and restored her dead son back to life. The Gospels are filled with accounts of Jesus seeing hungry, lost, hurting people and reaching out to meet their needs. How are we going to minister to a world full of lonely people if we haven't first looked to see them?

JAYNE V. CLARK

SEPTEMBER 27

HEBREWS 10:1–14

A greater mercy drew him back. Destined for the priesthood, Aaron had a bright future. Then, while Moses is on Mount Sinai, Aaron leads the people into rebellion against God. Aaron had every advantage and threw them all away. Yet, God accepts a sacrifice that atones for his sin. God's acceptance is demonstrated when his glory appears at the end of Aaron's ordination as high priest. Fire came out from his presence and consumed the burnt offering Aaron had prepared—instead of consuming Aaron. He was a high priest who could sympathize with their weaknesses because he knew what it was to fail. But he also knew what it was to experience a greater mercy that drew him back to God.

Leviticus was written for sinners. It lays out all the ways people disrupt fellowship between themselves and God and what to do when that fellowship is broken. There is a faithful way to deal with your faithlessness. You can be faithful even after you've failed to be perfect. Inserting Aaron's ordination account among the laws reinforces the restorative nature of the book. Essentially God is saying, "If Aaron can sin as badly as he did and not only be forgiven but installed as high priest, then there is hope for you. You can still be my people and I will wholeheartedly receive you."

WILLIAM P. SMITH

SEPTEMBER 28

PSALM 27

You don't see the deliverance? Be strong and take heart. The words are familiar. They are the words forever linked to Joshua, who heard them from Moses (Deuteronomy 3:28; 31:6–7, 23) and passed them on to the people (Joshua 1:6–7, 9, 18). The historical context is the transition in leadership from Moses to Joshua and the upcoming battles for the Promised Land. The fact that this psalm is composed in Jerusalem—*in* the Promised Land—makes David's confidence unshakable.

Sandwiched around the exhortation to be strong and take heart is the encouragement to wait for the Lord. Wait, wait patiently for the Lord. That is the summary of this psalm of confidence. Once again, we are taken into the mind of God in that, while anxiety prefers immediate deliverance, God might delay it, giving us time to trust him and wait by faith. So the psalmist will wait with confidence, which is to wait by faith. His God is absolutely reliable. While a very reliable human deliverer might encounter accidents and other unforeseen events on his way to our deliverance, God is never waylaid. No one can interfere with his care and deliverance.

EDWARD T. WELCH

HEBREWS 13:20–21

Our fallen experience need not control us. All of the words God uses to describe himself—King, Shepherd, Master, Savior, and God—have disappointing human parallels. In each of these examples, it does not make sense to say that life experience dictates a person's reality. On the contrary, the very experience of disappointing and distorted images can make you long to know the real King, Shepherd, Master, Savior, and God! You might say, "My pastor never taught me about God. How I rejoice that Hebrews 13:20–21 is true, that the great Shepherd of the sheep shed his blood for me and teaches me to do his will." "My boss is manipulative and deceptive. How I rejoice that Ephesians 6:5–8 is becoming true in me and I can serve Christ with integrity instead of being bitter or fearful!" "The God I grew up hearing about seemed like a remote killjoy. Praise the real God that Psalm 36 is true, and he is an immediate refuge and a fountain of love, light, and joy!" Clearly, our fallen experience need not control us.

DAVID POWLISON

SEPTEMBER 30

GENESIS 50:15–21

We are functioning as a judge when we remain bitter against someone. We assess the evidence against someone, render a verdict, and declare him guilty. James challenges our judgmentalism: "There is only one Lawgiver and Judge, the one who is able to save and destroy. But you—who are you to judge your neighbor?" (James 4:12). Or consider Paul's words in Romans 12:19: "Do not take revenge, my friends, but leave room for God's wrath, for it is written: 'It is mine to avenge; I will repay,' says the Lord." Revenge is wrong not because evil acts do not warrant revenge, they do; but because this is God's job, not ours. We must trust God to be God and to bring justice in his time and in his way.

In Genesis 50, Joseph's brothers feared that their now powerful brother might avenge their treachery to him in their younger years. The chapter opens with Jacob's funeral. They attempted to appease Joseph by seeking his forgiveness, but the timing seems suspiciously contrived, and they apparently fabricated their deceased father's words. When they arrived, they threw themselves down before Joseph as slaves. Joseph's merciful response reflected his knowledge of God: "Don't be afraid. Am I in the place of God?" (Genesis 50:19). Joseph understood that judgment is God's role, not ours. Joseph could extend grace because his God was in control of his life.

ROBERT D. JONES

OCTOBER 1

GENESIS 3:1–19

The most popular simplistic approach to change focuses on external circumstances. "I need more money." "If I could change my looks, my life would be better." "If I could get married, life would sing." "If I could get out of this marriage and find someone who appreciates me, I wouldn't be so depressed." "If my children respected me the way they should, I would be nicer."

In the garden just after the fall, Adam was the first to employ this approach by blaming Eve (and God) for his own sin: "It was the woman you gave me." It's the other person's fault. If it is not another person, it's something else—the hard day at work that leads me to snap at you; the lack of money that leads me to cheat on my taxes. In every difficult situation, temptation abounds to blame others.

This approach to change is not only deceptive, but hollow as well. It misses my need for Christ's redeeming grace, and it places the blame for my sin at God's doorstep! We blame God for placing the problem person or circumstance in our life. We question God's wisdom, goodness, and character. Obviously, with this approach, the grace of God will not be sought or received.

TIMOTHY S. LANE AND PAUL DAVID TRIPP

October 2

Colossians 2:6–15

On the cross Christ paid the debt for every selfish desire, thought, word, or deed to which you will ever give yourself. You no longer have to be afraid to own up to your selfishness. You do not have to whitewash your thoughts and motives. You do not have to cover your sin by blaming others or by self-atoning logic. You do not have to give yourself to acts of penance (self-atonement) that make you feel better about yourself. You do not have to search for biblical passages that will give ease to your conscience. No, your debt has been fully paid. Your punishment has been borne by Another. There is One who has taken your place and been condemned instead of you. Paul says, "He forgave us all our sins, having canceled the written code, with its regulations, that was against us and that stood opposed to us; he took it away, nailing it to the cross" (Colossians 2:13b–14). As God's child, you have been forgiven for every act of self-focused independence and rebellion. You have been freed from the debt of your every failure to love God above all else and your neighbor as yourself. You no longer need to live in hiding. Forgiving grace welcomes you out of the darkness to lift the burden of refusal, guilt, fear, and shame off of your shoulders. You have been invited to confess and receive the forgiveness that is yours.

PAUL DAVID TRIPP

OCTOBER 3

PSALM 56

Fears are loud and demanding. Even when you know they are irrational, they can still control you. It is hard to argue with feelings that are so intense, and easy to be loyal to our inaccurate interpretations. Claim as your own some of the psalms that are journals of fear. For example, Psalm 46 talks about treacherous circumstances, but it still keeps circling around to the same refrain: "The LORD Almighty is with us; the God of Jacob is our fortress" (Psalm 46:7, 11). Psalm 56 describes being slandered and attacked, but the psalmist calms his heart: "When I am afraid, I will trust in you" (Psalm 56:3). As you meditate on some of the psalms that speak about fear, you will find that you too will be able to make quicker transitions from fear to faith (see Psalm 57:4–5).

There are two basic steps in dealing with fears. First, confess them as unbelief. Isn't it true that much of our fear is our hearts saying, "Lord, I don't believe you," or "Lord, my desires want something other than what you promised"? Second, examine Scripture and be confident in the love and faithfulness of Jesus. Ask someone who is confident in Jesus to give reasons for his or her confidence. What are your fears? Where is your trust?

EDWARD T. WELCH

October 4

Psalm 42

Seek him. Hope is the constant companion of perseverance. God's Word gives you daily encouragement. In fact, all Scripture is his means of sustaining you in the battle. "For everything that was written in the past was written to teach us, so that through endurance and the encouragement of the Scriptures we might have hope" (Romans 15:4). Your hope is that God hears, that he finds great worth in perseverance, that he rewards those who seek him (Hebrews 11:6), that he blesses those who persevere (James 1:12), that he is faithful to all his promises. Your hope comes when you begin to fix your eyes on Jesus, the One who is invisible (Hebrews 11:27).

Sound impossible? If you cannot be aroused to hope, you are in good company. There was a point in Job's life when he said, "What strength do I have, that I should still hope? What prospects, that I should be patient?" (Job 6:11). But even in his despair, Job continued to seek his God. So, at least, seek him. If even that seems too much, ride on someone else's hope for as long as you need. Let your friends or family read Scripture to you. Let them tell you about their hope and confidence in Christ. There are many different ways of doing battle. Call out to the persevering God who gives endurance (Romans 15:5). He will answer you.

EDWARD T. WELCH

OCTOBER 5

PSALM 37

God's greatest mercy to humanity is revealed in his curse of the serpent. Remember that we, his images, are not simple signposts that point to the glory of God—we are his companions. God wants to relate to his creatures. This is an astounding thing. It requires a sin-soaked heart and mind to make it dull and boring. God wants to be friends with you. He does not create human servants to do his dirty work or feed some twisted craving. He creates people in his own likeness and treats them like his children. He provides for them, visits them, and speaks to them. He longs for relationship. Rebellion shatters his glory and it also breaks this special relationship. And to this rejection, which no human tale of unrequited love can equal, God responds with grace.

In cursing the serpent, God, in effect, says to his wayward offspring, "You chose to build an alliance against me, but I love you too much to let it stand. You are my children and you may not continue in rebellion against me. I'm stepping in for your good. I won't let you be friends with Satan!"

God won't let you have what will surely destroy you. God uses his power to act in your best interests. Confronted with treasonous disloyalty, he commits himself to rebuilding relationships with his people.

WILLIAM P. SMITH

OCTOBER 6

PSALM 139

God wants to know what's on your heart. He wants you to need him, to go to him, and to plead with him about your real problems. He wants you to tell him all about your troubles—the health problems, the financial worries, the straying child, the struggling church, and the grief and loss you have experienced. He wants you to confess to him the sins that drive your sinful anxiety—the idols that have hijacked your life. He wants you to ask for his forgiveness for your lack of trust and faith, and for desiring his good gifts more than him. Begin with total honesty and say, "Lord, I don't understand; help me to understand you." Admit to him that, although your words say you believe he is in control, your anxious thoughts reveal the truth: You still desire to be in control. Ask God to teach you how to close the gap between what you say you believe and how you think and function on a day-by-day basis. God will use your honest confession to build a relationship with him that will give you true and lasting peace. Your growing and deepening relationship with God is what will transform your anxious thoughts into humble faith and trust.

DAVID POWLISON

OCTOBER 7

PSALM 130

Rescue from what? Deliverance comes, but, as is God's custom, it comes in a way we couldn't have predicted. To be honest, at first glance it seems like a lame rescue attempt. The psalmist is given what appears to be a flimsy lifeline: his God is the one who forgives sins.

This one takes some reflection. We don't have evidence that the psalmist's sin caused his suffering. How is he going to take hope in the fact that he is forgiven? How will that rescue him? It seems like a pat spiritual answer to a life or death predicament. If you heard that from a friend, you *might* say "thanks" but you certainly wouldn't turn in that direction for help again. On the hierarchy of needs, physical survival seems more basic than spiritual encouragement. But the psalmist is clear on this. He is, without apology, presenting forgiveness of sins as the deepest answer of all. To appreciate the psalm's guidance on this, we have to believe that sin is a problem in our lives. In fact, to really be led by the psalm, we must realize that sin is our deepest problem. Robert Fleming, a persecuted Scottish minister who lived from 1630–1694, said, "In the worst of times, there is still more cause to complain of an evil heart than of an evil world."

EDWARD T. WELCH

OCTOBER 8

PSALM 31

Groaning is the default language of every Christian between coming to Christ and entering the final kingdom. Notice Paul's logic in Romans 8:22–25. We are *supposed* to groan because there are things that we have been promised but do not yet have. We are supposed to groan because the full expression of God's kingdom has not yet come. We are supposed to groan because we are not yet all that God shed the blood of his Son for us to become. We are supposed to groan because the temporary pleasures of this physical world do not satisfy us; they always leave a void in our hearts. We are supposed to groan because in every situation and circumstance we see the damage that sin has done and is doing. We are supposed to groan because we recognize how we each give in to the temptation to seek in the physical world what we can only find in the Lord and what will only be fulfilled in eternity. This side of eternity, groaning is meant to be the default language of the big kingdom. When we groan for these reasons, we get it right. This kind of groaning is only present in people who are submitting little kingdom desires to big kingdom interests.

PAUL DAVID TRIPP

OCTOBER 9

MATTHEW 9:1–13

Your growth and change are the Creator's intent. Throughout history, God has used hardships to reveal people's hearts, and this unveiling has had a purpose. You have to see what is in your heart before you can set out to change it. Notice how those who have medicated away their hardships with illegal drugs, alcohol, or sex can seem immature. Find a person who has weathered storms rather than avoided them and you will find someone who is wise.

Personal growth and change are not always easy, but they are essential to true humanness. They are the Creator's intent. You can see it taking place in animals, plants, and people. The difference with human beings is that we grow physically and spiritually. When we grow in the right direction, it is right and good. The Hebrew word *shalom* captures it: peace, wholeness, realignment rather than dislocation. Spiritual growth just feels right. For example, depression can feel like the severe pain of someone dying of cancer, but it can also be like the pain of surgery, which indicates that we are getting better. If both pains could be physically measured, they might be identical in their intensity but the pain from surgery will seem less severe to the sufferer than the pain of cancer. The pain from surgery is making you better; the other is a sign that you are worse.

EDWARD T. WELCH

OCTOBER 10

MATTHEW 18:21–35

Forgiveness is costly. Regardless of how big or small the offense, canceling a debt and absorbing the cost is going to hurt. But the parable shows us that not forgiving also has a price, and it is higher than the price forgiveness demands. This is where we must let the truth override our feelings since it often feels good to hold onto an offense. That good feeling, contrasted with the pain of forgiving, blinds us to the bill we're running up spiritually. Jesus clearly says that an abiding unwillingness to forgive will cost you eternally! God will treat you the same way you treat others. An entrenched refusal to forgive is a sign that you have not known God's amazing forgiveness yourself. Your ugly behavior reveals the ugly condition of your heart. In addition, holding onto an offense will make you a bitter and unloving person, and you will inevitably damage all your relationships. No matter which way you choose, you will pay a price. Which price are you willing to pay?

TIMOTHY S. LANE AND PAUL DAVID TRIPP

October 11

Mark 10:35–45

If our relationships are going to make us like Christ, and if Christian community is going to flourish, it is going to take lots of people who relish being demoted in the eyes of the world. Imagine human beings who naturally want position, power, and recognition being transformed into people who gladly throw off self-glory and self-love to be servants in the image of Jesus. This is what will turn average relationships into something glorious. Serving others is a simple way of consolidating all the Bible's "one another" passages under one big idea. When we serve one another, we carry one another's burdens in practical ways. We get our hands dirty as we come alongside people and pay attention to the details of their lives. If our professed commitment to Jesus does not lead us to resemble him in our actions, then we are mocking him and not representing him accurately to the world.

When you think about your relationships, how many of them ultimately revolve around making sure your concerns are heard and your self-defined "needs" are met? Start with those you love the most. You have to see how much of a servant you aren't before you can start to become one. That is the abiding irony of the Christian life. Up is down, life is death, and power is found and expressed in serving.

TIMOTHY S. LANE AND PAUL DAVID TRIPP

October 12

Luke 22:24–30

In the upper room in the final hours before Christ's capture he sits with his disciples as Messiah, Priest, and Lamb. He, in this moment and in the sacrificial moments to come, is instituting the New Covenant. There could be no more significant moment of redemptive importance. Yet, Luke tells us that in the middle of this moment of high and holy drama, the disciples are arguing about who of them is greatest! Are position, power, and affirmation of no consequence whatsoever? Of course not! But when they rise to the level of overwhelming the crashing significance of being welcomed into the kingdom of God, of eating at the table with the Lord of the universe, and of sitting on thrones built by him, then something has gone drastically wrong. In this moment the disciples are forsaking the transcendent glories of the kingdom of God for the pseudo-glory of personal power and position.

True humanity is always connected to glory, and true glory can only be found in the One who is glory, the Lord. God calls me to find personal glory in his glory, and in so doing, to be committed to community, stewardship, and truth glory as well.

PAUL DAVID TRIPP

OCTOBER 13

LEVITICUS 8

If there is a fire in your office building, you have to make a faith-based choice. If you believe that the person who wrote the guidelines was competent and dedicated to your best interests, you will follow the instructions to the letter. If not, you will trust yourself to find your own way out.

The same is true of Leviticus. Leviticus reflects God's desire to be friends with you. Read it as an invitation from him to be restored. If you believe God's invitation of friendship, you will do what he says. You'll come quickly to him when you fail, confident that he will receive you. If, however, you believe that he would never befriend such a disappointment as yourself, and that you'll never be good enough, you won't come.

The true foundation of Leviticus is faith. You would only do the things Leviticus prescribes if you trusted that God is who he says he is. Before Aaron could serve as high priest, he had to believe that, according to God's word, he had been purified. Before you can confidently rely on Christ's power in you, you have to believe that he has already created a way for you to deal with your sin.

WILLIAM P. SMITH

ROMANS 6:1–14

God's grace blows a hole in your self-contained kingdom, and in his redemptive love he reaches in and pulls you out, again and again. Paul says it this way: "He has delivered us from the domain of darkness and transferred us to the kingdom of his beloved Son, in whom we have redemption, the forgiveness of sins" (Colossians 1:13–14 ESV).

On the cross Christ broke the power of the little kingdom. As God's children we no longer live under the domination of the little kingdom. We have been freed from our imprisonment to ourselves. Once we were only able to desire, think, speak, and act in a self-focused way, but now grace has broken that slavery and welcomed us to a new and better way of living. Christ endured the awful suffering and death of the cross, not just to ensure your future with him in eternity, but to *free* you in the here and now to live for something more transcendent than your present definition of personal happiness. The cross smashed the dominant power of the shadow glories of creation over your heart and freed your heart to run after the transcendent glory that you will only find in him.

PAUL DAVID TRIPP

OCTOBER 15

REVELATION 7:9–17

Step into this scene of eternity. Look around, listen carefully, and then look back on your life to understand what cannot be understood any other way. Revelation 7 allows us to see the Lamb on the throne and hear the voices of the saints who have completed their journey. Do you see yourself in the crowd? These saints are people just like you. Like you, they suffered the scorching heat of earthly life. Like you, they went through God's process of radical change. Now they have reached their final destination. They stand before God's throne, purified and free, with a full welcome into the presence of the King of kings and Lord of lords, their Savior, their Shepherd Lamb.

Picture yourself there, because in God's story, you are there. This is your destination. This is where God is taking you! You will make it through the heat! Someday you will stand before the throne. There will be a moment when your voice will be heard in the chorus of praise that will never end. Someday you will be convinced that it has all been worth it. Life looks dramatically different when examined through the lens of eternity.

TIMOTHY S. LANE AND PAUL DAVID TRIPP

OCTOBER 16

PSALM 94

We have good reasons to be anxious because there's trouble in this world. In the midst of trouble our hearts forget God, and we get attached to other masters—to all kinds of desires, needs, and beliefs. We get anxious for bad reasons, and we overreact even to the good reasons we have to be anxious. Living in a world where there is trouble, with hearts that quickly stray, means we will always be tempted to lose sight of God. When we lose sight of God, we try to control our world on our own, and become filled with worry. But don't despair: God, in his Word, gives you better and imperishable reasons for responding to the troubles of life in faith. You can learn to remember God instead of forgetting him. God wants us to know him so intimately and trust him so completely that our desire to fix our troubles in our own way will no longer consume us. As we grow in our love for God, we will experience the right kind of concern in the midst of our troubles. "When my anxious thoughts multiply within me, your consolations delight my soul" (Psalm 94:19 NASB).

DAVID POWLISON

OCTOBER 17

PSALM 73

When we want a good thing more than God, anger goes wrong. Sometimes we want good things. It's not wrong to want your husband to love and listen to you. It's not wrong to want your children to respect and obey you. It's not wrong to want your boss to be honest with you. It's not wrong to want a warm meal and a hot cup of coffee, or to get to your appointment rather than getting stuck in traffic. But when fulfilling your desires, even for a good thing, becomes more important than anything else, that's when it changes into a "desire of the flesh" (Galatians 5:16–17 ESV). You want it too much. When you don't get what you want, demand, believe you need, and think you deserve, your anger flares up. James, in the letter he wrote to the early church, said this about where our wrong anger comes from: "What causes fights and quarrels among you? Don't they come from your desires that battle within you? You want something but don't get it. You kill and covet, but you cannot have what you want. You quarrel and fight" (James 4:1–2). When you want anything—even a good thing—more than God, you will get angry when you don't get it or it's taken away from you.

DAVID POWLISON

OCTOBER 18

PSALM 5

Where do your "if onlys" lead? Plow your own heart by evaluating your desires, demands, fears, insecurities, wants, and expectations. Ask God to show you the areas in your life where you are struggling. Asking these questions will reveal what you treasure the most.

Let me mention three common struggles: anger, fear, and indispensability. When you see these things in your heart, turn to the Lord and find his grace, mercy, and help in your time of need (Hebrews 4:16). Against anger, meditate on the fact that God who did not spare his own Son, the most lavish gift of all, will not withhold from us what we really need (Romans 8:32). Against fear, hear Jesus say, "Do not be afraid, little flock, for your Father has been pleased to give you the kingdom" (Luke 12:32). Against a sense of indispensability and self-sufficiency, remember that God's strength is actually "made perfect in weakness" (2 Corinthians 12:9). Remember, you are made in the image of God. God wants to transform you so you will be a beautiful reflection of his image to the watching world. This transformation happens as you ask God every day for wisdom and power through his Spirit, and by faith depend on him for everything you need for life and godliness (2 Peter 1:3).

MICHAEL R. EMLET

OCTOBER 19

PSALM 19

What truly refreshes you? What gives you pure and simple pleasure? What helps you to lay your cares down and get a fresh perspective on life? What enables you to step back into the business and hardship of life with a new joy?

The Psalms revel in creation. We marvel at the unparalleled beauty of a sunrise and sunset, and even more at a Master Artist so creative that he will erase his art every day to begin again the next. So many simple, unstained pleasures: Collecting stones on a lakeshore. Watching autumn leaves drop. Innocent pleasures are a means to step away from what is hard, wearisome, or difficult in our lives into something restful and beautiful. They are not an escape from life's troubles, they are meant to refresh and strengthen us.

What makes such pleasures innocent? It is the fact that there is a greater pleasure. That greatest pleasure is the Maker of all the innocent ones. Is devotion to God one of your pleasures? The lesser innocent pleasures come because the greatest pleasure, God himself, is in his rightful place. Innocent pleasures don't pretend to save you or protect you. They don't promise you meaning and identity in life. They don't take life's fragility, pain, frustration, disappointment, and uncertainty and wash them away. They are not the giver of every good and perfect gift; they are just gifts you enjoy. They are innocent because they don't pretend to be anything more.

DAVID POWLISON

October 20

Matthew 6:1–15

How perfect for those who worry! Jesus says that our daily needs are important to our heavenly *Father*. There is something familiar in what Jesus says, but it should sound new. "Father" is not a new way to address God. God himself said, "How gladly would I treat you like sons and give you a desirable land, the most beautiful inheritance of any nation. I thought you would call me 'Father' and not turn away from following me" (Jeremiah 3:19). But there are only a handful of direct Old Testament references to God as Father. Jesus exceeds that number in the Sermon on the Mount alone. "Heavenly Father" is Jesus' preferred way to talk about God, and it is how he teaches us to address God in prayer. His emphasis on our Father encourages us to listen even more attentively.

The term *Father* immediately connotes care, compassion, and strength. In those days, the father was committed to protecting his children so that the family line could continue and the father's name would receive praise. The son or daughter was always welcome, always loved. Do you remember seeing pictures of John F. Kennedy's son John-John playing in the Oval Office? A father is to be respected and obeyed, even feared, but he is accessible and welcoming to his children. He delights in blessing them.

Edward T. Welch

OCTOBER 21

MATTHEW 18:21–35

To angry people, God says, "Confess your selfish anger; trust me and obey." Jesus told a story about a man who was forgiven a great debt—more than a lifetime's worth of wages. As soon as he was released from the debt, he tracked down a man who owed him the equivalent of a couple of dollars and demanded immediate payment. When the king heard about it, the ungrateful man's injustice so angered him that he withdrew his forgiveness and threw the man in prison. If the man's actions make you angry, realize that Jesus is also warning you—"This is how my heavenly Father will treat each of you unless you forgive your brother from your heart." Through Jesus, we have been forgiven for many lifetimes' worth of debt against our heavenly Father, yet we want those who slight us to pay up immediately.

When that story fits (and it fits us all at some time), it shows that we don't truly grasp God's grace and mercy to us through Christ. We treat others the way we think we have been treated. If we think God has been stingy with us, we will be stingy toward others. But there is another way. Those who know that they have been forgiven will be generous, eager to imitate Christ by covering the offenses of others (Proverbs 19:11).

EDWARD T. WELCH

October 22

Mark 9:14–29

Entrust him with your weak faith; he longs to supply what you lack. God is kind to people who shrink back from trusting him. There's a special place in his heart for those with little faith. Jesus invites you to say to him, along with the father of the epileptic boy, "I do believe; help me overcome my unbelief!" (Mark 9:24).

First, acknowledge your difficulty in trusting him; admit that you need his help to believe him. Second, consider where you've seen God prove his reliability to you. Remember when you first came to him and he received you. Or cast your mind back to that sin you carried around for months, afraid to admit it to yourself, much less to him. Remember how he flooded you with forgiveness and relief? You weren't sure he'd receive you, yet he did. Last, act on the faith God gives you. Living passively saps your will and cripples your belief that you can accomplish what God calls you to do. Living faithfully means that you actively respond to the faith God gives you.

Jesus wants us to live a faithful life that relies on him. If your faith is small because of fearfulness, ignorance, or arrogance, ask him to increase your faith so that you can carry out his desires faithfully. Along with Augustine, pray, "Grant what you command and command what you will."

WILLIAM P. SMITH

OCTOBER 23

LUKE 12:22–34

Fear always asks the same questions: "Who will you trust? Where will you turn when you are afraid or anxious?" The story of Scripture is one in which God demonstrates himself to be trustworthy, and then he invites wary people to trust him. Given such an attractive invitation, you would think that none could resist, but we all have our reasons for putting our trust in things we can see. In spite of our reluctance, God delights in speaking words of hope and comfort to fearful people. He reserves some of the most beautiful revelations of himself for the timid. He patiently reasons with them. He reminds them that he is God, and he promises that he will never leave them alone. He shares with them some of his names—the ones that only intimate friends know.

The best known name is Shepherd. The best known psalm for those who are afraid is Psalm 23. Its New Testament counterpart (Luke 12:22–34) is actually spoken by the Good Shepherd. You are probably familiar with this passage, but read it carefully. These are God's words to you. Notice how Jesus never tires of repeating his promises. Instead, he patiently reasons with fearful people. He is persuading you to trust him.

EDWARD T. WELCH

OCTOBER 24

JOHN 14:15–21

God gives you a new identity when you come to him through trusting in Jesus. You become part of the family of God. You are his dearly loved child (1 John 3:1). You have a perfect Father in heaven who loves you and wants to fill your life with the good gift of himself (Luke 11:13). Jesus experienced every form of suffering when he was in the world. "He was despised and rejected by men, a man of sorrows, and familiar with suffering" (Isaiah 53:3). He was betrayed and tortured. He is well acquainted with your grief, and he will never leave you (John 14:18).

God has a purpose for you that flows out of your life experience, a high and holy calling. Paul says that God "comforts us in all our troubles, so that we can comfort those in any trouble with the comfort we ourselves have received from God" (2 Corinthians 1:4). As you learn about how Jesus Christ meets, enters, and transforms your particular affliction in life, you can begin to help others who are facing all kinds of affliction. Your compassion, wisdom, and hope for redemption will bring the light of God to a world dying in darkness and suffering. Then you will be able to say along with Joseph: "As for you, you meant evil against me, but God meant it for good, to bring it about that many people should be kept alive, as they are today" (Genesis 50:20 ESV).

DAVID POWLISON

OCTOBER 25

GENESIS 2:4–25

Adam wasn't meant to live alone. Adam wasn't meant to be Adam's best friend. The community that Adam and Eve were meant to live in with one another was designed to be the beginning of a huge web of interdependent human relationships that would define much of the focus and energy of peoples' lives. Human beings' lives were meant to transcend the narrow glories of independence, autonomy, and self-sufficiency. We were created to have lives shaped by a constant pursuit of the glory of humble, dependent community. We were made to need one another, and this community was meant to exist in a variety of forms, including neighbor, family, friend, church, city, state, nation, brother, sister, parent, and spouse. This web of ongoing relationships daily calls us out of our insulation and isolation to experience a community glory that selfish, personal focus can never deliver. God makes Adam and Eve and immediately calls them to the transcendent glory of a world-reaching, generation-spanning, and history-encompassing community. This commitment to community was meant to be a major shaping focus of their day-by-day living. This act of God to immediately tie Adam and Eve into community with one another was a call to transcendence. It was a call to never shrink the size of their community to a functional community of one.

PAUL DAVID TRIPP

OCTOBER 26

GALATIANS 6:1–10

All true comfort has its source in the Lord (2 Corinthians 1:3–4). In grief, we often seek out other comforts: memories, material things, distractions. They all provide some measure of comfort but none can fill the one place where grief causes us to feel so empty—our hearts. Only one Person can provide the comfort that restores your heart—Jesus Christ. He knows your pain. He is able to touch you where you most need to be touched, in your heart. In all the things you do to get yourself through the shock and grief of loss, don't forget to run to the one place where true comfort can be found.

God likens the church to a physical body (1 Corinthians 12). He reminds us that life is a community project. In grief, it is tempting to turn inside yourself and avoid the community around you. You can't bear one more heartfelt condolence or one more conversation about how you are doing. But Paul tells us we should "bear one another's burdens" (Galatians 6:2 ESV) precisely because he knows that we will all encounter burdens too heavy to carry alone. Remember to cry out in weakness and ask for help. God never expected you to do this alone. Also, asking for help does not show a lack of faith. God promised to provide what you need to face what he calls you to face. Finally, those who help you will in turn be helped through helping you.

PAUL DAVID TRIPP

OCTOBER 27

EXODUS 32

The difference between life and death. At Mount Sinai newly liberated people met with God. He reminded them how he had rescued them and how he longed to make them his special people if they would keep his covenant. To this gracious offer, the people responded, "We will do everything the LORD has said" (Exodus 19:8).

Sadly, just a few weeks later, they broke their commitment, along with God's covenant, in spectacular fashion. Moses, recognizing the danger the Israelites faced, immediately placed himself between God and his people. In doing this he demonstrated something supernatural. He put his own comfort second to the need of God's people. He looked beyond their sin to the danger they were in. He cared about their plight when it would have been easier not to care. Interceding for them was not natural, but it was certainly necessary. Without it they were doomed. Having an intercessor who could deal "gently with those who [were] ignorant and [were] going astray" (Hebrews 5:2) meant the difference between life and death for them.

Whatever the reason, Moses interceded for his people simply because of their need. He knew that their actions required someone to speak for them or they would be destroyed. They needed someone to step in and rescue them. And that is the crucial need of sinful, confused, and unhappy people in all times and places.

WILLIAM P. SMITH

OCTOBER 28

EPHESIANS 3:14–21

King Jesus' coronation ceremony was unlike any other. While earthly kings received gifts, Jesus gave gifts. More specifically, he gave a gift. He poured out his Spirit on his people. When someone is full of "grace and power" (Acts 6:8), that is the same as saying that the person is full of the Holy Spirit (Acts 6:5). When we receive gifts, they are called either gifts of grace (Ephesians 4:7) or gifts of the Spirit (1 Corinthians 12:4). When we receive grace, we receive the Spirit of grace (Hebrews 10:29). To receive grace is to receive the Spirit; to receive the Spirit is to be given the kingdom of the Spirit; to receive the kingdom of the Spirit is to receive everything imaginable under the reign of King Jesus, including: love, joy, adoption as God's children, patience, gentleness, power to fight sin, goodness, self-control, fruitfulness, peace, the mind of God, freedom, faithfulness, no condemnation, truth, unity, power to serve others, presence of God, promise of future perfection, wisdom, and life.

Are you worried about the future? You are looking at tomorrow as if it was a final exam and you haven't yet taken the class. Of course you panic at the thought. But you haven't considered that you will go through the class before you have to take the final. You will be given all the grace you need when you need it.

EDWARD T. WELCH

OCTOBER 29

DEUTERONOMY 10:12–22

What fills the eyes of your heart? Our thoughts can be so dominated by the necessary tasks of the day, by the difficulties we face, or by the people around us, that we lose our consciousness of the Lord of Glory who has drawn us into his transcendent purposes for the universe. Or our day can be kidnapped by anxious cravings and all the "what ifs" that worry is able to generate.

Big kingdom living really does start with remembering the King. This isn't some mystical spiritual exercise for the super spiritual. It is street-level worship. It is loving God more than my projects. It is caring more about his glory than about my schedule. It is caring that his grace is spread and his fame is known more than I care about the next sale, the next promotion, an immaculate house, or a fun lunch with my friends. Ask yourself, when you start your day, what "unseen" thing draws and motivates you? Do you see God? Are you drawn toward him? Do you desire that your day be his day? Do you recognize his grace, power, and sovereignty in your life?

PAUL DAVID TRIPP

OCTOBER 30

Psalm 8

We never stop imaging God. When we use a phrase like, "he's the spitting image of his father," we usually mean that the son displays the physical characteristics of his earthly father. He looks (and perhaps acts) like his dad. In a similar, but far more profound way, we resemble the God of the universe, both in his character and actions. You are created in the image of God (Genesis 1:26–28; Psalm 8:4–8). God made us to reflect his image to the world. We don't do this perfectly because of sin and disease, but no matter what, we never stop imaging God!

The gospel is about renewing the true image of God through Jesus (Ephesians 4:24; Colossians 3:10). This process is not derailed by illness or disability. Instead, God uses these things to make us more like him. God promises he will complete the work he began in each of us (Philippians 1:6). This means that God is doing his transforming work in you no matter what challenges you face. He is perfecting the character of Christ in you in the midst of your struggles.

MICHAEL R. EMLET

OCTOBER 31

You know where hope lies. One of the many ways God can bring good out of evil is by making you truly helpful to others who are struggling. Think about all you have to offer others. You know exactly what it's like for them. You know the allure of the sin. You know the struggle (with guilt, with numbness, with anger, with regret). You know where hope lies—in Jesus. You can become that unique creation of God, a person who is simultaneously compassionate and clear-minded. In a small way, you can become the way God is toward you. He will use you in the lives of others because you are actually becoming more like him! Be alert for the opportunities you have to come alongside others who are struggling as you have. Because of your experience, you will be able to challenge them with God's truth and comfort them with God's mercy in a way that few others can.

God is able to redeem your life and make you into a person who loves him and reaches out to others with his love. When you come to God in confession and ask him for mercy, he promises that he will do "immeasurably more than all we ask or imagine, according to his power that is at work within us" (Ephesians 3:20).

DAVID POWLISON

November 1

Psalm 32

Asking for forgiveness is so hard because of what it says about life and what it says about me. You cannot ask for forgiveness without acknowledging that there is something in life that is more important than the progress of your own kingdom. You cannot seek forgiveness without owning the fact that you were created for the glory of another. You cannot make honest, humble confession without acknowledging that there are more important things in life than getting your own way and being happy. You cannot admit a wrong without being hit with the fact that there are bigger things in life than how you feel and how you feel about how you feel. You see, it's our sturdy allegiance to our own kingdom that makes us unwilling to confess that we have gotten in the way of God's kingdom on earth.

Asking for forgiveness is hard because you have to admit to why you need it so frequently. When you seek forgiveness, you are confessing that you still forget why you were put on earth and granted the amazing gift of God's grace. You are admitting that you forget that every gift you have been given is to be invested in his kingdom.

PAUL DAVID TRIPP

November 2

Matthew 6:25–34

What is God calling you to do about today's trouble? To help you answer that question, imagine two circles: one six feet in diameter and another six inches in diameter. What you need to do today is in the little six-inch circle. Whatever is in the larger six-foot circle you have to leave in God's hands, because you can't control or do anything about those worries.

In every area of your life where there is trouble, God is calling you to a small step of faith and love. He is not calling you to solve what is wrong. What God is calling you to do is always less than the bad things that might happen. Your troubles do not rest on your shoulders. You are living in a world where there is trouble, but you are in relationship with a God who is in charge of his world. He has a purpose for you in every situation where there is trouble: God is calling you to be constructive in a very small corner of his world. There is an ecology motto: "Think globally, act locally." Apply this motto to your day-to-day life. Think globally by remembering every day that God is in charge of the world, and he is watching over his sheep. And then act locally by asking God each day to show you what small, constructive thing he is calling you to do.

DAVID POWLISON

November 3

Ephesians 3:14–21

When you notice how difficult really loving others is, you need to remember and experience once again all the riches that are already yours in Christ. You have a present relationship with him! He has given you so much relational wealth that you can readily afford to give it away. And since you are giving out of your excess, you don't need to wheedle a handout from anyone else. If you catch yourself doing that, take a moment and pray through Ephesians 3:14–19, "that out of his glorious riches he may strengthen you with power through his Spirit in your inner being, so that Christ may dwell in your hearts through faith." Ask Jesus to fill your heart with the knowledge of the breadth, length, height, and depth of his love for you. Ask him to fill you with joy in the inheritance you already have from him. As he answers that prayer, you will be able to genuinely love the difficult people in your life.

WILLIAM P. SMITH

NOVEMBER 4

LUKE 9:18–27

The cross sticks out in Scripture. It seems crazy, like the greatest aberrant moment of all of history. It seems like a big mistake, a very bad joke. Surely nothing good could come out of God taking on human life and then being publicly, viciously, and unjustly mutilated. There were no positive connotations to the cross. It was the most horrible punishment reserved for the lowliest and vilest of criminals. It was a public shame on a hill outside of the city, and it always ended in death.

Yet the cross is not a bad joke. It is history's most beautiful paradox. The death of the Messiah was the only way he could give life to those who would believe in him. The hope of the cross is in its willing sacrifice of One for the sake of another. This is exactly what Christ's call to daily take up your cross is about. The one who sacrificed his life so that we might have life now calls his disciples to sacrifice their lives for him. In a world that only understands the kingdom of self, living for the big kingdom of Christ will always require suffering and sacrifice. What are you unwilling to offer? Which of your pleasures would you refuse to nail to your daily cross?

PAUL DAVID TRIPP

LUKE 14:25–35

Christ doesn't just ask for some of our things. He doesn't ask for the majority of our things. He doesn't say, "I want the best of your things." He doesn't warn us that there are going to be times when he will take precious things from us. No, his call from the outset is this: "Any of you who does not give up everything that he has cannot be my disciple." Why is his call so all-inclusive?

Jesus looks at the large crowd and sees people in the midst of a raging personal war. He understands that each one is a worshiper—each of their lives is always shaped by the pursuit of the treasure that has come to rule their hearts. He knows that what they treasure will shape their decisions, actions, and words. And he knows that they will make incredible personal sacrifices to get, keep, and enjoy whatever it is that they treasure. So, in asking his followers to sacrifice everything, he is not calling them to live without anything. No, he is calling them to empty themselves of every other treasure but him. He is saying, "If you are going to be my disciple, I must be the treasure that gives shape and direction to everything you decide, say, and do."

PAUL DAVID TRIPP

November 6

Psalm 81

Your job is simply to believe. When children don't get what they want when they want it, they have a hard time believing that their parents truly love them. But parents know about a more sophisticated love. They know that catering to their children's wishes is not always in their children's best interests. Sometimes it is best for them to go to bed, even though their friends are still outside playing. But just try to persuade children of your love at those times! All you can do is remind them that you love them. "My child, you will have to trust that I love you this time, because I know it doesn't feel that way."

God is good and he is generous. He is not stingy. He commands his people not to covet because it is a form of denying his generosity. He is not trying to hold out on you until you are whipped into shape. Demons would have you believe such things. He invites us to the most lavish of banquets, and all he requires is that we are hungry and bring nothing (Isaiah 55:1–3). This is not a religious attempt to drum up some good feelings. It *is* harder to be surprised by the goodness and generosity of God when you feel so miserable. The goal is simply to remind you of the truth.

Edward T. Welch

November 7

Psalm 55

The details of how faith works in spiritual warfare are well known but easily forgotten. First, *remember that you have an enemy*. Follow the lead of wise people who begin each day by actually saying, "Today, I must be alert that I have an enemy." Ask others to remind you, and be quick to remind others. Realize that you are walking where rebels are known to be in the area. Their lives are devoted to your destruction.

Second, *assume that warfare rages*. Don't even bother looking for signs of warfare. Just assume that you are in the thick of it. If you want evidence, don't look for it in the intensity of your depression. Satan will use your pain as a venue to employ well-worn strategies like these: Are you hopeless? Do you believe God is aloof and distant? Do you question God's love? Do you question God's forgiveness? Do you see no point in knowing Christ better? Remember that Satan will always attack the character of God.

Are you listening to wise counsel and Scripture? If not, it is a sure sign that you are losing some spiritual skirmishes. Listening is a mark of humility, and Satan can't successfully fight against it.

Edward T. Welch

November 8

Psalm 27

Hope opens our eyes so that we, like the psalmist, can see the ongoing work of God. The psalmist says, "I am still confident of this: I will see the goodness of the LORD in the land of the living" (Psalm 27:13). The truth of God's story is that he is on the move right now. He is changing us, enlarging his church, and bringing all history to a climax.

The book of Revelation is the best-known teaching that God is at work. It is written to people who are going through great suffering, wondering if evil actually wins so that the church gradually is brought to nothing. To encourage them, God parts the curtain of heaven so his people can see that the armies of God are on the move *now*. God both is winning and has won. When you know that God's strategy is playing out perfectly, you see much more.

When you look around at yourself and the world around you, it is easy to be pessimistic because the future doesn't always look very promising. But when you know the conclusion—that the church will win and Christ will reign—you are able to see the Spirit of God move in the details. Ask God to open your eyes so you can see his goodness in the land of the living.

EDWARD T. WELCH

November 9

Philippians 4:4–13

God taught Paul a secret we all need to know: the secret of contentment. Contentment, unlike indifference, is the godly opposite of worrying and obsessing. When you worry, you're trying to hold onto what you might lose, or you're grabbing for what you don't have. Indifference means you are trying not to care about what you don't have or might lose. But that's not contentment. Contentment offers a fundamental stability that comes from knowing that the all-powerful Lord of the universe is near. He is listening to your cries and guarding you day and night. Paul learned contentment by depending on this Lord. He said, "I can do everything through him who gives me strength" (Philippians 4:13). Paul knew that, no matter how the circumstances of his life changed, God would be his constant, faithful, loving protector.

How can you live with the same confidence that Paul had in God? The antidote to anxiety is not some mental trick like, "Rehearse some Bible truth. Say this calming promise over and over to yourself. Remind yourself that you are a child of God; and your anxiety will disappear." God is after bigger game. You are his child, and he wants a relationship with you. He wants you to talk to him. He intends for your anxiety, your troubles, and your response to your troubles to drive you to him.

DAVID POWLISON

NOVEMBER 10

MATTHEW 4:1–11

If we have any doubts about how the world is organized into kingdoms and how these kingdoms are ruled by spiritual heads, take a look at what happens immediately after Jesus is proclaimed as the rightful heir to the true throne (Matthew 3:16): spiritual battle breaks out (Matthew 4). Satan tempts Jesus with promises of food, authority, and power, but Jesus defeats him by spiritual means. That is, he trusts his Father and obeys him. When Jesus casts demons out of man, he is announcing that "the kingdom of God has come upon you" (Matthew 12:22–28). And notice what happens even today whenever the reality of the kingdom of Christ is proclaimed: The Evil One quickly tries to snatch away what was sown in the heart (Matthew 13:19).

All we can see with the naked eye is our own particular frets and fears, but there is something much bigger taking place. Worries are a way that we doubt the King's presence and power. Our doubts could come from our own stubborn commitment to the myth of personal autonomy, or they may come from satanic accusations that question God's generosity and our unworthiness. Either way, anxiety and worry are spiritual wake-up calls that must be handled by spiritual means.

EDWARD T. WELCH

November 11

Matthew 22:1–14

Scripture provides more than one picture of life after death; a judgment seat isn't the only one. Equally prominent in Scripture, if not more so, is the wedding banquet.

If you feel at times like a spiritual street person, destitute and homeless, then you are invited. If you are spiritually superior, smug, or indifferent, then be warned. It is the outcasts and those who come as needy children who eat at the banquet table. How can this be? Outcasts and those with a glaring sense of their own spiritual neediness can only put their trust in someone other than themselves. This is what God requires—that we trust in him alone.

Our trust in Christ is never perfect, but it is one sign that we belong to Christ and that the work of the cross is applied to us. In part this means we are cleansed. Robes that were once blemished and hands that were bloody because of our murderous ways are washed. They are white, and white is the color of a bride beautifully dressed for her husband (Revelation 21:2). We are intended to be the bride of Christ, and when we belong to him we are intended to hear, "As a bridegroom rejoices over his bride, so will your God rejoice over you" (Isaiah 62:5). How do you qualify to be a bride? Simply acknowledge that you need cleansing and beauty from Christ.

Edward T. Welch

NOVEMBER 12

LUKE 6:27–36

Jesus said, "Love your enemies, do good to those who hate you, bless those who curse you, pray for those who mistreat you. . . . Be merciful, just as your Father is merciful" (Luke 6:27–28, 36). Notice the pair of motives that bookend the section—love and mercy, even toward our enemies. As a recipient of God's saving love and mercy in Jesus, how do we in turn show love and mercy to our enemies?

First pray, asking God to give you a heart of love and mercy, to help you better understand and apply his Word, to give you wisdom to know what to do and what not to do, and to make you more like Jesus. Ask God to work in the offender's heart, to lead him or her to repentance. Next, bless your enemy by speaking well to him and about him. Let the Scriptures guide you: "Do not let any unwholesome talk come out of your mouths, but only what is helpful for building others up according to their needs, that it may benefit those who listen" (Ephesians 4:29). Finally, demonstrate Christlike kindness by not repaying evil for evil and by taking positive actions.

God's grace in Jesus can teach you how to "be kind and compassionate to one another, forgiving each other, just as in Christ God forgave you" (Ephesians 4:31–32).

ROBERT D. JONES

NOVEMBER 13

LUKE 17:1–10

When the cross shapes my relationships, I respond to the sin and weakness of others with grace. Do you hold people to higher standards than you hold yourself? Do you tend to forget you are a sinner, while remembering that others are? Do you fail to overlook minor offenses? Do you spend more time catching people doing wrong than doing right? Do people feel accepted and loved by you, or criticized and judged? How do you tend to respond to the weaknesses, sins, and failures of those around you?

The cross enables me to serve others out of a heart of compassion, gentleness, forbearance, kindness, patience, and love. The closer I get to people, the more these attitudes are needed, because that is when I am affected by their weaknesses and sin (and vice versa). The closer we are to one another, the more our hearts are revealed. Thus we all need to ask, "What attitudes shape my closest relationships?" Christ lives in us to rescue us from ourselves, so that we can be loving and gracious with one another even though we are sinners. Every time I lay aside my own desires to minister to another, I am living out the results of Christ's death on the cross.

TIMOTHY S. LANE AND PAUL DAVID TRIPP

November 14

Psalm 63

Jesus was being accosted by the Tempter—Satan himself—when he cited this passage (Matthew 4:4). Fittingly, Jesus hadn't eaten for forty days. No doubt, food was his primary need. But in the midst of near starvation, he said that there was something more important than food: to be strengthened by the Spirit of God as he rested on the very words of the Father. Spiritual food can seem unsatisfying at first, but have you ever had someone say to you, "I love you"? Wouldn't you gladly pass on a buffet in order to hear such words? In Jesus' case, this spiritual food was more important than physical life itself. Now we begin to understand how God remains faithful to his promises even when his people go hungry. The physical food points to something better.

The apostle Paul often went hungry but he saw absolutely no contradiction between that and God's generous care for his truest needs. Paul knew that, no matter how well fed, the physical body was inevitably going to die. But a fed spirit is satisfied for this life and the life to come. To make it more personal, if Paul had God, what else did he really need?

EDWARD T. WELCH

NOVEMBER 15

PSALM 25

Praying through Psalm 25 will lead you out of your world of sin and guilt. In verse 3 David prays, "No one whose hope is in you will ever be put to shame." Then he asks God to help him turn from his sins. He doesn't want to end his life a failure, so he prays, "Show me your ways, O LORD, teach me your paths; guide me in your truth and teach me, for you are God my Savior" (Psalm 25:4–5). David asks God to "remember . . . your great mercy and love" (Psalm 25:6). He wants God to look at his life through the lens of his compassion, goodness, and forgiveness.

In verse 11 David prays, "Forgive my iniquity, though it is great." This is the heart of what it means to go to God—a radical giving of your life into the hands of another. David is pleading with God on the basis of his character to pardon him, change him, and teach him.

David goes on to pray about all the problems that bring temptation into his life. Pray this psalm to God and insert your troubles, your sins, and your need for forgiveness into it. As you pray, God will begin to reverse the turning inward that sin, guilt, and hardship bring. And he will draw you to himself—to the one who, for his name's sake and by his mercy, must and will work in you.

DAVID POWLISON

NOVEMBER 16

PSALM 23

Whatever your future, you are called to live by faith today. Jesus says, "Therefore do not worry about tomorrow, for tomorrow will worry about itself. Each day has enough trouble of its own" (Matthew 6:34). Jesus wants you to depend on him one day at a time. Learn not to worry about tomorrow. To do this you must meditate on who Jesus is.

More than any other passage, Psalm 23 brought Jesus to life for me in my struggles with fatigue. The psalm is full of promises—he provides, he restores my soul, he is with me, his goodness and mercy pursue me all of my days. Make this psalm your own. Jesus, your good Shepherd, will fill you with confidence. God doesn't meet us the way we want, but he does restore us. No matter what you are facing, you have a Shepherd who is with you, restoring you, and bringing good things—himself—into your life. Learn to trust him, and you truly have something worth living and dying for.

DAVID POWLISON

NOVEMBER 17

PSALM 13

The reasons for suffering are among "the secret things" that belong to the Lord. But "the things revealed belong to us" (Deuteronomy 29:29). God isn't only talking about his laws; he's also talking about his promises, his purposes, his revelation of himself in Jesus and the Word. What has been revealed is given so you can live. What hasn't been revealed is a secret thing. Instead of trusting in your knowledge, you have to trust in God's love and goodness. This is a lesson you will have to learn and relearn throughout your life. Your relationship with God is what brings peace, not having every question answered. C. S. Lewis wrote that our need for God is revealed in our "growing awareness that our whole being . . . is one vast need, incomplete, preparatory, empty yet cluttered, crying out for him who can untie things that are now knotted together and tie up things that are still dangling loose" (C. S. Lewis, *The Four Loves* [New York: Harcourt Brace, 1960], p. 3).

Suffering puts you in a place where all you can do is rely on God, the only one who can untie the things that are knotted together and tie up things that are dangling loose. You have to say, along with the apostle Peter, "Lord, to whom shall we go? You have the words of eternal life. We believe and know that you are the Holy One of God" (John 6:68–69).

DAVID POWLISON

NOVEMBER 18

ISAIAH 51:1–11

Each day we should remind ourselves of the utter simplicity of God's comfort and call. First, God comforts us with his presence and power and calls us to trust him. We are to entrust to God the things we cannot control. Second, God calls us to obey, and promises to bless us as we do. In good and bad circumstances, we must ask, "What has God called me to do and what has he provided in Christ to enable me to do it?"

I can admit my faults with no need to minimize, hide, or give way to paralyzing guilt. I can confess that I need to grow without beating myself up. I can cry out when life is hard but accept responsibility for the way I deal with it. I don't have to cover my sin, polish my reputation, and keep a record of my successes. I can look at my tomorrows with enthusiasm and hope. Yes, I am still a flawed person in a broken world. But my view of myself is not dark and depressed because the gospel has infused it with hope. Christ is with me and in me, and I will never be in a situation where he isn't redemptively active. Though change is needed in many ways, I am not discouraged. I am in the middle of a work of personal transformation. This process is often painful, but always beneficial.

TIMOTHY S. LANE AND PAUL DAVID TRIPP

NOVEMBER 19

PHILIPPIANS 1:3–11

The complete forgiveness that Christ provides means I no longer need to be afraid to look at myself in the mirror of God's Word. I no longer need to defend or excuse myself, to rationalize away my sinful choices, or shift the blame to someone or something else. I no longer need to deny or avoid my sin. Why? Because if the God of forgiveness, wisdom, and power actually lives in me, why would I be afraid to face my weaknesses and sin? Instead, I can be committed to grow in self-understanding. I can be glad that God's Word is a mirror into my heart and that God puts people in my life to help me to see myself more accurately. I can be excited about my potential to learn, change, and grow.

I will also seek godly help. The cross opens me up to the resources of God's grace. One of those resources is the body of Christ. I will not live independently. I will take advantage of biblical teaching available to me. I will seek the fellowship of a small group. I will pursue the wisdom of mature brothers and sisters. I will try to benefit from the accountability a close friend can provide. And I will take advantage of all of these resources by being honest about my struggles of heart and behavior.

TIMOTHY S. LANE AND PAUL DAVID TRIPP

NOVEMBER 20

LUKE 6:43–45

Word problems are heart problems. Christ said, "The good man brings good things out of the good stored up in his heart, and the evil man brings evil things out of the evil stored up in his heart. *For out of the overflow of his heart his mouth speaks*" (Luke 6:45, authors' emphasis). Our problem with words is not primarily a matter of vocabulary, skill, or timing. Have you ever said, "Oops, I didn't mean to say that!" Often it would be more accurate to say, "I'm sorry I said what I meant!" If the thought, attitude, desire, emotion, or purpose hadn't been in your heart, it wouldn't have come out of your mouth. Christ isn't saying that people never put their feet in their mouth and say something stupid. We all have. But he is asking us to own the connection between our thoughts, desires, and words. The real problem with your communication is *what* you want to say and *why* you want to say it, which ultimately has nothing to do with your language skills. Christ reveals that the *what* and the *why* are shaped by the heart. Therefore, if we hope to transform the way we talk with one another, the heart must change first.

TIMOTHY S. LANE AND PAUL DAVID TRIPP

November 21

Luke 19:1–10

Zacchaeus was lost. In his hometown, on a road he knew well, he was desperately lost. He just didn't realize how far gone he was. He wanted to see Jesus. He couldn't get through the crowd, so he climbed a tree for a better look.

There's something about post-adolescents in trees that suggests the dangerous and the ridiculous. Zacchaeus, a wealthy, feared government official, set himself up to be ridiculed for the rest of his life. Even today Sunday school songs immortalize this man's peculiar behavior! So here's this little man, who probably already had endured his share of insults regarding his height, providing raw material for new, embarrassing stories. Why is he doing this?

It could have been simple curiosity that drove him to go looking for Jesus, but curiosity is not enough to drive someone to such desperate behavior. Something else drove Zacchaeus. Despite his wealth, his life was not going well. We're not told what was wrong, but as you consider the lengths he went to, you realize he wanted something more—something that even his wealth couldn't give him. He was dissatisfied with his life and his dissatisfaction drove him to seek out Jesus.

WILLIAM P. SMITH

NOVEMBER 22

MATTHEW 8:18–27

Thanksgiving is gratitude for a benefit we have received. Joy includes gratitude, but its true delight is in the beauty of God and the deep goodness in all the things that come from him. Joy draws attention outward with a nonpossessive appreciation for something that is good. For example, you are in a boat and about to die. The winds have whipped the waters into a maelstrom that will engulf you within minutes. Jesus speaks a word and the waters are still. No one, however, thanks him. They are all too amazed (Matthew 8:23–27). This amazement at Jesus' power is the beginning of joy. It is not primarily self-referential. It is more than satisfied to contemplate the majesty of the One who just spoke.

Another example: You are blind. Jesus is coming and you call out for mercy. When he stops, he asks what you want. You ask for sight. When he gives it to you, you don't simply thank him, you follow him. This, too, is the beginning of joy. Your attention is captured by the Giver more than the benefit received (Matthew 20:29–34).

The words *thanks* and *thanksgiving* can be found dozens of times in Scripture. The words *joy, gladness, rejoice,* and *enjoy* can be found hundreds of times.

EDWARD T. WELCH

November 23

Isaiah 30:12–18

Don't do anything; just sit there! Sit and learn who God really is. You are drowning under layers of wrong thinking about God. Start with the truth that Jesus is God. Everything you want to know about the true God can be found in him. So keep your eyes peeled for Jesus. Read about Jesus in the Gospels. Keep in mind that Jesus is the King who got off his throne, humbled himself, came to earth, and died an awful, shameful death for you (Philippians 2:6–11). His death paid the penalty in full for you. You are tempted to think that you have to pay some of it yourself because no one has ever offered such forgiveness and love to you. But God is not like a person. He pays it all. You just say "thank you." Whenever you think you have to pay him back, stop immediately. That might sound very religious, but it is your old religion talking. The true gospel is that you have been given an extravagant gift of forgiveness. It does sound too good to be true, but it is true. Hold out your hands and show Jesus that you have nothing to bring to him. All he asks of you is that you admit that you have nothing to bring and he has brought everything for you.

EDWARD T. WELCH

November 24

Galatians 5:16–26

"I want my way! My will be done!" Anger goes wrong when we get angry about things that don't matter. God's anger is always holy and pure because what he says is wrong *is* wrong, and what he says matters *does* matter. One difference between our anger and God's anger is that, since we aren't always holy and pure, we often get angry at things that aren't true wrongs and don't really matter to anyone but us. If you throw a tantrum when you are served cold food in a restaurant, or curse when you are stuck in traffic—these are not things that really matter in God's world. God explains to us in the Bible why we get angry at things that don't really matter to anyone but us. The apostle Paul uses the phrase "the desire of the flesh" (Galatians 5:16–17 ESV) to describe where our wrong anger comes from. You and I get angry because of what we desire (what we expect, want, and believe we need) to happen in a certain situation or relationship. Think about the last time you got angry. Underneath your angry feelings, words, and actions is what you wanted but didn't get. Respect, affirmation, power, convenience, cooperation, help, money, comfort, intimacy, peace, pleasure, identity, safety . . . what is it that you want? And how do you respond when you don't get it? Anger going wrong loudly tells the world, "I want my way! My will be done!"

David Powlison

NOVEMBER 25

DEUTERONOMY 8

God knows exactly what he is doing! The wilderness wanderings were not a sign of Moses' poor leadership. They were not a sign of God's forgetfulness, faithlessness, or weakness. Yet this was how the children of Israel interpreted their circumstances. They doubted God so intensely that they actually considered returning to Egypt! Deuteronomy 8 tells us that God had a purpose for each trial. In each one, God sought to do three things for the Israelites: to teach, humble, and discipline them. Why?

First, God was preparing them for the spiritual obstacles they would face in the sufferings and blessings of the Promised Land. They needed to experience trials in order to understand that no matter what things looked like, God's hand would sustain them. Like all sinners, the Israelites could easily drift into autonomy and self-sufficiency. Second, they needed to see the propensity of their own hearts to drift away from trusting God and obeying his commands. Third, they needed to see regular demonstrations of God's power, so that they would not fear the things they could not defeat on their own.

These trials did not call God's character into question; rather, they stand as signs of his covenant-keeping love. His eyes are on each of his children and his ears are attentive to each cry.

TIMOTHY S. LANE AND PAUL DAVID TRIPP

NOVEMBER 26

EPHESIANS 1:3–14

The Bible is filled with reminders of God's grace for us in Christ: friendships, the sacraments, Scripture, worship, and prayer. They keep the wonder of his glory and mercy before us. God calls us into relationships with other believers in the body of Christ. As they speak into our lives and walk alongside us and we do the same for them, we are living reminders of God's grace and forgiveness.

When we celebrate the sacraments of baptism or the Lord's Supper, God reminds us of his redeeming grace. His Word lovingly reminds us of his deep compassion and never-ending mercy. Worship and prayer, when linked, reignite the newness of the gospel in us.

So often, Christians live as if God's forgiveness is not very amazing. Some even act as if it is God's job to forgive. When that happens, the desire, ability, and commitment to forgive others wane. Forgiving others and asking for forgiveness are supernatural works of grace. They only happen when God's forgiveness captivates our hearts.

Can you say those frightful but liberating and God-honoring words: "I was wrong. I sinned against you. Will you forgive me?" Or, "Yes, I forgive you!" To say either with biblical clarity, honesty, and sincerity is a sign that the Holy Spirit is at work in your life. It is evidence that you are a partaker of the wonderful forgiveness that is yours because Jesus absorbed the cost of your sins.

TIMOTHY S. LANE

NOVEMBER 27

Exodus 3

"Who am I, that I should go to Pharaoh and bring the Israelites out of Egypt?" Moses asks when God appoints him to deliver the Israelites from Pharaoh's tyranny. God responds, "I will be with you." Is that a satisfying answer? Moses didn't think so and he proposed that God find someone else. I agree. If God wants me to take on Pharaoh, I want a weapon I can hold and control. Instead, God promises to be with me. What good is that! And that's when it hits me: What more could God offer me? Yet somehow, I don't believe it's enough.

Consider how God's promises to Israel are deeply and completely fulfilled in Christ. The Israelites feared losing Moses, but we never lose our Deliverer. He lives today interceding for us. He has poured out his Holy Spirit into us so that we are never separated from him. We walk through life with One who promises he will never leave us or forsake us; we can connect with him at any moment. Do your reactions to life's challenges show that you believe he is all you will ever need, or do they reveal that you long for something more?

WILLIAM P. SMITH

NOVEMBER 28

EPHESIANS 4:25–32

Anger responds to an incident: "I'm angry about what you did." Bitterness goes deeper to form an attitude—a settled stance or posture—against the perpetrator: "I'm bitter at you, because you are an evil person." We store that hurt in our heart, nurture it, and let it grow to the point where we look with hostility at the offender.

What hope do you and I have to escape the sorrow, slavery, and soul impoverishment that resentment brings? The answer is found in Jesus. Jesus comes to us in our mistreatment and remains with us to help us. As one who was sinned against severely, he understands mistreatment. The Scriptures tell us that he came to save his own people but they did not receive him (John 1:11). "He was despised and rejected by men, a man of sorrows, and familiar with suffering" (Isaiah 53:3). Jesus was sinned against severely: mocked, taunted, punched, spit upon, abandoned, and crucified. Paul calls us to "get rid of all bitterness, rage and anger, brawling and slander, along with every form of malice." The antidote to bitterness? "Be kind and compassionate to one another, forgiving each other, just as in Christ God forgave you" (Ephesians 4:31–32). Paul calls us to have our minds consciously controlled by God's forgiveness through Jesus' death on the cross. As we grasp the mighty work of our incarnate, crucified, and risen Lord, we are moved to forgive others.

ROBERT D. JONES

November 29

Galatians 2:15–21

It is not enough for Paul to say that the death of Christ made him new. He says that when he died, the old Paul was not replaced with a new and improved version of Paul, but with Christ himself! He's not simply saying that the new Paul is better at controlling the sin in his heart. He is saying that where sin once controlled, Christ now rules! Our hearts, once under the domination of sin, are now the dwelling place of Christ, the ultimate source of righteousness, wisdom, grace, power, and love.

Here is the gospel of our potential. It was necessary for us to die with Christ so that he could live forever in our hearts. The old sinful me has died. But it has not been replaced with a better me. The replacement is Christ! My heart is new, because Christ lives there. My heart is alive, because Christ lives there to give it life. My heart can respond to life in new ways because it is no longer dominated by sin, but liberated by the gracious rule of Christ. That is why I have the potential for amazing change and growth in my heart and life.

Timothy S. Lane and Paul David Tripp

NOVEMBER 30

PSALM 4

What was God seeking to produce by the cross? Was his goal a kingdom of unangry people? No, the cross was meant to produce people who are angry every day. Jesus died to produce a culture of people who are so in love with him, so committed to his righteous cause, and so distressed by what sin has done to them and their world, that they cannot help but be angry every day. This is not the old, selfish, unholy anger. These people are able to be good *and* angry at the same time.

Jesus died not only to free you from your anger, but to enable you to take up his righteous anger. He died so that you would not rage inside because people and circumstances loom as constant obstacles to the realization of your little kingdom cravings. He died so that you would not be a captive to the self-absorbed anger of your claustrophobic little kingdom. He died so that you would be angry with sin and the way it has harmed you and everyone around you. He died so that you would be angry at the way sin has damaged the world you live in. He died so that your anger would be holy and pleasing to him. He died so that your anger would propel you to act in deeds of mercy, love, forgiveness, compassion, restoration, and peace.

PAUL DAVID TRIPP

December 1

Psalm 29

When you sin you worship something besides God, e.g., comfort, success, control, power, pleasure. Fight against temptation by admitting to God that your behavior is wrong—the result of forgetting your identity in Christ and finding your identity in what you believe you need besides him. Don't be discouraged when you notice what's captured your heart instead of Jesus. Name it, confess it to God, and ask for forgiveness. Remember, "If we confess our sins, he is faithful and just to forgive us our sins and to cleanse us from all unrighteousness" (1 John 1:9). Even though you have loved something more than God, Jesus is still completely committed to you. He lived, died, was raised, and sent his Spirit for you. Right now he is praying for you, and one day he will come to rescue you completely. Make every effort to remember who you are in Christ. You are not a slave to sin; instead, you belong to Christ (Galatians 2:20). He is more committed to you than you are to yourself. He is more satisfying and attractive than anything else in this world. Begin to have a conversation with your Redeemer. Interact with him as you bring your sins before him and as you tell him about your struggles. He understands what it is like to live in a broken world as a human, and he will give you mercy and grace as you ask (Hebrews 4:14–16).

Timothy S. Lane

DECEMBER 2

PSALM 119:89–96

When you hear the words *Psalm 119*, what are your first associations? I suspect that your heart does not immediately come up with the following: "Psalm 119 is where I go to learn how to open my heart about what matters, to the person I most trust. I affirm what I most deeply love. I express pure delight. I lay my sufferings and uncertainties on the table. I cry out in need and shout for joy. I hear how to be forthright without self-righteousness. I hear how to be weak without self-pity. I learn how true honesty talks with God: fresh, personal, and direct; never formulaic, abstract, or vague. I hear firsthand how Truth and honesty meet and talk it over. This Truth is never denatured, rigid, or inhuman. This honesty never whines, boasts, rages, or gets defensive. I leave the conversation nourished by the sweetest hope imaginable. I hear how to give full expression to what it means to be human, in honest relationship with the Person who made humanness in his image."

Such a response reflects that Truth has grappled with everything you think, feel, do, experience, and need, changing the way you process life. And you have grappled with Truth. Now you can say what you're really thinking because self-centeredness has been washed away! Psalm 119 is about life's painful realities, the gifts of God, and how those two meet to find life's highest delight.

DAVID POWLISON

DECEMBER 3

PSALM 103

Living a God-centered life has not been left in a cloud of mystery for us. God has given us his Word as a functional guide for our everyday living. We do not need to be confused about what it means to be a God-centered neighbor, parent, spouse, friend, worker, or citizen. We do not need to fret over what it means to handle our possessions, finances, grief, anger, opportunities, and responsibilities in a godly way. We do not need to be confused about what we are to do with our thoughts, what should control our desires, or where we should place our hopes. God has precisely revealed his will for our daily living in his Word. Our principal job in life is not to uncover mystery. Our principal job is to obey what has already been revealed. Our job as we awake each morning is not to figure out how we would like to respond to what is on our plate. The commands, directives, and principles of God's Word are meant to guide us in how we live to serve him.

PAUL DAVID TRIPP

DECEMBER 4

MATTHEW 27:45–54

Atonement was made by the high priest once a year. After careful cleansing, attired in special garments, the high priest entered the Most Holy Place, which was separated from the rest of the temple by a heavy curtain. In this room the high priest sprinkled the blood of sacrificed animals on the atonement cover of the ark. This was done according to God's detailed instructions; to do it carelessly would result in immediate death.

Under this system of ritual cleansing and sacrifice there are daily reminders that your sinfulness requires bloodshed, and that an impenetrable curtain stands between you and God because of your sin. Not a moment passes without an acute awareness that seeing God face to face would kill you. There is hope because God provides cleansing so that he can live among his people. However, the unending bloodshed and that curtain are constant reminders of a debt that is never repaid.

When Jesus was crucified and the temple curtain was torn in two, God's message was unmistakable: his people had been forgiven once and for all. The obstacle of sin was removed. There was no longer a need for separation between God and his people. Likewise, death, the ultimate form of separation and punishment, is no longer our final destiny. Along with Jesus himself, the dead came out of their graves with new life. Now nothing separates God from his people. We can approach him without fear.

WINSTON T. SMITH

DECEMBER 5

MATTHEW 13:44–46

There are different ways to enter the kingdom. Some people stumble upon it, some search for it. Whatever way we find it, we are hooked once we do. One man was working in the fields, found something of inestimable worth, buried it again, and gave up everything he had to buy the field. The other man had been looking for one precious pearl his entire life. When he found it, of course he gave up everything else for it. Both men happily gave up everything they owned to have something much better.

You can't imagine either of them second-guessing themselves. There is no wavering, no regret. Notice the joy of the man who found the treasure. The kingdom was announced as a kingdom of joy (Luke 2:10); those who are brought into it can know a joy that can never be taken away (John 16:22). Such joy can sound like the impossible dream and, indeed, it might be a long way off. But like everything else in Scripture that seems too good to be true, let it arouse and inspire you. Don't write it off as impossible. Let it be a vision and hope that invades your prayers.

EDWARD T. WELCH

DECEMBER 6

LUKE 15:11–32

The father wasn't interested in meeting his son halfway. God gave us this story to help us understand him better. In the ancient Near East, the children's job description was to enhance the reputation—the glory—of the father. The father cared for the children and blessed them so they could continue the family line. The children honored the father by loving and obeying him. Clearly, this child was not a dutiful son. To make matters worse, the father was a prominent person who lived in a culture where everyone was watching. The actions of the son would and did bring great shame. Who could have predicted that the father, on hearing the news that his son might be returning, would run to meet him? Important people don't run anywhere. That's the job of servants. If an important person ran toward anyone, it would be undignified and, in this case, compound his shame. This father, however, threw reputation to the wind. He wasn't interested in meeting his son halfway, even though that would have been embarrassment enough to a normal father. In his delight, he ran until he embraced his bedraggled son and kissed him.

EDWARD T. WELCH

December 7

James 1:1–18

If temptation comes from our circumstances, then we can deal with temptation by changing our circumstances, right? Circumstances do bring temptation into our lives, but God says in James that we succumb to temptation because of what's inside of us (what we desire, fear, etc.), not because of what's outside of us (our circumstances). When James talks about hard circumstances in chapter 1 he uses a Greek word that can be translated test, trial, or trap: "Consider it pure joy, my brothers, whenever you face trials of many kinds" (James 1:2); "Blessed is the man who perseveres under trial" (James 1:12). Here James describes circumstances as a trial or test that God allows for the purpose of growing us in grace.

But the translation of the Greek word changes in verses 13–15 to tempt: "When tempted, no one should say, 'God is tempting me.' For God cannot be tempted by evil, nor does he tempt anyone; but each one is tempted when, by his own evil desire, he is dragged away and enticed."

God sends circumstances into our lives to test us so we will grow in grace, not to trap us. Any circumstance is either a test that will help us to grow or a trap that leads to sin. What makes the difference? It's your inner condition in the midst of the circumstance. No circumstance makes you sin; you sin because what you want leads you to sin.

TIMOTHY S. LANE

DECEMBER 8

Self-examination—a work of grace in itself—precedes the redemptive promises in James 4:4–6. These verses enable us to "purify our hearts" (James 4:8) since that is where the real problem lies. They brim with hope. Verse 4 restates what verses 1–3 outlined. Because you have made something more important than God, you are in an extramarital relationship, spiritually speaking. You have become an unfaithful bride to your true husband, Jesus. While this is a negative assessment, notice how this verse talks about your relationship with God. If you belong to Jesus, you are in a marriage relationship with him! This is not because of anything you have done, but because of his mercy and grace. These verses call you to remember your true identity. In addition, verse 5 says that when you stray, God is a jealous lover who will not let you share your love and affection with another. He sends his Spirit to reclaim your heart's devotion and then gives you even more grace when you humble yourself (James 4:6)! James is saying that even God's children can stray from their love and devotion to God. Yet when you do, he loves you so much that he will not sit by and tolerate it. Instead, he pursues you with a holy love so that you will be captivated by his love for you at the very moment you are being unfaithful.

TIMOTHY S. LANE

DECEMBER 9

JEREMIAH 31:31–34

All roads in Scripture lead to Jesus. All the oaths God makes eventually have their guarantee and fulfillment in him (Hebrews 7:22). He is the one who writes the last will and testament and willingly dies so that the promises can have their full effect. He is the High Priest who makes the final sacrifice for sin so that another sacrifice never has to be made. The sacrifice, of course, is himself. His blood puts an end to the sacrificial system and ushers in an ever-better series of promises. "I will put my law in their minds and write it on their hearts. I will be their God, and they will be my people. . . . they will all know me, from the least of them to the greatest. . . . I will forgive their wickedness and will remember their sins no more" (Jeremiah 31:33–34).

This is the covenant of peace that he secured by his own death. This is his assurance that he will never leave us (Ezekiel 37:26–28). All this is unprecedented. When someone makes a promise to you, it is often because he did something wrong. But God makes promises to us because *we* did something wrong, and we cannot believe we could ever receive such mercy and grace. The apostle Paul put it this way: "For no matter how many promises God has made, they are 'Yes' in Christ" (2 Corinthians 1:20).

EDWARD T. WELCH

December 10

Hebrews 11

Real faith is lived within the context of being a deeply flawed person. Romanticized versions of biblical heroes can keep us from connecting with Christ. We make more of these saints than they are and then wonder why we cannot relate to them and their faith! Recognizing that our spiritual forerunners were deeply flawed does not mean that you can get comfortable with your failings. God still expects you to obey him. Instead, you lose your fear of acknowledging your failings. This allows you to develop greater confidence in the love God has for you despite your lack of faith.

Recognizing the patriarchs' failings causes you to look forward to Christ. When you read the Old Testament, you start looking for the One who will finally get it all completely right. You keep looking for him and you keep being disappointed. And you should be. Like you, these people had no righteousness in themselves. None of them were the Messiah and none of them could live a godly life apart from him. Part of the buildup of the Old Testament is a greater longing for the promised One.

WILLIAM P. SMITH

DECEMBER 11

ISAIAH 44:1–8

God's story goes from eternity to eternity. It starts with, "In the beginning, God." He is the Creator and we are his creatures. Immediately this retelling subverts all other stories. Other stories are always looking for ways to humanize God and deify us, but God's story exalts him and brings appropriate humility to us as his creatures. All wisdom starts here. If you miss it, you are on the wrong path and without hope.

Words of comfort often begin with God reaffirming that he is the Creator and we are his creatures. God's self-revelation as Creator is a comfort because it reminds us that there is no other god who can thwart God's intent. His plans will prosper. Isaiah reminds those listening that they are not God. They are God's offspring, who owe allegiance to him and no other.

The story continues. He creates a people for himself but his people choose a different story. Yet God continues with his plan and pursues wayward creatures. There is hope throughout, but sin and death are prominent. That is why the authentic story of hope hinges on the resurrection of Jesus. It is God's answer to a hopeless world.

EDWARD T. WELCH

DECEMBER 12

EXODUS 16:13–36

The Sabbath was a weekly tutorial for anxious people. Imagine that you are self-employed with very tight financial margins. Miss a day's work and your competitors get the upper hand. Miss a day's pay and you wonder if you will be able to buy groceries. Time is money. Now consider an agrarian economy. Here time might mean survival. Delay planting and you might miss the rain. Take a day off in the midst of harvest and your produce might overripen or even rot. With these risks in mind, the Sabbath was a big deal. It was a test. God was saying through it, "I am the Creator God who will care for your needs. Embedded in the rhythm of your week will be an opportunity to rest. You will do this because I rested on the Sabbath, and you will do it because I continue to be at work on your behalf on the Sabbath."

Just when you think you are getting the knack of the manna and are not worrying about tomorrow, you are told to trust your heavenly Father for today *and* tomorrow. Once again, we can't help but be astonished at God's strategy. Worry and fear are about danger, perceived needs, and being out of control. By incorporating the Sabbath into the normal rhythms of life he gives us weekly opportunities to say, "You, God, are in control, and I will practice trusting you by honoring your Sabbath and resting today."

EDWARD T. WELCH

DECEMBER 13

EPHESIANS 6:10–18

The world, the flesh, and the devil are three basic elements to temptation. The world includes our past, our strengths and weaknesses, and our relationships. These things don't determine our behavior, but they do make us more susceptible to respond in a certain way. For example, if you grew up in a verbally abusive home and experiencing little love, then that external pressure might make you susceptible to anger, bitterness, and despair. Suppose, on the other hand, you grew up in a loving family. This external reality, though a blessing, could still lead someone to be ungrateful, demanding, and proud.

The flesh is comprised of "evil desires" (James 1:14). How does the flesh interact with the world? Suppose you live for the approval of others. When you are criticized, your desire for approval could lead you to lash out in anger, or become depressed and isolated, or you might work even harder to gain approval. The external criticism was the occasion for how you responded, but what caused your particular response was the condition of your heart.

The devil uses the world and the flesh to trap you into sin, and then accuses you of being a hopeless case. Peter says, "The devil prowls around like a roaring lion looking for someone to devour" (1 Peter 5:8). Thankfully, the Spirit says, "The one who is in you is greater than the one who is in the world" (1 John 4:4).

TIMOTHY S. LANE

DECEMBER 14

PSALM 40

Your anger can be transformed. How do you learn to let go of your wrong anger and express your just anger constructively? Evaluate your wrong anger by asking: What is happening around you when you get angry? When did you get angry at something that doesn't really matter, or because you had made a good thing more important than God? What were your expectations (what did you want, need, demand) when you became angry? This question about your motives brings God into the discussion, because it reveals what hijacked God's place in your heart. Your answer will show you where you need God's help the most.

James says that sinful desires are the cause of our anger (James 4:1–2). If you remember that this is God's kingdom and not yours, the way you deal with your anger will be hugely affected. When you add to that an understanding of your real sins, then you will also see how God, in Christ, is tenderhearted and forgiving to you. Your anger will be transformed. Remembering the height, the depth, the width, and the length of God's love and mercy toward you will put your circumstances and your angry response in the right perspective (Ephesians 3:14–19). Meditating on your need for mercy and God's forgiveness will remind you that no matter what is making you angry, it's so much less than what you have been given in Christ.

DAVID POWLISON

December 15

Psalm 147

There are two reasons You don't turn to God. One, you believe he will take away something you need— something you trust in. Two, you don't believe you are good enough to come to God. The truth is, all you have to do is turn to him and speak honestly, and he will meet you. God meets the hurt with compassion (Psalm 147:3). God meets the angry and promises justice (Romans 12:19). God meets the self-loathing by taking their shame on himself. "Therefore, there is now no condemnation for those who are in Christ Jesus." And, "anyone who trusts in him will never be put to shame" (Romans 8:1; 10:11).

You expected judgment and a deaf ear; you get the God who loves you and hears you. If you want a relationship with God, respond to him in the same way you respond to someone who loves you, someone you have been avoiding. Tell God that you have been wrong. Confess your sins. Confess that your world is about you rather than him. Confess that you are living as if you know better than God. Confess that you are trying to save your own life rather than lose it (Matthew 10:39). Confess that you are trying to make life work apart from Jesus.

Edward T. Welch

DECEMBER 16

PSALM 131

"But I have stilled and quieted my soul; like a weaned child with its mother, like a weaned child is my soul within me" (Psalm 131:2).

How do you purify your heart? How does a proud heart become humble? Not by doing penance. Not by beating on yourself or resolving to mend your ways. You can do all those things and still be proud. You cannot destroy the tumult of self-will by sheer will: "I will stop being irritable. I will stop being fretful. I will stop imposing my will on the universe." Can the leopard change his spots? You are not strong enough; you are too strong. The only way you can wrestle yourself to is by the promises of God. You need help the way a drowning person needs help from outside himself to rescue him.

Only one thing is strong enough to overpower a stormy life: what God promises to do in and through Jesus Christ. It is by great and precious promises that we escape the corruption that is in the world by lust (2 Peter 1:4). From God's side we escape ourselves by being loved by Jesus Christ through the powerful presence of the Holy Spirit. From our side, we escape ourselves by learning a lifestyle of intelligent repentance, genuine faith, and specific obedience.

DAVID POWLISON

December 17

Psalm 115

All that's left to do is trust God. But that just happens to be the hardest thing for a human being to do. If it were natural to us, everyone would happily follow Jesus, and divided allegiances would be an aberration. But trust isn't natural, and divided allegiances are the norm. We are all guilty of little faith and, to make things worse, it isn't enough to simply understand this. Acknowledging the diagnosis does not automatically lead to a cure. You can confess it, and worry will creep in even during your confession! The cure is not to simply know what the problem is. The cure is to know the one we are called to trust. Keep looking at the triune God and how he has revealed himself throughout history. Don't spend your time focusing on your wavering allegiances.

How do you seek the kingdom? When you seek the King, you are seeking his kingdom. This kingdom includes everything that comes from him. It includes his law, his grace and mercy, his blessings of life, adoption, and holiness, and all his promises throughout Scripture. Those who seek him feed on his Word and seek to imitate him.

Are you worried? Jesus says there is nothing to worry about. It isn't our kingdom, it is God's. We take our cue from the King, and the King is not fretting over anything. He is in complete control.

EDWARD T. WELCH

DECEMBER 18

MATTHEW 16:21–28

Sin in its essence is self-focused. Sin causes my heart to be ruled by personal desire and felt need. Sin makes me want to set my own rules for me and others. Sin will even cause me to co-opt the grace of God for the purposes of my own agenda. Sin makes me want to write my own story and to have God endorse it. Sin makes me demanding and impatient. Sin causes me to wrap both of my hands around my life and do anything I can to preserve it for my own purpose.

Christ, on the other hand, not only calls us to be willing participants in our own death, but he also lays out the logic behind his call. It is found in this one profound big kingdom principle: *Try to save your life and you will lose it, but lose your life for Christ's sake and you will find it.* To jealously hold on to my dream of what I want to accomplish, experience, and enjoy is to guarantee that I will never ever experience true life. Instead, I will experience the slow and progressive shrinking of my soul until there is no life left. Our life cannot be found outside of our relationship to the Lord. If I am seeking life outside of the One who *is* life, I am effectively committing spiritual suicide.

PAUL DAVID TRIPP

DECEMBER 19

MARK 12:28–34

In the Bible, "heart" describes who we are at our core. When the Bible talks about the Christian life, it talks about loving God with all of our hearts. God is not content to live on the periphery of our lives. He will settle for nothing short of the center!

This is in stark contrast to other popular views of the Christian life. For most non-Christians (as well as many Christians), the Christian life is a matter of keeping the rules. God does have concerns about a person's behavior, but the Bible gives us a much more redemptive picture of a believer's life. It describes the Christian life in terms of a new relationship with God that brims with hope and flows from the core of our being into our daily lives! A Christian is someone whose life has been invaded by the holy love of God. God intends to create in us a pure love that flows from a new heart. We have seen that God even uses the metaphor of marriage to describe our intensely personal relationship with him. Marriage only begins to describe the relationship he wants to have with us, but it helps us understand why we obey God's commands and pursue a life of holiness.

TIMOTHY S. LANE AND PAUL DAVID TRIPP

DECEMBER 20

MATTHEW 12:46–50

Loneliness was born at the fall (Genesis 3:1–13). The perfect union Adam and Eve had enjoyed with God and with each other was destroyed when they chose to disobey God. Sin separated them from God and from each other. The real solution to loneliness lies in our union with Christ, which leads to our union with one another. When God created Eve, he created marriage; but more than that, he created community. Marriage is a form of community, perhaps its most basic and elemental form. Community requires people coming together. In marriage it happens literally. Community usually involves the group expanding. In marriage this happens by bearing children.

When God called Abram to follow him, he told him that his descendants would outnumber the grains of sand on the seashore and that all the nations of the earth would be blessed through him (Genesis 12:1–3; 13:16). God always had in mind a community made up of those from every tribe and language and people and nation.

When Jesus was told that his mother and brothers wanted to speak to him, he said, "Who is my mother, and who are my brothers? . . . Whoever does the will of my Father in heaven is my brother and sister and mother" (Matthew 12:48, 50). Jesus was redefining and enlarging the meaning of family. It's still based on blood—but it's his shed blood.

JAYNE V. CLARK

DECEMBER 21

ISAIAH 49:14–18

"Praise be to the God and Father of our Lord Jesus Christ, the Father of compassion and the God of all comfort, who comforts us in all our troubles, so that we can comfort those in any trouble with the comfort we ourselves have received from God" (2 Corinthians 1:3–4). The comfort God has given you is not only his loving ministry to you, it is his call to you to minister to others. You have experienced the pain of loss, but you have also begun to experience the comfort that only the Lord can give. You know how easy it is for grief to give way to doubt, anger, envy, and fear. You know how easy it is to isolate yourself and to want to give up; but you know the things God has given for help, hope, comfort, and strength. God now calls you to share this comfort with others. Who near you is discouraged and ready to quit? Who is struggling to hold onto hope? Who is dealing with the pain of disappointment? Who is struggling with problems so large that they can't see God? You are God's agent of help and hope. God entered your darkness, not just to give your heart rest, but to equip you to share that rest with others.

PAUL DAVID TRIPP

DECEMBER 22

GALATIANS 5:1–6

Jesus defines me, not my particular calling or vocation. While a Christian should never minimize personal gifts, past problems, or current struggles, these do not displace his or her more fundamental identity of being in Christ. "I am a new creation in Christ who happens to be a businesswoman, pastor, or parent." "I am a Christian who was hurt by someone in my past, who struggles with depression, who struggles with anger." My fundamental identity in the cross of Christ supersedes whatever struggle I am going through now.

Do you know what it means to live a cross-centered life on a daily basis? Some Christians think that the cross is what you need to become a Christian and get to heaven. They think, I need my sins forgiven so that I escape God's judgment when I die. But once that is taken care of, what matters is that I follow Christ's example. I need to roll up my sleeves and get to work! The tricky thing about this perspective is that it is partially correct. Once you become a Christian, you do participate in your ongoing growth. You do actively pursue the obedience that comes from faith (see Romans 1:5; 16:26; Galatians 5:6). You do engage in spiritual warfare! However, you are never to minimize your continuing need for the mercy and power of Christ in the process of becoming like him.

TIMOTHY S. LANE AND PAUL DAVID TRIPP

DECEMBER 23

2 CORINTHIANS 5:11–21

God wants to make us people who are more interested in what he wants for us than what we want for ourselves. He will not relent until we are free from our slavery to an agenda of personal happiness. And he calls us to speak in a way that has this reconciliation agenda in view.

Your words are always in pursuit of some kind of kingdom. You are either speaking as a mini-king, seeking to establish your will in your relationships and circumstances; or you are speaking as an ambassador, seeking to be part of what the *King* is doing. There is no end to the battle of words when two mini-kings talk to each other! When our words reflect the self-focused desires of our hearts rather than God's work of reconciliation, there is no end to our struggle. When we use words to establish our will rather than submit to God's, we plunge into difficulty. As sinners we want what we want when we want it, and we often see others as obstacles. We treat words as if they belong to us, to be used to get what we want. When we face how powerful our self-interest is, we are confronted by the truth that only a change in our hearts can produce a change in our words.

TIMOTHY S. LANE AND PAUL DAVID TRIPP

December 24

Romans 8:18–30

Life is filled with struggle and pain. The image of child-birth in Romans 8:20–22 reminds us that this pain is a part of a process. Now is painful because then won't be. It is only because a child will be born then that a mother experiences pain now. The example of childbirth reminds us that there is a redemptive purpose at work in the pain, but that does not make the pain go away! Understanding the hope of the gospel doesn't produce stoicism or denial. You don't deal with pain by minimizing it. Paul is clear: there is pain and we shouldn't be shocked when it comes our way. Where are you experiencing it right now?

As you consider these verses, notice that Paul uses a similar phrase in each one. Frustration, decay, and pain are true of "the creation," an all-encompassing category that includes everything but God. Everything else has been touched by sin and the fall. Nothing I am involved with, nothing that surrounds me, functions the way it was originally intended. Everything is broken in some way. You see it everywhere.

TIMOTHY S. LANE AND PAUL DAVID TRIPP

DECEMBER 25

Isaiah 32

The bright and shining hope of the Old Testament, as it chronicles the failed kingdoms of man, is that a King was coming who would establish his kingdom and reign in justice and righteousness forever. (See Isaiah 9:6–9; Isaiah 32; Ezekiel 37:24ff; Zechariah 9:9–13.) The Old Testament calls the people of God to shift their hope from the flawed rule of human kings to the promise of One who would rule without sin forever. The Old Testament is a detailed history of how God accomplished all the necessary steps leading to the coming of the Promised King. At the same time it chronicles the irresistible tendency that sinners have to opt for self-rule, even in the face of the promise of this benevolent King. The Old Testament ends with God's people waiting, looking, and hoping for the King.

The Gospels announce the coming of the King and the establishment of his kingdom. This is the backdrop of every teaching of Christ, every miracle, and every provision. The long-awaited time had come. Matthew has an announcement or description of the kingdom in every chapter. The Epistles detail the glorious hope that sinners find in the Savior-King's rule of grace. The entire Bible is the story of Christ the King. He *is* the One who alone is worthy of standing at the center of the kingdom of God.

Paul David Tripp

DECEMBER 26

PSALM 24

What will happen if you rest for a day? "For in six days the LORD made the heavens and the earth, the sea, and all that is in them, but he rested on the seventh day. Therefore the LORD blessed the Sabbath day and made it holy" (Exodus 20:11). To hear this as a call to imitate God, remember that God made humankind in his "image" (Genesis 1:27), and as his image bearers we must serve God and live in a way that represents him well. In part, our Sabbath rest symbolizes his Sabbath rest. You may be willing to tip your hat to God's power and glory, but his ability to manage all things effortlessly doesn't mean you're able to do the same. A day of rest may sound wonderful—until you realize how much farther behind you would fall if you lost that day to "catch up."

This points us to other reasons for observing the Sabbath. God's command to rest forces us to acknowledge that God isn't just in perfect control of his world, but ours as well. Resting means acknowledging that our world belongs to him and we must entrust our well-being into his hands. If you rest for a day, will God keep your life from falling apart? Rest then is an exercise in faith. Resting should be a way of living out the truth that our world belongs to God. We must trust that he is in loving control of it.

WINSTON T. SMITH

DECEMBER 27

2 CORINTHIANS 4:7–18

Trouble exposes what's really going on in your heart and mind. In your trouble you can turn to God for help, or you can turn away from God. What is going on in your heart as you struggle? Do you demand certain things from life: "I want _____. I fear its opposite." The Bible calls these demands "desires of the sinful nature" (Galatians 5:16; Ephesians 2:3; 1 John 2:16). Desires or cravings of the sinful nature are not just sexual or financial. They're anything you want more than the living God. These are your god-substitutes—what you worship instead of God. There is only one thing to do when you feel trapped by your response to trouble. You turn. You turn away from your false identity and false desires toward the living God. Turn to him in repentance and ask for mercy. Turn to God every day and every moment. Turn to Jesus who sympathizes with your weakness. He has experienced your temptations, and he promises to help you in your time of need. This is what the life of faith is all about—noticing your sins and relying on Jesus for forgiveness and help. His death and resurrection guarantee that you will be forgiven and helped. They guarantee that one day your tears will be wiped away and you will be with God forever (Revelation 21:3–4).

DAVID POWLISON

DECEMBER 28

HEBREWS 12:18–29

They needed a mediator. At Mount Sinai, the Israelites saw God's power and glory, but forgot the underlying grace and kindness that seasons the way he uses his awesome power. What they needed—and what they had—was a mediator who could speak for God to them. They needed someone who would stand between them and God, someone who would help them understand God and know how to respond to him. They needed to know that God did not desire for them to live in abject terror, that he was approachable. At the same moment, they needed to be exhorted not to take him lightly but to obey him with reverent fear.

God chose a mediator who would meet their exact need at that precise moment. You too have a Mediator who is also your God. As he saw the desperate need of Jerusalem, Jesus longed to gather his people under his protection. His people rejected him, but do you see his great love for them? His heart and his longing have not changed. He does not rule with terror. Rather, he invites you to come to him with reverent confidence when you need his mercy and his help—because he is just like his Father.

WILLIAM P. SMITH

DECEMBER 29

HEBREWS 4:12–16

Guilt is part of the human condition in this broken world. And once you become a Christian, you don't stop sinning, so you need to deal with the guilt that comes from your continuing struggle with sin. Hebrews 4:12–16 gives a clear picture of how Jesus has freed us from our guilt. These verses are both sobering and encouraging. We will give an account one day because we are accountable, and there is a standard. God is the one before whom we are accountable, and our lives will be compared against his perfect character. This is why we feel guilty, because deep down we know we are guilty. What can free us from our guilt?

God himself frees us. He sent his one and only Son, Jesus, to die a terrible and undeserved death for us. Jesus is our Great High Priest who offered himself and became the sacrifice for our sins. The answer to our guilt is found in his life, death, and resurrection. "But God demonstrates his own love for us in this: While we were still sinners, Christ died for us" (Romans 5:8). Jesus came and died in our place. He was our substitute. Because he was without sin, he was able to pay the penalty for our sins. His death for us means we can be free from guilt and reconciled to God. Jesus' death is the only real answer to our guilt.

TIMOTHY S. LANE

DECEMBER 30

MATTHEW 6:25–34

"Is not life more important than food, and the body more important than clothes?" Every question and sentence from Jesus will be good for hours of meditation, especially this one. Jesus' question implies, "Yes, there is something more important." Even if I forget the Old Testament commentary about the manna story, which says that manna is really about being sustained by the very words of God, Jesus has already talked about what is more important: "Blessed are the poor in spirit, for theirs is the *kingdom of heaven*" (Matthew 5:3, author's emphasis). "Your kingdom come" (Matthew 6:10). "Store up for yourselves treasures in heaven" (Matthew 6:20).

Why am I so concerned about a meal, which will fill me for about an hour, when the kingdom is coming? One of the strategies for dealing with worry is to be overtaken by something more important than the object of your worries. Jesus is showing us what is more important. A new kingdom was being inaugurated, and it was present even as Jesus spoke those words because he is its King. This new kingdom is so beautiful and important that it can override our worries about everyday concerns like food and clothing.

EDWARD T. WELCH

DECEMBER 31

REVELATION 22:1–21

God's story is a great story. We, however, are people of habit. Change does not come easily or quickly. We stubbornly cling to past interpretations and old stories even when God's universal story is much better. The reason is not that we lack education and knowledge, but that we overflow with pride. You have been crafting your own story for years. It isn't original, having been pieced together with scraps from your culture and people you admired, with your own unique twists. But it is your own. To adopt a different story, with a different hero, means that we must say, "I was wrong." Given the options, many of us opt to stay with our old story.

Deep change is rarely a matter of knowledge. It is a matter of repentance. We have chosen a path apart from God; repentance is the process of turning back. We have chosen a different story, filled with subtle lies about God, questioning his love, care and compassion. Repentance means to renounce our story and believe that there is only one Storyteller. God alone is authorized to interpret our lives.

EDWARD T. WELCH

SOURCE INDEX

January 1.   Paul David Tripp, *Age of Opportunity* (Phillipsburg, NJ: P&R, 2001), 104.

January 2.   Paul David Tripp, *A Quest for More* (Greensboro, NC: New Growth, 2008), 160–61.

January 3.   William P. Smith, *Caught Off Guard* (Greensboro, NC: New Growth, 2007), 74–75.

January 4.   Edward T. Welch, *Depression* (Greensboro, NC: New Growth, 2011), 225–26.

January 5.   Timothy S. Lane, *Conflict* (Greensboro, NC: New Growth, 2006), 15–19.

January 6.   William P. Smith, *How to Love Difficult People* (Greensboro, NC: New Growth, 2008), 9, 11–12.

January 7.   Edward T. Welch, *Running Scared* (Greensboro, NC: New Growth, 2007), 127.

January 8.   Edward T. Welch, *Depression* (Greensboro, NC: New Growth, 2011), 56.

January 9.   Edward T. Welch, *Depression* (Greensboro, NC: New Growth, 2011), 98–99.

January 10.   William P. Smith, *When Bad Things Happen* (Greensboro, NC: New Growth, 2008), 12–13.

January 11.   Michael R. Emlet, *CrossTalk* (Greensboro, NC: New Growth, 2009), 5–6.

January 12.   Paul David Tripp, *Grief* (Greensboro, NC: New Growth, 2010), 9–10.

January 13.   Michael R. Emlet, *Chronic Pain* (Greensboro, NC: New Growth, 2010), 13–14.

January 14.	William P. Smith, *Caught Off Guard* (Greensboro, NC: New Growth, 2007), 116.
January 15.	David Powlison, *Overcoming Anxiety* (Greensboro, NC: New Growth, 2008), 12–13.
January 16.	Paul David Tripp and Timothy S. Lane, *Relationships: A Mess Worth Making* (Greensboro, NC: New Growth, 2008), 12.
January 17.	David Powlison, *Speaking Truth in Love* (Greensboro, NC: New Growth, 2005), 65–66.
January 18.	Edward T. Welch, *Depression* (Greensboro, NC: New Growth, 2011), 69–70.
January 19.	Edward T. Welch, *Depression* (Greensboro, NC: New Growth, 2011), 72–73.
January 20.	Edward T. Welch, *Running Scared* (Greensboro, NC: New Growth, 2007), 72–73.
January 21.	Paul David Tripp, *A Quest for More* (Greensboro, NC: New Growth, 2008), 74–75.
January 22.	William P. Smith, *Caught Off Guard* (Greensboro, NC: New Growth, 2007), 18–19.
January 23.	Edward T. Welch, *Depression* (Greensboro, NC: New Growth, 2011), 35–36.
January 24.	Edward T. Welch, *Depression* (Greensboro, NC: New Growth, 2011), 64–65.
January 25.	Edward T. Welch, *Depression* (Greensboro, NC: New Growth, 2011), 247.
January 26.	Edward T. Welch, *Depression* (Greensboro, NC: New Growth, 2011), 142–43.

January 27.	Edward T. Welch, *Depression* (Greensboro, NC: New Growth, 2011), 122–23.
January 28.	David Powlison, *Grieving a Suicide* (Greensboro, NC: New Growth, 2010), 9–10.
January 29.	Edward T. Welch, *Depression* (Greensboro, NC: New Growth, 2011), 30–31.
January 30.	Edward T. Welch, *Eating Disorders* (Greensboro, NC: New Growth, 2008), 11–13.
January 31.	Edward T. Welch, *Running Scared* (Greensboro, NC: New Growth, 2007), 268–69.
February 1.	Robert D. Jones, *Freedom from Resentment* (Greensboro, NC: New Growth, 2010), 11–12.
February 2.	Edward T. Welch, *Depression* (Greensboro, NC: New Growth, 2011), 121–22.
February 3.	Edward T. Welch, *Depression* (Greensboro, NC: New Growth, 2011), 44–45.
February 4.	Timothy S. Lane, *Conflict* (Greensboro, NC: New Growth, 2006), 13–14.
February 5.	Paul David Tripp and Timothy S. Lane, *How People Change* (Greensboro, NC: New Growth, 2008), 13–14.
February 6.	Edward T. Welch, *Running Scared* (Greensboro, NC: New Growth, 2007), 230–32.
February 7.	Paul David Tripp and Timothy S. Lane, *How People Change* (Greensboro, NC: New Growth, 2008), 88, 90.
February 8.	Paul David Tripp, *A Quest for More* (Greensboro, NC: New Growth, 2008), 171–72.

February 9.   William P. Smith, *Caught Off Guard* (Greensboro, NC: New Growth, 2007), 60.

February 10.   Paul David Tripp and Timothy S. Lane, *Relationships: A Mess Worth Making* (Greensboro, NC: New Growth, 2008), 56–57.

February 11.   Edward T. Welch, *Depression* (Greensboro, NC: New Growth, 2011), 30–31.

February 12.   William P. Smith, *How to Love Difficult People* (Greensboro, NC: New Growth, 2008), 4–6.

February 13.   William P. Smith, *Caught Off Guard* (Greensboro, NC: New Growth, 2007), 28–29.

February 14.   Paul David Tripp and Timothy S. Lane, *Relationships: A Mess Worth Making* (Greensboro, NC: New Growth, 2008), 59–60.

February 15.   Timothy S. Lane, *Forgiving Others* (Greensboro, NC: New Growth, 2004), 9–10.

February 16.   Paul David Tripp, *A Quest for More* (Greensboro, NC: New Growth, 2008), 115–16.

February 17.   Edward T. Welch, *Depression* (Greensboro, NC: New Growth, 2011), 104–5.

February 18.   Paul David Tripp, *Helping Your Adopted Child* (Greensboro, NC: New Growth, 2008), 12–13.

February 19.   Paul David Tripp, *Grief* (Greensboro, NC: New Growth, 2010), 7–8.

February 20.   Timothy S. Lane, *Temptation* (Greensboro, NC: New Growth, 2010), 30–32.

February 21.   Edward T. Welch, *Depression* (Greensboro, NC: New Growth, 2011), 38–39.

February 22.   Paul David Tripp and Timothy S. Lane, *How People Change* (Greensboro, NC: New Growth, 2008), 25–26.

February 23.   Paul David Tripp and Timothy S. Lane, *How People Change* (Greensboro, NC: New Growth, 2008), 6–7.

February 24.   Paul David Tripp and Timothy S. Lane, *How People Change* (Greensboro, NC: New Growth, 2008), 22–23.

February 25.   Robert D. Jones, *Freedom from Resentment* (Greensboro, NC: New Growth, 2010), 24–26.

February 26.   Winston T. Smith, *Marriage Matters* (Greensboro, NC: New Growth, 2010), 26–27.

February 27.   Paul David Tripp, *A Quest for More* (Greensboro, NC: New Growth, 2008), 54–56.

February 28.   Edward T. Welch, *Depression* (Greensboro, NC: New Growth, 2011), 55–56.

February 29.   Edward T. Welch, *Running Scared* (Greensboro, NC: New Growth, 2007), 139–40.

March 1.   Edward T. Welch, *Depression* (Greensboro, NC: New Growth, 2011), 60–61.

March 2.   Edward T. Welch, *Running Scared* (Greensboro, NC: New Growth, 2007), 153–54.

March 3.   Paul David Tripp, *Grief* (Greensboro, NC: New Growth, 2010), 11–12.

March 4.	Paul David Tripp, *A Quest for More* (Greensboro, NC: New Growth, 2008), 202–3.
March 5.	David Powlison, *Grieving a Suicide* (Greensboro, NC: New Growth, 2010), 12–14.
March 6.	Paul David Tripp and Timothy S. Lane, *How People Change* (Greensboro, NC: New Growth, 2008), 16.
March 7.	Paul David Tripp, *Grief* (Greensboro, NC: New Growth, 2010), 10–11.
March 8.	William P. Smith, *How to Love Difficult People* (Greensboro, NC: New Growth, 2008), 6–7.
March 9.	Winston T. Smith, *Marriage Matters* (Greensboro, NC: New Growth, 2010), 104–5.
March 10.	Paul David Tripp and Timothy S. Lane, *How People Change* (Greensboro, NC: New Growth, 2008), 189.
March 11.	Winston T. Smith, *Burned Out* (Greensboro, NC: New Growth, 2010), 21–23.
March 12.	Edward T. Welch, *Depression* (Greensboro, NC: New Growth, 2011), 134–35.
March 13.	David Powlison, *Renewing Marital Intimacy* (Greensboro, NC: New Growth, 2008), 9–10.
March 14.	Timothy S. Lane, *Conflict* (Greensboro, NC: New Growth, 2006), 19–20.
March 15.	Paul David Tripp and Timothy S. Lane, *How People Change* (Greensboro, NC: New Growth, 2008), 43–44.

March 16. Jayne V. Clark, *Single and Lonely* (Greensboro, NC: New Growth, 2009), 10–11.

March 17. Edward T. Welch, *Depression* (Greensboro, NC: New Growth, 2011), 49–50, 52–53.

March 18. Paul David Tripp, *A Quest for More* (Greensboro, NC: New Growth, 2008), 27–28.

March 19. Paul David Tripp and Timothy S. Lane, *Relationships: A Mess Worth Making* (Greensboro, NC: New Growth, 2008), 72.

March 20. Edward T. Welch, *Running Scared* (Greensboro, NC: New Growth, 2007), 129–31.

March 21. Paul David Tripp, *A Quest for More* (Greensboro, NC: New Growth, 2008), 81–82.

March 22. Edward T. Welch, *Running Scared* (Greensboro, NC: New Growth, 2007), 120–21.

March 23. Edward T. Welch, *Running Scared* (Greensboro, NC: New Growth, 2007), 109.

March 24. William P. Smith, *How to Love Difficult People* (Greensboro, NC: New Growth, 2008), 7–8.

March 25. Edward T. Welch, *Depression* (Greensboro, NC: New Growth, 2011), 65–66.

March 26. Paul David Tripp and Timothy S. Lane, *Relationships: A Mess Worth Making* (Greensboro, NC: New Growth, 2008), 56.

March 27. David Powlison, *Facing Death with Hope* (Greensboro, NC: New Growth, 2008), 19–21.

March 28.   David Powlison, *Life Beyond Your Parents'
              Mistakes* (Greensboro, NC: New Growth,
              2010), 10, 12–13.

March 29.   William P. Smith, *Caught Off Guard*
              (Greensboro, NC: New Growth, 2007),
              35–37.

March 30.   William P. Smith, *Caught Off Guard*
              (Greensboro, NC: New Growth, 2007),
              66–67.

March 31.   Paul David Tripp, *Grief* (Greensboro, NC:
              New Growth, 2010), 19–20.

April 1.   Paul David Tripp, *A Quest for More*
              (Greensboro, NC: New Growth, 2008),
              178.

April 2.   Paul David Tripp and Timothy S. Lane,
              How People Change (Greensboro, NC: New
              Growth, 2008), 190.

April 3.   William P. Smith, *How to Love Difficult
              People* (Greensboro, NC: New Growth,
              2008), 18–20.

April 4.   Paul David Tripp, *A Quest for More*
              (Greensboro, NC: New Growth, 2008),
              44–46.

April 5.   Paul David Tripp and Timothy S. Lane, *Re-
              lationships: A Mess Worth Making* (Greens-
              boro, NC: New Growth, 2008), 46–48.

April 6.   David Powlison, *Breaking the Addictive
              Cycle* (Greensboro, NC: New Growth,
              2010), 13–15.

April 7.   Paul David Tripp, *A Quest for More*
              (Greensboro, NC: New Growth, 2008),
              69–70.

April 8.	Edward T. Welch, *Depression* (Greensboro, NC: New Growth, 2011), 36–37.
April 9.	Edward T. Welch, *Running Scared* (Greensboro, NC: New Growth, 2007), 143.
April 10.	Edward T. Welch, *Depression* (Greensboro, NC: New Growth, 2011), 240–41.
April 11.	Edward T. Welch, *Running Scared* (Greensboro, NC: New Growth, 2007), 188–89.
April 12.	Paul David Tripp, *A Quest for More* (Greensboro, NC: New Growth, 2008), 52–53.
April 13.	Paul David Tripp and Timothy S. Lane, *Relationships: A Mess Worth Making* (Greensboro, NC: New Growth, 2008), 97.
April 14.	Edward T. Welch, *Depression* (Greensboro, NC: New Growth, 2011), 78–79.
April 15.	Winston T. Smith, *Burned Out* (Greensboro, NC: New Growth, 2010), 16–17.
April 16.	Edward T. Welch, *Depression* (Greensboro, NC: New Growth, 2011), 73–74.
April 17.	Winston T. Smith, *Burned Out* (Greensboro, NC: New Growth, 2010), 25–27.
April 18.	Paul David Tripp, *A Quest for More* (Greensboro, NC: New Growth, 2008), 120–21.
April 19.	William P. Smith, *Caught Off Guard* (Greensboro, NC: New Growth, 2007), 48–49.
April 20.	Edward T. Welch, *Depression* (Greensboro, NC: New Growth, 2011), 152–53.

May 3.   David Powlison, *Speaking Truth in Love* (Greensboro, NC: New Growth, 2005), 6.

May 4.   Edward T. Welch, *When People Are Big and God Is Small* (Phillipsburg, NJ: P&R, 1997), 129.

May 5.   Timothy S. Lane, *Temptation* (Greensboro, NC: New Growth, 2010), 27–28.

May 6.   Paul David Tripp, *Grief* (Greensboro, NC: New Growth, 2010), 14–15.

May 7.   Paul David Tripp and Timothy S. Lane, *How People Change* (Greensboro, NC: New Growth, 2008), 14–15.

May 8.   Paul David Tripp and Timothy S. Lane, *How People Change* (Greensboro, NC: New Growth, 2008), 113.

May 9.   Paul David Tripp and Timothy S. Lane, *How People Change* (Greensboro, NC: New Growth, 2008), 191–92.

May 10.   Edward T. Welch, *Running Scared* (Greensboro, NC: New Growth, 2007), 133–34.

May 11.   Edward T. Welch, *Depression* (Greensboro, NC: New Growth, 2011), 232–33.

May 12.   Paul David Tripp and Timothy S. Lane, *Relationships: A Mess Worth Making* (Greensboro, NC: New Growth, 2008), 98–99.

May 13.   Edward T. Welch, *Depression* (Greensboro, NC: New Growth, 2011), 163–64.

May 14.   Edward T. Welch, *Depression* (Greensboro, NC: New Growth, 2011), 244–45.

May 15.   David Powlison, *Speaking Truth in Love* (Greensboro, NC: New Growth, 2005), 64.

May 16.	David Powlison, *Facing Death with Hope* (Greensboro, NC: New Growth, 2008), 12–13.
May 17.	Edward T. Welch, *Running Scared* (Greensboro, NC: New Growth, 2007), 196–97.
May 18.	Edward T. Welch, *Depression* (Greensboro, NC: New Growth, 2011), 43–44.
May 19.	Edward T. Welch, *Depression* (Greensboro, NC: New Growth, 2011), 155–56.
May 20.	Edward T. Welch, *Depression* (Greensboro, NC: New Growth, 2011), 80–81.
May 21.	Paul David Tripp, *A Quest for More* (Greensboro, NC: New Growth, 2008), 126–27.
May 22.	Edward T. Welch, *Depression* (Greensboro, NC: New Growth, 2011), 74–75.
May 23.	Edward T. Welch, *Running Scared* (Greensboro, NC: New Growth, 2007), 75.
May 24.	Paul David Tripp, *A Quest for More* (Greensboro, NC: New Growth, 2008), 16–18.
May 25.	Paul David Tripp and Timothy S. Lane, *How People Change* (Greensboro, NC: New Growth, 2008), 15.
May 26.	Paul David Tripp and Timothy S. Lane, *Relationships: A Mess Worth Making* (Greensboro, NC: New Growth, 2008), 97–98.
May 27.	David Powlison, *Facing Death with Hope* (Greensboro, NC: New Growth, 2008), 7–8.

May 28.	David Powlison, *Overcoming Anxiety* (Greensboro, NC: New Growth, 2008), 10–11.
May 29.	Edward T. Welch, *Running Scared* (Greensboro, NC: New Growth, 2007), 93.
May 30.	Paul David Tripp, *A Quest for More* (Greensboro, NC: New Growth, 2008), 127–28.
May 31.	David Powlison, *Overcoming Anxiety* (Greensboro, NC: New Growth, 2008), 16–17.
June 1.	David Powlison, *Renewing Marital Intimacy* (Greensboro, NC: New Growth, 2008), 11–12.
June 2.	David Powlison, *Life Beyond Your Parents' Mistakes* (Greensboro, NC: New Growth, 2010), 4–5.
June 3.	Winston T. Smith, *Marriage Matters* (Greensboro, NC: New Growth, 2010), 10–11.
June 4.	Edward T. Welch, *Running Scared* (Greensboro, NC: New Growth, 2007), 264.
June 5.	David Powlison, *I'm Exhausted* (Greensboro, NC: New Growth, 2010), 13–14.
June 6.	William P. Smith, *Caught Off Guard* (Greensboro, NC: New Growth, 2007), 112–13.
June 7.	Robert D. Jones, *Single Parents* (Greensboro, NC: New Growth, 2008), 4–5.
June 8.	David Powlison, *Life Beyond Your Parents' Mistakes* (Greensboro, NC: New Growth, 2010), 18–19.

June 9.   William P. Smith, *Caught Off Guard*
           (Greensboro, NC: New Growth, 2007),
           21.

June 10.   William P. Smith, *Caught Off Guard*
           (Greensboro, NC: New Growth, 2007),
           121.

June 11.   Timothy S. Lane, *Forgiving Others* (Greens-
           boro, NC: New Growth, 2004), 8–9.

June 12.   Edward T. Welch, *Depression* (Greensboro,
           NC: New Growth, 2011), 109–10.

June 13.   David Powlison, *Life Beyond Your Parents'
           Mistakes* (Greensboro, NC: New Growth,
           2010), 10–11.

June 14.   David Powlison, *Overcoming Anxiety*
           (Greensboro, NC: New Growth, 2008),
           11–12.

June 15.   Timothy S. Lane, *Temptation* (Greensboro,
           NC: New Growth, 2010), 24–25.

June 16.   Edward T. Welch, *Depression* (Greensboro,
           NC: New Growth, 2011), 75–76.

June 17.   David Powlison, *Overcoming Anxiety*
           (Greensboro, NC: New Growth, 2008),
           6–8.

June 18.   Edward T. Welch, *Running Scared* (Greens-
           boro, NC: New Growth, 2007), 229–30.

June 19.   Paul David Tripp and Timothy S. Lane, *Re-
           lationships: A Mess Worth Making* (Greens-
           boro, NC: New Growth, 2008), 113.

June 20.   Paul David Tripp and Timothy S. Lane,
           How People Change (Greensboro, NC: New
           Growth, 2008), 44–45.

June 21.   Winston T. Smith, *Help for Stepfamilies* (Greensboro, NC: New Growth, 2008), 10–11.

June 22.   Paul David Tripp and Timothy S. Lane, *How People Change* (Greensboro, NC: New Growth, 2008), 150–51.

June 23.   David Powlison, *Controlling Anger* (Greensboro, NC: New Growth, 2008), 11–12.

June 24.   William P. Smith, *Caught Off Guard* (Greensboro, NC: New Growth, 2007), 67–68.

June 25.   William P. Smith, *Caught Off Guard* (Greensboro, NC: New Growth, 2007), 12.

June 26.   Paul David Tripp, *A Quest for More* (Greensboro, NC: New Growth, 2008), 158–59.

June 27.   Paul David Tripp, *Instruments in the Redeemer's Hands* (Phillipsburg, NJ: P&R, 2002), 23–24.

June 28.   Paul David Tripp and Timothy S. Lane, *How People Change* (Greensboro, NC: New Growth, 2008), 141–42.

June 29.   William P. Smith, *When Bad Things Happen* (Greensboro, NC: New Growth, 2008), 10–11.

June 30.   David Powlison, *Controlling Anger* (Greensboro, NC: New Growth, 2008), 22–23.

July 1.   Edward T. Welch, *Depression* (Greensboro, NC: New Growth, 2011), 113.

July 2.   David Powlison, *Controlling Anger* (Greensboro, NC: New Growth, 2008), 20–21.

July 3.   Edward T. Welch, *Living with an Angry Spouse* (Greensboro, NC: New Growth, 2008), 7–9.

July 4.   David Powlison, *Grieving a Suicide* (Greensboro, NC: New Growth, 2010), 5–6.

July 5.   Paul David Tripp and Timothy S. Lane, *How People Change* (Greensboro, NC: New Growth, 2008), 99–100.

July 6.   Timothy S. Lane, *Conflict* (Greensboro, NC: New Growth, 2006), 14–15.

July 7.   Edward T. Welch, *Running Scared* (Greensboro, NC: New Growth, 2007), 196.

July 8.   Paul David Tripp, *A Quest for More* (Greensboro, NC: New Growth, 2008), 21–22.

July 9.   Paul David Tripp, *A Quest for More* (Greensboro, NC: New Growth, 2008), 167–68.

July 10.   Paul David Tripp and Timothy S. Lane, *How People Change* (Greensboro, NC: New Growth, 2008), 34.

July 11.   Paul David Tripp and Timothy S. Lane, *Relationships: A Mess Worth Making* (Greensboro, NC: New Growth, 2008), 46.

July 12.   Paul David Tripp and Timothy S. Lane, *Relationships: A Mess Worth Making* (Greensboro, NC: New Growth, 2008), 48–49.

July 13.   Winston T. Smith, *Burned Out* (Greensboro, NC: New Growth, 2010), 5–8.

July 14.   Robert D. Jones, *Freedom from Resentment* (Greensboro, NC: New Growth, 2010), 15–16.

July 15.   Paul David Tripp, *A Quest for More* (Greensboro, NC: New Growth, 2008), 114.

July 16.   Paul David Tripp, *A Quest for More* (Greensboro, NC: New Growth, 2008), 53–54.

July 17.   William P. Smith, *When Bad Things Happen* (Greensboro, NC: New Growth, 2008), 9–10.

July 18.   David Powlison, *Speaking Truth in Love* (Greensboro, NC: New Growth, 2005), 64–65.

July 19.   David Powlison, *Facing Death with Hope* (Greensboro, NC: New Growth, 2008), 11–12.

July 20.   Edward T. Welch, *Running Scared* (Greensboro, NC: New Growth, 2007), 150–51.

July 21.   David Powlison, *Overcoming Anxiety* (Greensboro, NC: New Growth, 2008), 21–22.

July 22.   William P. Smith, *When Bad Things Happen* (Greensboro, NC: New Growth, 2008), 14–17.

July 23.   Winston T. Smith, *Marriage Matters* (Greensboro, NC: New Growth, 2010), 28–29.

July 24.   Edward T. Welch, *Depression* (Greensboro, NC: New Growth, 2011), 4–5.

July 25.	Paul David Tripp, *A Quest for More* (Greensboro, NC: New Growth, 2008), 168.
July 26.	Edward T. Welch, *Running Scared* (Greensboro, NC: New Growth, 2007), 237–38.
July 27.	Edward T. Welch, *Depression* (Greensboro, NC: New Growth, 2011), 231–32.
July 28.	William P. Smith, *When Bad Things Happen* (Greensboro, NC: New Growth, 2008), 4–5.
July 29.	William P. Smith, *Caught Off Guard* (Greensboro, NC: New Growth, 2007), 97.
July 30.	Paul David Tripp and Timothy S. Lane, *How People Change* (Greensboro, NC: New Growth, 2008), 91–92.
July 31.	Paul David Tripp and Timothy S. Lane, *How People Change* (Greensboro, NC: New Growth, 2008), 5–6.
August 1.	Paul David Tripp and Timothy S. Lane, *How People Change* (Greensboro, NC: New Growth, 2008), 153–54.
August 2.	Paul David Tripp, *A Quest for More* (Greensboro, NC: New Growth, 2008), 42.
August 3.	William P. Smith, *When Bad Things Happen* (Greensboro, NC: New Growth, 2008), 11–12.
August 4.	Edward T. Welch, *Running Scared* (Greensboro, NC: New Growth, 2007), 226–27.

August 5.   Paul David Tripp and Timothy S. Lane, *Relationships: A Mess Worth Making* (Greensboro, NC: New Growth, 2008), 108–9.

August 6.   Winston T. Smith, *Marriage Matters* (Greensboro, NC: New Growth, 2010), 33.

August 7.   David Powlison, *Breaking the Addictive Cycle* (Greensboro, NC: New Growth, 2010), 25–27.

August 8.   Edward T. Welch, *Running Scared* (Greensboro, NC: New Growth, 2007), 223–24.

August 9.   Paul David Tripp and Timothy S. Lane, *How People Change* (Greensboro, NC: New Growth, 2008), 96.

August 10.   Paul David Tripp and Timothy S. Lane, *How People Change* (Greensboro, NC: New Growth, 2008), 44.

August 11.   Winston T. Smith, *Burned Out* (Greensboro, NC: New Growth, 2010), 23–25.

August 12.   David Powlison, *I'm Exhausted* (Greensboro, NC: New Growth, 2010), 14–16.

August 13.   James C. Petty, *When the Money Runs Out* (Greensboro, NC: New Growth, 2009), 12–14.

August 14.   David Powlison, *Controlling Anger* (Greensboro, NC: New Growth, 2008), 8–11.

August 15.   Edward T. Welch, *Running Scared* (Greensboro, NC: New Growth, 2007), 165–67.

August 16.   Paul David Tripp and Timothy S. Lane, *Relationships: A Mess Worth Making* (Greensboro, NC: New Growth, 2008), 111–12.

August 17.   Edward T. Welch, *Eating Disorders* (Greensboro, NC: New Growth, 2008), 9–11.

August 18.   Paul David Tripp, *A Quest for More* (Greensboro, NC: New Growth, 2008), 14–16.

August 19.   Edward T. Welch, *Living with an Angry Spouse* (Greensboro, NC: New Growth, 2008), 6–7.

August 20.   Edward T. Welch, *Depression* (Greensboro, NC: New Growth, 2011), 123–24.

August 21.   David Powlison, *Controlling Anger* (Greensboro, NC: New Growth, 2008), 9–10.

August 22.   Edward T. Welch, *Depression* (Greensboro, NC: New Growth, 2011), 114.

August 23.   Winston T. Smith, *Burned Out* (Greensboro, NC: New Growth, 2010), 9–13.

August 24.   William P. Smith, *Caught Off Guard* (Greensboro, NC: New Growth, 2007), 116–17.

August 25.   Edward T. Welch, *Depression* (Greensboro, NC: New Growth, 2011), 114–15.

August 26.   William P. Smith, *Caught Off Guard* (Greensboro, NC: New Growth, 2007), 6–7.

August 27.   Timothy S. Lane, *Conflict* (Greensboro, NC: New Growth, 2006), 8–11.

August 28.   Timothy S. Lane, *Family Feuds* (Greensboro, NC: New Growth, 2008), 10–11.

August 29.   Winston T. Smith, *Marriage Matters* (Greensboro, NC: New Growth, 2010), 21.

August 30.	Paul David Tripp and Timothy S. Lane, *How People Change* (Greensboro, NC: New Growth, 2008), 35–36.
August 31.	James C. Petty, *When the Money Runs Out* (Greensboro, NC: New Growth, 2009), 6–7.
September 1.	Paul David Tripp, *A Quest for More* (Greensboro, NC: New Growth, 2008), 79–80.
September 2.	David Powlison, *Speaking Truth in Love* (Greensboro, NC: New Growth, 2005), 30–31.
September 3.	David Powlison, *I'm Exhausted* (Greensboro, NC: New Growth, 2010), 8–9.
September 4.	Edward T. Welch, *Running Scared* (Greensboro, NC: New Growth, 2007), 62–63.
September 5.	Edward T. Welch, *Depression* (Greensboro, NC: New Growth, 2011), 67–68.
September 6.	Paul David Tripp and Timothy S. Lane, *How People Change* (Greensboro, NC: New Growth, 2008), 15.
September 7.	Paul David Tripp and Timothy S. Lane, *How People Change* (Greensboro, NC: New Growth, 2008), 22.
September 8.	Paul David Tripp, *A Quest for More* (Greensboro, NC: New Growth, 2008), 105–6.
September 9.	Paul David Tripp and Timothy S. Lane, *How People Change* (Greensboro, NC: New Growth, 2008), 26–27.
September 10.	Timothy S. Lane, *Conflict* (Greensboro, NC: New Growth, 2006), 3–4.

September 11.   Edward T. Welch, *Depression* (Greensboro, NC: New Growth, 2011), 162–63.

September 12.   Edward T. Welch, *Depression* (Greensboro, NC: New Growth, 2011), 34–35.

September 13.   Edward T. Welch, *Running Scared* (Greensboro, NC: New Growth, 2007), 163–64.

September 14.   Edward T. Welch, *Running Scared* (Greensboro, NC: New Growth, 2007), 76–77.

September 15.   Paul David Tripp, *A Quest for More* (Greensboro, NC: New Growth, 2008), 181–82.

September 16.   Edward T. Welch, *Running Scared* (Greensboro, NC: New Growth, 2007), 96–97.

September 17.   Winston T. Smith, *Marriage Matters* (Greensboro, NC: New Growth, 2010), 17–18.

September 18.   Paul David Tripp, *A Quest for More* (Greensboro, NC: New Growth, 2008), 58.

September 19.   Edward T. Welch, *Depression* (Greensboro, NC: New Growth, 2011), 112.

September 20.   Edward T. Welch, *Running Scared* (Greensboro, NC: New Growth, 2007), 194–95.

September 21.   Paul David Tripp and Timothy S. Lane, *Relationships: A Mess Worth Making* (Greensboro, NC: New Growth, 2008), 45–46.

September 22.   David Powlison, *Facing Death with Hope* (Greensboro, NC: New Growth, 2008), 8–9.

September 23.   Paul David Tripp and Timothy S. Lane, *Relationships: A Mess Worth Making* (Greensboro, NC: New Growth, 2008), 125–26.

October 6.   David Powlison, *Overcoming Anxiety* (Greensboro, NC: New Growth, 2008), 15–16.

October 7.   Edward T. Welch, *Depression* (Greensboro, NC: New Growth, 2011), 61–62.

October 8.   Paul David Tripp, *A Quest for More* (Greensboro, NC: New Growth, 2008), 136–37.

October 9.   Edward T. Welch, *Depression* (Greensboro, NC: New Growth, 2011), 119–20.

October 10.   Paul David Tripp and Timothy S. Lane, *Relationships: A Mess Worth Making* (Greensboro, NC: New Growth, 2008), 96.

October 11.   Paul David Tripp and Timothy S. Lane, *Relationships: A Mess Worth Making* (Greensboro, NC: New Growth, 2008), 119.

October 12.   Paul David Tripp, *A Quest for More* (Greensboro, NC: New Growth, 2008), 32–33.

October 13.   William P. Smith, *Caught Off Guard* (Greensboro, NC: New Growth, 2007), 107–8.

October 14.   Paul David Tripp, *A Quest for More* (Greensboro, NC: New Growth, 2008), 68–69.

October 15.   Paul David Tripp and Timothy S. Lane, *How People Change* (Greensboro, NC: New Growth, 2008), 39–40.

October 16.   David Powlison, *Overcoming Anxiety* (Greensboro, NC: New Growth, 2008), 8–9.

October 17.	David Powlison, *Controlling Anger* (Greensboro, NC: New Growth, 2008), 6–7.
October 18.	Michael R. Emlet, *Help for the Caregiver* (Greensboro, NC: New Growth, 2008), 11, 20.
October 19.	David Powlison, *Breaking the Addictive Cycle* (Greensboro, NC: New Growth, 2010), 6–8.
October 20.	Edward T. Welch, *Running Scared* (Greensboro, NC: New Growth, 2007), 107.
October 21.	Edward T. Welch, *Depression* (Greensboro, NC: New Growth, 2011), 145.
October 22.	William P. Smith, *Caught Off Guard* (Greensboro, NC: New Growth, 2007), 70–71.
October 23.	Edward T. Welch, *Depression* (Greensboro, NC: New Growth, 2011), 130–31.
October 24.	David Powlison, *Recovering From Child Abuse* (Greensboro, NC: New Growth, 2008), 4–5, 23–24.
October 25.	Paul David Tripp, *A Quest for More* (Greensboro, NC: New Growth, 2008), 20–21.
October 26.	Paul David Tripp, *Grief* (Greensboro, NC: New Growth, 2010), 15–16, 18–19.
October 27.	William P. Smith, *Caught Off Guard* (Greensboro, NC: New Growth, 2007), 94–96.
October 28.	Edward T. Welch, *Running Scared* (Greensboro, NC: New Growth, 2007), 143–45.

October 29.   Paul David Tripp, *A Quest for More* (Greensboro, NC: New Growth, 2008), 128–29.

October 30.   Michael R. Emlet, *Help for the Caregiver* (Greensboro, NC: New Growth, 2008), 4–5.

October 31.   David Powlison, *Healing After Abortion* (Greensboro, NC: New Growth, 2008), 22–23.

November 1.   Paul David Tripp, *A Quest for More* (Greensboro, NC: New Growth, 2008), 156–58.

November 2.   David Powlison, *Overcoming Anxiety* (Greensboro, NC: New Growth, 2008), 17–20.

November 3.   William P. Smith, *How to Love Difficult People* (Greensboro, NC: New Growth, 2008), 20–21.

November 4.   Paul David Tripp, *A Quest for More* (Greensboro, NC: New Growth, 2008), 115.

November 5.   Paul David Tripp, *A Quest for More* (Greensboro, NC: New Growth, 2008), 179.

November 6.   Edward T. Welch, *Depression* (Greensboro, NC: New Growth, 2011), 39–40.

November 7.   Edward T. Welch, *Depression* (Greensboro, NC: New Growth, 2011), 54.

November 8.   Edward T. Welch, *Depression* (Greensboro, NC: New Growth, 2011), 233–34.

November 9.   David Powlison, *Overcoming Anxiety*
               (Greensboro, NC: New Growth, 2008),
               13–15.

November 10.   Edward T. Welch, *Running Scared* (Greens-
               boro, NC: New Growth, 2007), 118.

November 11.   Edward T. Welch, *Running Scared* (Greens-
               boro, NC: New Growth, 2007), 233–34.

November 12.   Robert D. Jones, *Freedom from Resentment*
               (Greensboro, NC: New Growth, 2010),
               29–31.

November 13.   Paul David Tripp and Timothy S. Lane,
               How People Change (Greensboro, NC: New
               Growth, 2008), 192–93.

November 14.   Edward T. Welch, *Running Scared* (Greens-
               boro, NC: New Growth, 2007), 79.

November 15.   David Powlison, *Breaking Pornography
               Addiction* (Greensboro, NC: New Growth,
               2008), 16–17.

November 16.   David Powlison, *I'm Exhausted* (Greens-
               boro, NC: New Growth, 2010), 17–18.

November 17.   David Powlison, *Grieving a Suicide*
               (Greensboro, NC: New Growth, 2010),
               6–8.

November 18.   Paul David Tripp and Timothy S. Lane,
               How People Change (Greensboro, NC: New
               Growth, 2008), 127.

November 19.   Paul David Tripp and Timothy S. Lane,
               How People Change (Greensboro, NC: New
               Growth, 2008), 190.

November 20.   Paul David Tripp and Timothy S. Lane, *Re-
               lationships: A Mess Worth Making* (Greens-
               boro, NC: New Growth, 2008), 72.

November 21. William P. Smith, *Caught Off Guard* (Greensboro, NC: New Growth, 2007), 4–5.

November 22. Edward T. Welch, *Depression* (Greensboro, NC: New Growth, 2011), 240.

November 23. Edward T. Welch, *Eating Disorders* (Greensboro, NC: New Growth, 2008), 17–18.

November 24. David Powlison, *Controlling Anger* (Greensboro, NC: New Growth, 2008), 5–6.

November 25. Paul David Tripp and Timothy S. Lane, *How People Change* (Greensboro, NC: New Growth, 2008), 114.

November 26. Timothy S. Lane, *Forgiving Others* (Greensboro, NC: New Growth, 2004), 20–23.

November 27. William P. Smith, *Caught Off Guard* (Greensboro, NC: New Growth, 2007), 114–15.

November 28. Robert D. Jones, *Freedom from Resentment* (Greensboro, NC: New Growth, 2010), 5–7.

November 29. Paul David Tripp and Timothy S. Lane, *How People Change* (Greensboro, NC: New Growth, 2008), 151.

November 30. Paul David Tripp, *A Quest for More* (Greensboro, NC: New Growth, 2008), 190–91.

December 1. Timothy S. Lane, *Temptation* (Greensboro, NC: New Growth, 2010), 19–21.

December 2. David Powlison, *Speaking Truth in Love* (Greensboro, NC: New Growth, 2005), 11–12.

December 3. Paul David Tripp, *A Quest for More* (Greensboro, NC: New Growth, 2008), 127.

December 4. Winston T. Smith, *Marriage Matters* (Greensboro, NC: New Growth, 2010), 165–66.

December 5. Edward T. Welch, *Running Scared* (Greensboro, NC: New Growth, 2007), 164–65.

December 6. Edward T. Welch, *Running Scared* (Greensboro, NC: New Growth, 2007), 66–67.

December 7. Timothy S. Lane, *Temptation* (Greensboro, NC: New Growth, 2010), 5–8.

December 8. Timothy S. Lane, *Conflict* (Greensboro, NC: New Growth, 2006), 11–13.

December 9. Edward T. Welch, *Running Scared* (Greensboro, NC: New Growth, 2007), 260–62.

December 10. William P. Smith, *Caught Off Guard* (Greensboro, NC: New Growth, 2007), 29–31.

December 11. Edward T. Welch, *Depression* (Greensboro, NC: New Growth, 2011), 228–29.

December 12. Edward T. Welch, *Running Scared* (Greensboro, NC: New Growth, 2007), 78.

December 13. Timothy S. Lane, *Temptation* (Greensboro, NC: New Growth, 2010), 10–13.

December 14. David Powlison, *Controlling Anger* (Greensboro, NC: New Growth, 2008), 17–20.

December 15. Edward T. Welch, *Eating Disorders* (Greensboro, NC: New Growth, 2008), 15–16.

December 16. David Powlison, *Seeing with New Eyes* (Phillipsburg, NJ: P&R, 2003), 81.

December 17.   Edward T. Welch, *Running Scared* (Greensboro, NC: New Growth, 2007), 110.

December 18.   Paul David Tripp, *A Quest for More* (Greensboro, NC: New Growth, 2008), 117.

December 19.   Paul David Tripp and Timothy S. Lane, *How People Change* (Greensboro, NC: New Growth, 2008), 172.

December 20.   Jayne V. Clark, *Single and Lonely* (Greensboro, NC: New Growth, 2009), 6–9.

December 21.   Paul David Tripp, *Grief* (Greensboro, NC: New Growth, 2010), 23–24.

December 22.   Paul David Tripp and Timothy S. Lane, *How People Change* (Greensboro, NC: New Growth, 2008), 159–60.

December 23.   Paul David Tripp and Timothy S. Lane, *Relationships: A Mess Worth Making* (Greensboro, NC: New Growth, 2008), 73–74.

December 24.   Paul David Tripp and Timothy S. Lane, *How People Change* (Greensboro, NC: New Growth, 2008), 108–9.

December 25.   Paul David Tripp, *A Quest for More* (Greensboro, NC: New Growth, 2008), 98–99.

December 26.   Winston T. Smith, *Burned Out* (Greensboro, NC: New Growth, 2010), 8–9.

December 27.   David Powlison, *I'm Exhausted* (Greensboro, NC: New Growth, 2010), 9, 12–13.

December 28.   William P. Smith, *Caught Off Guard* (Greensboro, NC: New Growth, 2007), 54–55.

December 29.   Timothy S. Lane, *Freedom From Guilt* (Greensboro, NC: New Growth, 2008), 8–11.

December 30.   Edward T. Welch, *Running Scared* (Greensboro, NC: New Growth, 2007), 106.

December 31.   Edward T. Welch, *Depression* (Greensboro, NC: New Growth, 2011), 234.

PERMISSIONS

January 1 excerpt taken from *Age of Opportunity* by Paul David Tripp (ISBN 978-0-87552-605-8), p. 104.

May 4 excerpt taken from *When People Are Big and God Is Small* by Edward T. Welch (ISBN 978-0-87552-600-3), p. 129.

June 27 excerpt taken from *Instruments in the Redeemers' Hands* by Paul David Tripp (ISBN 978-0-87552-607-2), pp. 23–24.

December 16 excerpt taken from *Seeing with New Eyes* by David Powlison (ISBN 978-0-87552-608-9), pp. 80–81.

Quotes used with permission of P&R Publishing Co., PO Box 817, Phillipsburg NJ 08865, www.prpbooks.com.

Scripture Index

SCRIPTURE INDEX

ption of the soap-
he soaplands will
ent, you go in and
you do in a hotel.
ived just on time,
bears (she will be
horts) and escorts
f you are early or
o wait in a lounge
sually a television

o when you enter
move your shoes.
ds you a towel to
u to a steam box,
oor, leaving only
ng, she will check
me other kind of
our brow. When
e will let you out
ot-bath.
es, the girl then
down on a small
m top to bottom,
umerous buckets
directs you to lie
e-down to begin
oes to your neck
minues.
ce of any of the
are famous, you
face-up. Her ac-
here will be no
. The girls can
English to make
eign customers.

they have to make, and that is why they like to have these professional women on hand when they are wheeling and dealing or have just finished a hard piece of business.

The Shimbashi geisha district is one of the best known of the more than two dozen listed districts in Tokyo, and at the last count included seventy geisha *ryotei*. Guests who call in geisha are charged by the hour, with the rate depending on the class and popularity of the individual geisha. It is said that top geisha from Shimbashi as well as the Akasaka and Yanagibashi districts earn between $150,000 and $300,000 a year. But only a small percentage of this is net income because their expenses are very high.

Geisha generally work in teams of three or four. A geisha dinner party usually lasts from three to four hours and a bill of several thousand dollars is not unusual. Geisha from less prestigious districts are not as expensive.

Licensed geisha are not prostitutes, although it is common for them to form sexual liaisons with exclusive patrons.

In addition to the registered and licensed geisha, there are large numbers of women—often referred to as "instant geisha"—who are utilized by second- and third-class *ryotei* as well as by some traditional-style restaurants that cater to foreign visitors. These women do not follow the strict etiquette code of the professional geisha.

Coffee Shop Culture

Coffee shops play an important role in Japan, both day and night. Because the Japanese do not generally meet or entertain friends or business associates at home, and because there are no private offices in most Japanese companies, coffee shops are used as a universal meeting place in Japan. Some are small nooks that seat only ten or twelve people, while others cover entire floors

Many coffee shops have distinctive t
the type of music featured, the uniform
and so on. Some employ only good-loo
have all-male staffs. There are thousan⸤
Japan's major cities, so the visitor gene
lem finding one. The best guide is an c
be very small and inconspicuous—that
there is no telling what the front is g⸤

After the visitor in Japan has dined,
of theater entertainment. Japan ha
world's top film producers since the l
over eight thousand theaters in the cc
nese directors have gained internati
number of Japanese films such as *Th*
Rashomon (rah-show-moan) are consic
masterpieces of cinema art.

Most of Japan's entertainment dist
ber of first- and second-run theaters
ment Center in Tokyo's Asakusa Wa
aters), and there are dozens of othe
terminal areas. Some first-run theatei
nese films include English subtitles fc
foreign viewers who do not understa

Besides the movie theaters, Tokyo ⸤
lar kabuki, noh, and bunraku or p
Kabuki plays are mostly classical d⸤
actors perform all the roles while c
styled, colorful costumes.

The puppet plays of Japan are kat
best puppet theaters and handlers h
in Osaka, while Tokyo is recognized
The visitor to Japan who fails to tal
mance has missed one of the world⸤
theatrical experiences. Noh dramas ⸤

For the uninitiated, a detailed descri
land routine should be useful. Most of
accept reservations by phone. In any ev
walk up to a registration counter, just a⸤
If you have a reservation and have arr
your masseuse almost immediately ap
wearing a short robe over her bra and s
you to her private bath-massage room.
have no appointment, you may be asked
area where there will be magazines and ⸤
set.

The first thing you are instructed to c
the tiny vestibule of the bath-room is to r⸤
Then the girl helps you undress and ha⸤
wrap around your waist. She escorts yo
guides you into it, and closes the hatch-c
your head exposed. While you are steam⸤
the hot-water bath, offer you beer or sc
refreshment, and wipe the sweat from ⸤
you indicate that you have had enough s
of the box and direct you to enter the h

After letting you soak for a few minu
directs you to get out of the tub and sit
stool. She then proceeds to scrub you frc
front and back. She rinses you off with ⸤
of fresh hot water, towels you dry, then
down on the massage bunk—usually fac
with. She then massages you from your ⸤
and fingertips for some twenty to thirty

If you are going to be offered a choi
special services for which the soaplands
will know shortly after she has you turn
tions will become intimate enough that
doubt when the next move is up to yo
invariably communicate well enough in
their services and their rates known to fo

The Kimono and the Yukata

The Japanese *kimono* (kee-moe-no) and its simplified offspring the *yukata* (yuu-kah-tah) are two of Japan's most valuable tourist attractions. The predecessor of the kimono was imported from China more than a thousand years ago. After modifying it to fit their tastes, the Japanese adopted it as the national female costume of the country.

The kimono is still very much in evidence as the official, formal wear of Japanese women, and is worn regularly at parties, weddings, festivals, and holidays. It is also commonly worn by maids in inns, by geisha, by some cabaret hostesses*, and by shop clerks and office girls on several annual occasions. Elevator girls and maids in large, name hotels also wear kimono on special days, and because of the contrast with their Western surroundings, appear all the more exotic.

There is a provocative mystique surrounding the kimono. Its patterns and colors are closely related to the age of the wearer. The most brilliant colors and elaborate patterns are worn by young, single girls. But such provocative seductiveness is considered inappropriate for women after they marry, and their kimono are more subdued. The

---

*The percentage of cabaret hostesses wearing kimono has been declining since the mid-1960s, when half of them favored the national costume, apparently because of their expense and the complicated steps involved in putting them on. Of the 36,000 hostesses presently working in Tokyo's Ginza district, only around three hundred of them regularly wear kimono, according to kimono materials dealers. These dealers say that nowadays only *mama-sans* (the female managers of cabarets) and the top-earning hostesses wear kimono (one of whom says she spends $100 a day to have a professional dresser come to her apartment to help her don her kimono before leaving for work). As a result of this change, one department store on the Ginza that used to sell materials for 3,500 kimono each day, and devoted two whole floors to their display, now sells two or three a day. The material for a kimono costs from two hundred thousand to five hundred thousand yen (about $1,300 to $3,300).

older the wearer, generally the more conservative the colors and patterns of the kimono.

Young Japanese girls and women today still like the kimono because the sensuous patterns and beautiful materials of which they are made accent their youth and glorify their charms, thereby acting as a powerful stimulant to the male sex.

The yukata, originally an undergarment for the kimono and now used by both men and women as a bathrobe, nightgown, and the national leisure costume, is not only more comfortable and convenient than the kimono, it is also sexier. I think it is one of the most seductive garments a woman can wear.

The summer yukata consists of a single, thin layer of decorated cotton cloth that snuggles the body kimono-fashion, both concealing and revealing the figure at the same time. Its sexiness is considerably heightened by its connection with the bath, bed, and hot-spring resort spas. Traditionally yukata were worn without any undergarments, and there is always the intriguing question of whether the present-day wearer follows tradition.

In winter, a kind of yukata wrap called *dotera* (doe-tay-rah) may be worn over the yukata.

To fully appreciate the role the yukata plays in life in Japan, you must experience it yourself. The intimacy it generates, particularly when you are in a ryokan in a resort noted for its scenic beauty and romantic history, is almost magical.

Both the kimono and the yukata have a remarkable psychological effect on Japanese girls and women. Because of the nature of the two garments, worn wrapped around the body robe-fashion, from ankle to neck, the wearer is forced to move in a restrained and graceful manner. This has a remarkably feminizing influence on the wearer as well as itself presenting an image of charged femininity.

In addition to making the wearer look more feminine, and making it more difficult for her to act in other than a feminine manner without appearing grossly vulgar, the kimono and the yukata are representative of the traditional manners and values of Old Japan, and when they are wearing them the women are strongly affected by this influence.

When the Japanese girl or woman changes from Western dress to a kimono or yukata it is like stepping out of one culture into another. Not only her appearance but her attitude and behavior as well undergo subtle changes.

While most Westerners react favorably to the exotic and sensual attractions of the kimono, they are inclined to regard it as simply too restricting. But its formidability is misleading. The large arm holes give direct access to the area of the breasts, and the skirt of the garment can be flipped open to the waist in a matter of seconds.

The yukata is even more erotic. Although completely concealing, it reveals while covering, and can be opened from top to bottom in one quick motion—or shed completely in two movements.

Many Western visitors to Japan, perhaps out of a sense of embarrassment, are reluctant to wear the yukata even inside their ryokan. This is another of the many times when you are in Japan that you should put aside such feelings and wholeheartedly enter into the spirit of the place and the occasion.

The Sensational Hot-Spring Spas

Japan has more known hot-spring spas than any other country, and hundreds of them have been in use since ancient times. There are over 1,100 spas whose waters have recognized medicinal value.

A number of Japan's best-known cities owe their prominence to hot-springs (Atami, Ito, Unzen, and Beppu among them), and several hundred small towns and communities throughout the ilsands are built around natural hot-springs which serve as their primary economic resource.

Most of the country's famous winter ski resorts, including Zao and Akakura, are built over giant hot-springs which often seem more popular than the adjoining snow-covered slopes.

One of Japan's most spectacular and famous hot-spring resorts is *Noboribetsu* (no-boe-ree-bate-sue) in Hokkaido. Located in a large ravine formed by the Kusurisambetsu River in a section of the Shikotsu-Toya National Park (about an hour and a half train ride from Sapporo), the spa includes eleven large hot-springs. Each of the springs has a complex of inns surrounding it, and a different mineral content, so the visitor can choose the one he or she believes will be the most beneficial—or visit them all!

Mixed-sex bathing is the rule in Noboribetsu, and some of the baths, which look like huge pool-pocked gardens, will accommodate over one hundred bathers at a time without crowding. This is an especially good place for the visitor to get his first taste of mixed bathing because the steam rising up from the pools of hot water keeps visibility in the baths low at all times.

The most popular of the hot-springs near Tokyo are Atami, Hakone, Ito, Nasu, Kinugawa, and Shiobara. Atami, less than an hour from Tokyo by express train, is perched on the side of half of an extinct volcano—the other half collapsed into the sea ages ago—and has dozens of hot-spring inns and hotels. It has long been noted as a honeymoon spot, a hideaway for weekend lovers, and a favorite place to hold company parties.

Hakone, a large district that includes *Ashi-no Ko* (ah-she-no koe) or Hakone Lake, has fourteen spas within its boundaries: Yumoto, Tonosawa, Miyanoshita, Dogashima, Sokokura, Kowakidani, Kiga, Gora, Ubako, Sengokuhara, Ashinoyu, Yunohanazawa, Ohiradai, and Moto-Hakone— all located in areas so superbly scenic that any attempt to describe their settings quickly become redundant with superlatives.

The entire Hakone district lies within the crater of an extinct volcano that measures approximately twenty-five miles in circumference. Inside the crater are several volcanic peaks, two rivers, a great lake, and a total of seventeen communities.

Most of the hot-spring spas of Hakone are perched on the rim or just below the rim of the ancient crater, affording visitors spectacular views of lower mountain ranges, valleys, and gorges. Several of the most noted spa inns and hotels have unobstructed views of the towering pinnacle of Mt. Fuji, which dwarfs everything within two hundred miles.

Hakone is about the same distance from Tokyo as Atami—a little over an hour by train and about ninety minutes by toll turnpike. It is a much larger area than Atami, and offers a larger variety of activities—boating, fishing, water-skiing, and golf courses that are unsurpassed for surrounding scenery.

Beppu (bape-puu), facing the Inland Sea on the northern coast of Kyushu (que-shuu), is the best known of the many hot springs on the southernmost of Japan's four main islands. There are actually eight hot-spring spas in this district, plus a large number of boiling "mud ponds" (called "hells" in Japanese) which have long been used as mud baths for their therapeutic value. One of the most amazing of these "hells" is vermilion in color, maintains a constant temperature of 93 degrees centigrade, and is an estimated five hundred feet deep.

At least one hot-spring spa should be a must on every visitor's itinerary, and you will be shortchanging yourself if you don't spend some time at two or three of the more spectacular ones. A tour devoted exclusively to ten or twenty of Japan's most famous hot springs would be an incomparable experience.

As the term suggests, hot-spring spas are places to go to play and relax. You can pick your spa according to the season (some are high in the mountains, others are at seaside) and according to what you want to do in addition to bathing—play golf, ski, hike, swim, fish, go boating, or just laze the time away in the baths.

You can even pick your spa on the basis of the mineral content of the water, since there are many kinds that are recommended for different things. Wherever you go, a spa is no place to go alone. A companion is absolutely essential to make the experience complete.

Return of the Public Baths

With the coming of affluence to Japan in the 1960s and 1970s, the venerable institution of the *sento* (sin-toe) or public baths went into a rapid decline as new apartments and homes generally had built-in bathtubs and showers. In 1964, the peak year, there were 23,000 *sento* nationwide. By 1987 this had fallen to approximately 11,000.

But the prophets who predicted the total demise of the neighborhood public baths did not take into consideration the entrepreneurial spirit of the bathhouse operators or the long Japanese tradition of bathing as a recreational and social experience as well as a hygiene practice.

A Ministry of Health and Welfare survey shows that the surviving bathhouses are rapidly adding a variety of facilities and services to attract more clients and increase their cash flow. One *sento* in Osaka has a sauna, an "electric bath," an open-air tub on the roof, plus a water slide for children in the main bath area. The bathhouse is so popular people from other neighborhoods drive to it. Tsurunoyu, a *sento* in Tokyo's Koto Ward, features a variety show three times a month. Other bathhouses have workout rooms and aerobic classes, etc.

Given Japan's long history in combining bathing facilities with various forms of pleasure, a much safer prediction would probably be that the *sento* will continue to make a comeback in numbers as well as in variety of services as they redefine their image and role to fit the times. The visitor who wants to experience this aspect of traditional Japan will have no trouble in being directed to a public bath.

The Landscaped Gardens

Japan's landscaped gardens are one of the most distinctive features of the country, and add a special dimension to its enjoyment. No one knows when the art of landscape gardening appeared in Japan, but it was already commonplace in 720 A.D. when the *Chronicles of Japan*, the first history, was compiled—attesting to the existence long before then of a highly civilized style of living and the particular Japanese attachment to beauty in their surroundings.

For untold centuries, the Japanese gave landscaped gardens as much if not more consideration than the homes or buildings they surrounded. They have traditionally been an integral part of temples and shrines and the private homes of the more affluent, with the result that there are uncounted thousands of them beautifying the country.

Many of Japan's most famous landscaped gardens were created by noted Zen tea masters of the day. The garden of the *Chishaku-in* (chee-sha-kuu-een) Temple in Kyoto, for example, was originally laid out by Sen-no Rikyu (1521–1591), regarded as the greatest tea master of all. The celebrated garden of the *Katsura* (kot-sue-rah) Detached Palace in Kyoto was designed by another tea master, Enshu Kobori, whose other gardens include those of the famous Daitoku (die-toe-kuu), Kodai (koe-die), Nanzen (nahn-zen), and Chion (chee-own) Temples.

Among the most noted gardens in Tokyo are Korakuen (koe-rah-kuu-een), Rikugien (ree-kuu-ghee-een), Hyakkaen (h'yahk-kah-een), and Kiyosumi (kee-yoe-sue-me). Two of Tokyo's better-known restaurants, Chinzanso (cheen-zahn-soe) and Hannyaen (hahn-yah-een), both formerly mansions of feudal lords, include equally famous gardens.

National Parks

Because of their exceptional natural beauty, twenty-three large areas of Japan have been designated as national parks, and are regarded as irreplaceable national treasures by the people.

There are five such parks in Hokkaido, made up of volcanoes, hot springs, mountain lakes, and virgin forests. One of these five, *Daisetsuzan* (die-sate-sue-zahn), is the largest park in the country, covering 1,438 square miles. Honshu, the largest and the main island of Japan, has several national parks, including the famous Nikko-Bandai-Asahi, the Fuji-Hakone-Izu, and the Ise-Shima, with their mountains, volcanoes, lakes, rivers, forests, seacoasts, and offshore islets.

Japan's most unusual national park is the *Seto Naikai* (say-toe nie-kie) or Inland Sea, which is bounded by Kyushu, Shikoku, and the southern part of Honshu, and is made up mostly of water. This unbelievably scenic area has been known since ancient times as "A Sight Fit for the Eyes of a King."

Comparatively shallow (up to 120 feet), the Inland Sea is studded with some 950 islands that are mostly pine-tree covered and swarms with a wide variety of colorful sealife. The coastlines formed by the surrounding islands are marked by an incredible number of bays, coves, and inlets, hundreds of white-sand beaches, and an apron of green pine trees, twisted and gnarled from the action of the coastal winds.

Several luxury liners cruise the Inland Sea Park, leaving from Osaka and calling at Kobe, Takamatsu, Beppu, and some of the larger islands in the sea. Life on some of these islands has changed very little since the days of Old Japan, and afford the visitor another rare opportunity to step back in time.

In addition to the national parks, there are also twenty-seven quasi-national parks in Japan, plus over two hundred other parks that are maintained by prefectural governments.

One Vast Museum

A great part of the unusual charm of Japan derives from the presence of so much handicraft art. Until the introduction of industrial machines and modern technology into the country from 1868 onward, Japanese industry was primarily made up of artisans and craftsmen whose work was characterized by a high level of artistic excellence that had been handed down for centuries. The first Westerners to visit Japan often remarked that the whole country was one vast museum of handicraft arts.

The system responsible for the presence of so much

handicraft art in Japan was that of the master and the apprentice. Boys in their early teens or younger were apprenticed to skilled craftsmen for at least ten and sometimes for as long as thirty years. The standards of excellence that resulted from this system, which was guided aesthetically by the Zen concept of restrained natural beauty, were applied to everything the Japanese used in their daily lives, from soup bowls to paper fans.

The impression these handicrafted items make upon the foreign viewer is strongly enhanced by the fact that they are made of natural materials that have an extraordinary bucolic beauty of their own—bamboo, stone, potter's clay, handmade paper, wood, straw, plant fibers, and hand-worked metals.

Despite the abundance now of machine-made goods (which are functional but have little or no artistic merit), Japan's ancient handicrafts have managed to survive, and in some instances are even more conspicuous today because they stand out from assembly-line products. Items that are still made in the traditional manner include lacquerware, pottery, ceramics, and metal teapots. Such products can invariably be found in every inn and home in the land.

The presence of so much common art, seen also in the structure of the traditional-style homes, ryokan, restaurants, even the finishing and decor of Western buildings, gives off vibrations of naturalness, warmth, sincerity, and refinement that have a tranquilizing, sensual effect on the sensitive viewer.

The Traditions of Traveling

The Japanese of old, perhaps more than any other people, celebrated the beauty and the other attractions of their country in deed as well as in word. Their love of travel goes back to prehistoric times and is regarded as a national trait. Japanese literature compiled in the eighth century A.D. is replete with references to people traveling about the country, in groups and singly, for just about every purpose imaginable.

Buddhist monks had a great deal to do with popularizing travel in Japan. As early as the seventh century, when much of central and all of northern Honshu and Hokkaido were wild frontiers inhabited by *Ainu* (aye-nuu) tribesmen, Buddhist monks were making their way by foot to the remotest parts of the islands. Seeking out places of extraordinary beauty—on hills, in valleys and virtually inaccessible gorges, and on the highest mountains—they built thousands of temples (many of which still exist today), where they often spent the rest of their days in religious and artistic pursuits.

Shintoist priests were also great travelers because there is hardly a nob, hill, mountain, or attractive spot in between that does not have its Shinto shrine dating back hundreds of years. Still today there are over 140,000 listed Shinto shrines in the country.

As the greater of all these Buddhist temples and Shintoist shrines gained fame, usually through the extraordinary accomplishments of their founders or later heads, they began to attract followers who regularly made pilgrimages to visit them.

More important in the development of travel in Japan at this early date, however, was an action taken by the imperial government. In the latter part of the seventh century, the settled areas of the country were divided into provinces which were grouped together into "circuits" *(do)* that were assigned to supervisory officials and tax collectors. Each year these government officials, with retinues of various sizes, set out on these circuits—with the officials usually on horseback and their staffs walking—to make their rounds.

To facilitate traveling to the outlying districts and provinces of the country, the government developed and maintained a network of roads leading from the capital in Kyoto to every provincial village and town in the country.

Because the traffic was on foot, food stands, inns, and other facilities were established at short intervals along all of these national roads, giving Japan a roadway system that was comparable to the ones developed by the Chinese, the Romans, and the Incas.

The most famous of Japan's roads was known as the *To Kai Do* (toe kie doe), also written as Tokaido, or Eastern Sea Route, which passed through the provinces between Kyoto and the Kanto Plain (where Tokyo now stands), following the coastline except where it crossed peninsulas jutting out into the Pacific Ocean.

As the centuries passed, the traffic on these national roads continued to grow in volume and importance—particularly along the *To Kai Do* after 1192, when Kamakura just south of Tokyo became the capital city of the new shogunate system of government administration.

But this was nothing compared to what was to happen in the early 1600s, after Ieyasu Tokugawa became shogun and moved the shogunate government to his castle in Edo (present-day Tokyo). Ieyasu's grandson (and successor) issued an edict in 1638 that thereafter over two hundred of the country's provincial feudal lords, known as *Daimyo* (dime-yoe) or "Great Names," would keep their families in Edo and themselves spend every other year there in attendance at the shogun's court.

Each of the lords, along with a retinue of warriors and retainers, was thus required to travel on foot from their fiefs to Edo every other year. These troupes of marching lords and their retainers were known as *Daimyo Gyoretsu* (dime-yoe g'yoe-rate-sue) or "Processions of the Lords."

Each day these columns of lords, ladies, and warriors marched approximately thirty miles, stopping over every night at "post stations" interspersed along the way. There were fifty-three such post stations between the imperial capital in Kyoto and the shogunate capital in Edo. (These stations were immortalized by the great woodblock print artist Hiroshige, also known for his "Thirty-Six Views of Mt. Fuji." The prints were so common during the latter part of the Tokugawa period that they were often used as wrapping paper, which is said to be how the first ones reached Europe, where they came to be regarded as outstanding works of art.)

Maeda, the richest of the provincial lords, maintained four large mansions in Edo with a total staff of some 10,000 persons. When he came to Edo for his turn at the shogun's court, he brought several hundred additional warriors and retainers with him.

The samurai warriors of each lord were richly garbed in brilliant uniforms. Lesser retainers were dressed in apparel denoting their occupation and position. All were marked with the identifying crest of the clan to which they belonged. The lord himself usually rode in an enclosed palanquin carried by teams of men. Some of his warriors were mounted on horses; the rest of the procession marched in rigidly prescribed formation, preceded and flanked by guards.

It is estimated that ten percent of the annual income of the provincial lords was used on these yearly journeys to and from Edo—in a system that continued for over two hundred years and was undoubtedly the most distinctive and colorful feature of Japanese life for these many generations. (For more on the Processions of the Lords see The Traditions of Hospitality, Chapter VI.)

Despite many checkpoints on the roads connecting Edo with provincial cities, especially during the Tokugawa period, voluminous records show large numbers of people were constantly on the move. One of the highest adventures of this period was to travel the *To Kai Do* from Edo to Kyoto, and one of the first travel books written in Japan chronicles the misadventures of two rather irresponsible men from Edo named Yajiro and Kitahachi, making their way down the famous road, stopping at teahouses and inns along the way, getting in and out of trouble. Theirs was the original "road show," duplicated in the 1940s by Bob Hope and Bing Crosby in their famous "Road to" series of films.

In addition to the processions of the clan lords, shogunate officials, and representatives of the imperial court who were constantly on the road during the Tokugawa era, many other travelers, including priests and monks, peddlers, gamblers, entertainers, poets, masterless samurai, and merchants, used this extensive network of roads on a daily basis.

This tradition of traveling within Japan has continued. Annual student trips around the country are a part of the national educational system. Virtually every company in the country sponsors annual company trips as recreational outings for it employees. Associations of farmers and other rural organizations sponsor domestic trips for their members every year. Urban residents visit their ancestral towns or villages regularly—at least once a year if their parents still live there. Literally millions of other people make short-to-long trips each year to visit hot-spring spas or beaches or to go skiing or mountain-climbing. Pilgrimages to distant shrines and temples are also a popular activity in modern-day Japan. Honeymoon trips are a major industry.

All of this activity supports what is probably the most efficient hospitality industry in the world, and is the primary reason why traveling in Japan is so convenient and pleasant for visitors from abroad.

Touring by Car

It is now entirely feasible for foreign visitors who want to see Japan close-up to tour the country by car. There is an outstanding network of toll expressways, well marked by international signs. Good travel maps are plentiful, as are roadside services, from restaurants and toilets to motels, hotels, and inns.

The main thing car-tourers should keep in mind is to thoroughly familiarize themselves with Japan's highway signs and road maps, so they can travel from place to place with confidence, and not constantly be trying to figure out where they are and how they can get to their next destination.

Japan has several special advantages that have contributed to its emergence as one of the world's best leisure-time motoring countries. The first of these is that literally thousands of scenic and recreational areas have been developed and famous for hundreds of years. Second is that no matter where you are in the islands, you cannot be more than a short drive from not one or a few but dozens of places of historical, scenic, or recreational interest. There are hundreds of "Leisure Villages" and "Inland Isles" featuring villas, motels, drive-ins, service stations, and other facilities in some of the most scenic areas on the globe.

Rental cars are available from several large American and Japanese companies, as well as from joint U.S.-Japanese firms. Keep in mind that you need an international driver's license before you can rent a car in Japan. Such licenses are easy to obtain in your home country.

A word of warning, however. The streets and highways near Japan's major cities become jam-packed on holidays and weekends. You should definitely take this into consideration in your planning.

CHAPTER V

Bunka No Toge
Crossing the Cultural Barriers

A Rose Is Not a Rose

In Japan a rose is a *bara-no hana* (bah-rah-no hah-nah), which is "rose" by another name, but with roses as well as other things in Japan, the name is often where the similarity stops. Virtually everything you see, hear, eat, and otherwise experience physically in Japan today must be interpreted in its proper "Japanese" context.

One of the more conspicuous examples of what you see not being what you are supposed to get is the use of the English language in print advertisements, as product names, slogans, and various other labels.

It is natural for the visitor to look at English as English, and to expect it to make sense. This is one of the first and most common mistakes foreigners make in cross-cultural communications with the Japanese. In Japan, English is not used as just English. It is also used to create moods, as an exotic ingredient, to exude sophistication, to help the Japanese feel less provincial and more cosmopolitan, more international.

When used in this manner English does not have to

remain true to its original English-language meaning. That often is of no consequence whatsoever. The name of one popular soft drink immediately comes to mind: *Pocari Sweat* (poe-cah-ree). *Pocari* means nothing to the foreign visitor, but *sweat* is not something any English speaker would ever associate with a refreshing drink. (*Pocari* doesn't mean anything in Japanese, either. It was chosen as a brand name because it "sounds good" to Japanese ears.)

Many of the uses of English in Japan turn out to be humorous (from the viewpoint of foreigners). A popular toilet paper goes by the brand name of "My Fanny." I would like to believe that the creative expert who came up with this name understood the humor involved, but that is doubtful.

Even more pervasive and much more important in how visitors perceive Japan is the difference in the way Westerners and Japanese view human relations, including normal daily communication, the difference in priorities, the rationale for their actions, and so on.

Maintaining harmonious human relations is so important in Japan that this need has traditionally determined how the Japanese communicate with each other. The language is constructed and used first to maintain and enhance harmony and favorable relations, and second to communicate information.

This form of social ethics and etiquette is of course responsible for the famed ceremonial behavior and politeness of the Japanese—which is seen as very positive from the outside, but makes communicating with the Japanese very delicate, difficult, and often impossible in terms of Western logic.

The Japanese are, of course, acutely aware of the delicate nature of their interpersonal relations system, because it causes them more trouble and more frustration than it does foreigners. The foreigner is not always automatically expected to know and abide by Japanese rules of behavior, and in normal social situations can get by with only routine polite behavior. The Japanese themselves, however, have no such out. They are expected to follow every subtle twist and turn of special language use, body language, and overall attitude in all their dealings with each other.

Japanese attitudes toward foreigners have changed in recent years and are changing still. As their economic and political status rises, they have begun to expect more of foreigners—but more so in business than in the travel industry. In fact, there is a separate set of rules and behavior for travelers in Japan.

Foreign businessmen in Japan today, particularly those who are selling instead of buying, have to be much more knowledgeable and skilled in conducting (and that is the proper word) their relations with their clients, prospects, and government officials. This especially applies to foreigners called on to sell advertising or other services to Japanese companies, since the products are intangibles.*

While visitors are spared the more demanding social requirements in their own personal behavior in Japan, the degree and depth of their enjoyment of the Japanese lifestyle is greatly influenced by the extent that they can avoid judging everything they see by Western standards and get into the cultural spirit of things.

Breaking Out of Your Cocoon

The biggest problem facing Western tourists visiting Japan is not the language barrier or unfamiliarity with the Japa-

---

*For a detailed analysis of the business culture in Japan, see the author's *Japanese Etiquette and Ethics in Business* (Passport Books) and *How to Do Business with the Japanese* (NTC Business Books).

nese lifestyle. It is the limitations and restrictions imposed on them by their own culture. The visitor who has the best time in Japan is the one who can shed several layers of cultural skin and really get involved in the Japanese scene.

One of the most common daily experiences is, of course, eating. The visitor who refuses, for example, to try using *hashi* (hah-she), or chopsticks, is not only missing out on a new experience but some fun—as simple and as innocuous as this action may seen to be.

The challenge is for you to be fully conscious of the importance of letting yourself go and personally experiencing new things, new ways of sitting, eating, bathing, and so on.

An unbecoming number of Westerners who visit Japan expect—and often demand—the same kind and quality of accommodations and food that they are used to at home. As mentioned earlier, many of these people are so afraid to try anything new that they do little more than glimpse Japan in passing. Their trip abroad is little more than a change in geographical location.

Choosing a Western-style hotel over a *ryokan* inn, for example, just for the sake of familiarity and convenience, means that you automatically give up one of the most distinctive, interesting, and educational experiences in Japan.

Just making this choice requires a kind and quality of courage that many people no longer have. It is also unfortunately the kind of choice that the majority of people planning trips to Japan do not consider seriously or at all.

The blame for this does not belong entirely to travelers. For many decades, the travel industry has deliberately designed and constructed hotels and other tourist-oriented facilities to be essentially the same as the facilities they are used to at home—the idea being to offer travelers familiar accommodations and services . . . *to make sure they are comfortable and have a good time.*

The fact that this approach removes much of the adventure, fun, and benefit from the foreign experience is glossed over lightly by the travel industry, which takes the position that travelers can have their cake and eat it too (enjoy the comforts of home while having a marvelous time in a foreign country). A great deal of foreign travel thus becomes a one-dimensional affair, instead of the rich, cross-cultural experience that comes only from "going native."

Just as you cannot know or enjoy the taste of a mango or papaya without eating one, you cannot know or appreciate the pleasures of other lifestyles without physically experiencing them. Physical experience is totally different from intellectual experience—which, again, one can have from viewing a videotape.

Everyone who travels abroad should make a firm commitment in advance to go beyond the Western-style hotels and restaurants, and get away from the paved paths neatly laid out by the travel industry. This commitment should include learning some of the language, learning something about the history of the country, eating the food, and participating in living experiences.

I recall one 27-year-old American a few years ago who came to Japan as a tourist on vacation, intending to stay for two weeks. He was determined to see and experience the "real Japan" (which, I'm delighted to say, he read about in one of my books). To do so, he skipped Tokyo and went directly to a small fishing village near the end of Izu Peninsula.

There were no hotels or inns in the village. He wandered around until he found an old man sitting outside his home. Using a Japanese-English conversational dictionary, he managed to convey to the aged man that he wanted to stay in the village for a few days for no reason other than to enjoy the ambience of the life of its people.

The old man led him to a nearby house, the home of the head of the village, and in a few minutes he was invited in for tea and sweetened bean cakes. The wife of the village head and her young daughter, the only ones home, discussed the situation with the old man. Within a few minutes—with the aid of one of the girl's schoolbooks—they were able to tell the visitor that he could stay at their home.

A week later the man telephoned his employer in the U.S., quit his job, and spent the rest of the summer and fall in the village. He went out with the fishermen. He attended village meetings. He taught English to the children and wives of the fishermen. He went to weddings and funerals. On his way back to the U.S. he stopped over in Tokyo and told me it was the best time, the most satisfying time, and the best learning experience he had ever had.

Of course, this kind of spur-of-the-moment decision is beyond most of us, but it epitomizes the idea of what true cross-cultural experience is all about.

Even one day away from a scheduled trip, spent in a private home or visiting a school or some small village, can be the highlight of a trip, overshadowing the spectacular luxury of a great international hotel, the awe and appreciation inspired by a huge monument, temple, shrine, or castle. The simple secret of getting a lot out of a trip to Japan is to step outside your own cultural cocoon and live in the Japanese environment for as long as possible.

Getting Set for New Sensations

The first step in preparing for a sojourn inside "real Japan"—after you have made the commitment to do so—is to begin a crash course in the study of the Japanese language. This book (see *A Little Language Goes a Long Way*) will get you started. Another one that I recommend (without any embarrassment at all) is my own *Japanese in Plain English* (Passport Books). In addition to that book, I also recommend that you get a Japanese-language video or cassette tape. One of the best (and I think the most interesting) Japanese-language videos is called "Living Japanese," which is produced by Cross Cultural Communications in Tokyo.

"Living Japanese"—in the sense of both the living language and the Japanese lifestyle—does two things. It teaches the language and shows the life and work styles of the Japanese in a broad and comprehensive manner.

There are many other very good language books on Japan—one of the handiest being the conversational dictionary the young American used during his stay in the Izu Peninsula fishing village. Its title is *English-Japanese Conversation Dictionary*, written by the late Oreste and Elize Vaccari, who were pioneers in the publishing of Japanese-language teaching materials.

The second step, which can be taken simultaneously, is to get several other particular books on Japan that will round out your Japan orientation and provide you with specific information for day-to-day use. Since food is a daily necessity (as well as a major expense if you do not know where to eat in Japan), I recommend that the next book you buy be *Eating Cheap in Japan,* written by Kimiko Nagasawa and Camy Condon, and published by Shufunotomo.

Another valuable little book that is filled with useful Japanese-language sentences and hundreds of useful facts about everyday life in Japan, from using telephones and post offices to buying train tickets, is *Gaijin's Guide* (guyjeen), written by Janet Ashby and published by *The Japan Times.*

A very valuable *big* book is (again) one of mine: *The Japan Almanac,* which is an encyclopedic reader on things Japanese, covering some nine hundred topics that range from art, business, crafts, energy, fishing, gardening, history, martial arts and other sports to women and zen. Designed to be a one-volume reference on Japan, the book answers virtually all of the common questions one might have about Japan, plus several hundred others—included because they are unusually interesting and/or useful.

Going through these books will take several days (the smaller ones you will want to take with you on your trip), and each additional hour that you spend studying the Japanese language will contribute that much more to your enjoyment and the benefits that you will gain from your trip. It has often occurred to me that not being able to converse with someone, even on a very basic level, is something like taking a shower in a rubber suit that covers you from head to foot. You don't get the feel of the water.

The next step is to actually plan your trip, either on your own or with the help of a travel agent. If you want to plan your own trip, contact the nearest office of the Japan National Tourist Organization (JNTO). (For a list of the overseas offices of JNTO see the back of this book.) Tell the JNTO staff by phone or letter what you would like to see and do in Japan. They will send you all kinds of detailed current information. This includes pamphlets and booklets that describe many special services and facilities designed for non-tour-group travel in Japan.

The Sense of Safety

One of the great advantages of traveling on your own in Japan, either by yourself or with a friend or friends, is that you do not have to worry about personal security. Japan is one of the safest countries in the world. Incidents of public violence, muggings, purse-snatching, and the like are very, very rare. Women (and children) of all nationalities come and go as they please in Japan, day or night, in what could be described as the most disreputable parts of cities, without fearing for their safety. Of course one should exercise sensible caution just to avoid becoming the victim of some rare incident, but there is a great feeling of relief and comfort in the sure knowledge that you do not have to be constantly on guard against a threat of violence.

If you prefer to go to a travel agent for your arrangements, fine. They can be a great help to you at no cost (since their commissions come from the travel industry services). But if you want more than a canned package tour you must be willing and able to work with the agent to get what you want. This means, of course, that you have to *know* what your options are—that you can stay in modern hotel-type youth hostels or folk lodges as well as in luxury tourist hotels; that you can get excellent food in a *shokudo* (show-kuu-doe) at one-third to one-tenth of what it costs in a name hotel; that you can arrange to stay with Japanese families, etc.

Perhaps the most important thing in visiting Japan on an arranged tour is to make sure you have programmed in a goodly number of personal experiences to balance the sightseeing (which should be a minor part of your overall trip), along with lots of free time to do things on your own and to react to opportunities that invariably arise (to go somewhere not scheduled, to spend time with people, to stop running and smell the *bara*).

Of course, this is the kind of thing that is often incompatible with the travel industry system, which is designed to operate more like a space mission, with everything and everybody following prescribed moves. Some of the experiences and pleasures you can have in Japan might send you into orbit, but it is better to get there on your own instead of riding on a fast-moving rocket that someone else is controlling.

In summary, the challenge in getting the most out of traveling abroad today is to take time to prepare yourself for the trip, to either slow the system down or get off it entirely, and to include as much as possible of the personal and human touch in the experience.

Locking In the Memories

An ideal approach, which appears to be beyond the control of most of us, would be to travel to Japan by air and return by sea. There is no way in the near future that air or space travel could begin to compare with the special ambience and pleasures of shipboard travel no matter which way you are going—to or from.

But over and above the inherent benefits of taking a slow ship home (besides totally avoiding the debilitation of time-lag) is the opportunity it gives one to make the transition from Japan to your home country over a period of several days instead of hours, during which you are in between cultures and can contemplate and enjoy over and over again all of your best Japan experiences.

When you go both to and from even a distant country in just a few hours it takes away much of the prior anticipation and following contemplation. As we all know, in many things in life anticipating is often better than the real thing. Particularly in the case of a visit to a foreign country, no matter how intense the experience, it tends to lose something when we almost literally step out of one culture into another. The new and different experiences have not had time to become an integral part of us.

For many people, the rapid transition from Japan back

to their own home or office leaves them feeling as though the trip was just a dream that they could have imagined (at no expense and without the physical problems that come from abruptly changing time zones). Fortunately there are several ways besides going home by sea to counter this illusion of reality becoming unreal. But if you *can* force yourself to stop the world long enough to take an extra ten days or two weeks before re-entering your own sphere, do it. The benefits will enrich the rest of your life.

CHAPTER VI

Kogu No Dento
The Traditions of Hospitality

The Traveler as a Very Important Person

I do not know of any country in the world that treats travelers with more kindness, courtesy, generosity, respect, and all-around good service than Japan. The Japanese commonly refer to travelers as *O'kyaku* (oh-kyah-kuu) or "guests." And travelers are treated as special guests, with a type and quality of service generally reserved for Very Important People in the West.

The special kind of treatment afforded travelers in Japan came about for a number of reasons. One of the tenets of Buddhism, in which Japanese culture is steeped, is that all travelers are to be treated with the utmost respect and kindness. The Japanese have thus been conditioned in the "Good Samaritan" concept for more than a thousand years.

Shintoism, which is Japan's indigenous religion and predates Buddhism by well over a thousand years, teaches unselfish respect and service to other people.

It was, however, the appearance of the feudal shogunate system in 1192 A.D. and the subsequent proliferation of the

Samurai warrior class with their *Bushido* (buu-she-doe) "Way of the Warrior" ethics and practices that was the most important in shaping the attitudes and behavior of Japanese in all areas of their lives, including that of traveling.

The codes of behavior established by the shogunate government for the ruling Samurai class were very, very specific and very strict. The behavior and etiquette demanded of the lower classes was somewhat less restrictive, but was nevertheless very precise, especially when it came to their interaction with the Samurai class. Any breach of etiquette was a serious offense; some, in fact, called for the death sentence (which was often carried out on the spot by arrogant Samurai warriors).

The shogunate action that put the finishing touches on the attitude of the Japanese toward travelers occurred in 1635. In that year, the ruling Tokugawa shogun ordered all of the larger of the some 270 provincial lords around the country, known as *Daimyo* (dime-yoe) or "Great Names," to establish residences in Edo, the shogunate capital, to keep their families there at all times, and to spend every other year in Edo in attendance at the shogun's court.

The edict specified when each of the *Daimyo* would travel to Edo, the route they were to take, the number of retainers and warriors they were authorized to bring with them, the kinds of weapons they could carry, and even where they would stop at night. The number of overall retainers was based on the size and wealth of the particular fief.

The reasons for this edict were political: to in effect keep the families of the ambitious *Daimyo* as virtual hostages, to keep the *Daimyo* themselves away from their fiefs half of the time and in Edo where they would have less chance of plotting an insurrection against the shogun, and to keep them from building up the wealth they would need to raise a rebellion against the shogunate.

Thus began a system that was to become one of the most important political, economic, and social activities in Japan until the fall of the Tokugawa Shogunate in 1867. Virtually all travel in Japan during those long decades was by foot— only members of the imperial court in Kyoto, high personages in the Tokugawa Shogunate, some warriors, and messengers were allowed to ride horseback or be carried in palanquins, and there was no wheeled passenger transportation.

This meant that the various *Daimyo* were on the road for varying lengths of time—from a few days for those who were nearest Edo, to several weeks for those whose fiefs were in the farthest reaches of the kingdom. These troops of feudal lords, retainers, and warriors had the absolute right-of-way when they were on the road. Ordinary travelers were required to leave the road, move several yards off, and bow down to the ground while a procession was passing. (In the 1860s a party of foreigners out horseback riding near Yokohama failed to make way for a Daimyo procession. They were immediately attacked by the sword-wielding Samurai guards. One of them was cut down, and the others barely escaped with their lives.)

The inauguration of this system, known as *Sankin Kotai* (sahn-keen koe-tie) or "alternate attendance," resulted in one of the greatest construction booms ever to occur in any country up to that time. Thousands of new inns were built along all of the great walking roads that led to Edo from the provinces. Many of the processions included two hundred to five hundred people or more, requiring several inns to accommodate them. Within a very few years, Japan had the world's largest network of travelers' inns and Japanese-style hotels—a position it probably still holds today, despite the proliferation of motels in the U.S.

In addition to resulting in the rapid development of a vast network of travel facilities, the institution of the *Kotai*

Sankin system was to have a profound effect on the attitude and manners of the people employed in this new industry. The *Daimyo* were absolute rulers in their own domains, with the power of life and death over their subjects. This power accompanied them when they were on the road and could be applied to any commoner they encountered.

The Samurai warriors belonging to each of the fief clans were trained to perfection, fiercely loyal to their lords, and extraordinarily sensitive to any breach of prescribed etiquette toward themselves or their masters—and they had the authority to instantly attack and cut down any offender.

The behavior of the Samurai as well as the commoners during this long period was carefully prescribed, much of it in detailed written form and so precise, formal, and ceremonial that Miss Manners would have been considered an untutored barbarian.

The innkeepers, maids, and others involved in providing accommodations and services to the processions of the *Daimyo*, already well behaved from centuries of conditioning under the Samurai class, and already extraordinarily solicitous about the comfort and welfare of officials, superiors, and travelers, were required to follow even more explicit rules of behavior and to provide an even finer level of service for their lordly guests.

The penalty for faulty or indifferent service to the lords and their ranking retainers was far more serious than the loss of a tip. This, combined with their own conditioned response to treating customers as honored guests, raised the level of service in Japan's lodging business well above what existed anywhere else in the world.

This tradition of service still prevails in Japan's lodging industry in particular, and has been extended pretty much across the board to the entire travel industry, from its airlines and passenger ships to its tourist-oriented restaurants. Thus the traveler in Japan today, regardless of social status, falls heir to a tradition of service and hospitality that is unique.

After a few trips on Japan Air Lines or All-Nippon Airways, for example, it is extremely difficult to accept and be satisfied with the attitudes and behavior of Western flight attendants. The contrast is shocking.

These same traditions of service and hospitality are not limited to the transportation, lodging, and restaurant industries. They are characteristic of the Japanese at large, and are an important part of the attraction of life in Japan.

Hotel Heaven

Despite my advice to first-time visitors to Japan to take advantage of the opportunity to directly experience the traditional Japanese lifestyle by staying in *ryokan*, Western-style hotels are an important and impressive facet of the Japanese hospitality industry.

Taking all factors into consideration, the ideal approach is for the visitor to spend the first two or three days in Japan, and perhaps the last two or three as well, in Western-style hotels, putting up at choice Japanese inns in the interim. This gives the visitor time to rest up from the trip in familiar and comfortable surroundings and to be better prepared physically and emotionally to enjoy a totally different kind of experience in a traditional setting.

Japan's top hotels are in a class by themselves. They are, in fact, an outgrowth of the special luxury inns that were designed and reserved exclusively for the *Daimyo* lords and their chief retainers who had to spend so much of their lives on the road during the Tokugawa Shogunate period.

Each of the hundreds of stopovers on the roads leading to Edo had three classes of inns—the top class, called *Honjin* (hoan-jeen) which was for Very Important People, a second class called *Waki Honjin* (wah-kee hoan-jeen), or "Annex Honjin," for lower-ranking officials and personages, and finally the *hatago* (hah-tah-go) inns that accommodated ordinary travelers.

These luxurious *Honjin* were the predecessors of Japan's present-day luxury-class Western-style hotels, such as the Imperial, the Okura, the Akasaka Prince, and the Ana Hotel. In addition to the usual rooms, suites, conference rooms, and meeting halls, these hotels have anywhere from half a dozen to twenty or more restaurants on their premises, shopping arcades of fifteen to thirty or more individual shops, business service centers, travel agency offices, airline offices, bookshops, drugstores, and more.

Japan's top hotels are major social and entertainment centers, being used for numerous occasions such as weddings and receptions, and offering a variety of cultural and folk exhibits, nightclub-type shows and (in the case of the Imperial) theatrical performances.

While Japan's leading first-class hotels do not offer a new kind of experience, they are often a conspicuous improvement on an old experience, and they are certainly representative of modern-day Japan in all its sophisticated high-tech glory. (Not having to tip bellboys and other service staff in the hotels is another attractive point.)

Besides its internationally famous luxury hotels, Japan has an amazing number of first-class hotels that cater to the traveling public, along with another huge number of so-called businessmen's hotels, which are primarily designed for the hundreds of thousands of Japanese businessmen who are constantly traveling within the country and can't affort to, don't want to, or don't need to stay in a prestigious hotel for their image.

These businessmen's hotels are generally *just* hotels, with smaller rooms at one-half to one-fourth of the rates charged by the international hotels. They have all of the essentials (baths, showers, restaurants, laundry service), and are located near transportation terminals and business districts. They are also becoming more and more popular with foreign tourists and businessmen.

An important consideration in booking one of the first-class hotels is to find out where they are located in relation to primary transportation terminals, shopping areas, and entertainment districts. In Tokyo, for example, there are four areas where the main luxury and first-class hotels are concentrated: the downtown area (Hibiya-Ginza-Marunouchi), the Akasaka-Toranomon area, the West Shinjuku area, and the Shinagawa area.

If you want to be closer in and near major business, shopping, and entertainment areas at the same time, you will choose one of the Hibiya-Ginza-Marunouchi hotels (Tokyo Prince, Imperial, or Palace in the first-class or luxury category, or the Dai-Ichi, Ginza Tokyu, or Shiba Park Hotel if you are seeking more moderately priced accommodations).

In the Akasaka-Toronomon area, adjoining Government Center, the American Embassy, a major geisha inn and nightclub district, and only five to ten minutes from the Ginza and downtown areas, you have the Akasaka Prince, New Otani, Akasaka Tokyu, Capital Tokyu, and, up on a hill across the street from the U.S. Embassy, the famed Okura Hotel. Midway between these two areas is the spectacular Ana Hotel, which is part of the huge Ark Hills complex that includes adjoining executive apartments. This area is also only moments from Roppongi, one of the city's most popular entertainment and restaurant districts, where there are also a number of first-class hotels, including the Roppongi Prince.

In Shinjuku, which is some thirty to forty minutes from downtown, and is a major city in its own right with department stores, a huge concentration of shops, restaurants, and entertainment spots, there is the Tokyo Hilton International, the Keio Plaza, the Century Hyatt, the Washington, and the Shinjuku Prince. Since Shinjuku has become a major business center, these hotels are also popular among foreign businessmen visiting Tokyo.

The fourth major hotel district in Tokyo, Shinagawa, is about the same distance south of the center of Tokyo as Shinjuku is west. It is therefore only twenty to thirty minutes from the downtown area (as well as from most other major centers in Tokyo), but it is not in or immediately adjacent to major shopping or entertainment centers. Hotels in this area are the Pacific Meridien, the Takanawa Prince, the New Takanawa Hotel, and the Shinagawa Prince Hotel.

Other first-class hotels that are outside these districts but still within central Tokyo are the Grand Palace in Iidabashi and the Miyako Hotel Tokyo in Shiroganedai, near Meguro Station. The Sunshine Prince Hotel in Ikebukuro is in a category by itself. It is located in the Sunshine City Building, the tallest building in Japan, with hundreds of shops, restaurants, offices, and other services in the same huge complex.

There are so many businessmen's hotels in Tokyo that you can just about pick the spot you would like to be in or near, and there will be anywhere from a few to dozens of available choices. Some of the better-known ones: Ginza Dai-ei Hotel, Mitsui Urban Hotel (Ginza), Takanawa Tobu Hotel, Hotel Ibis (Roppongi), Hotel Sunroute (Shibuya), Shibuya Tokyu Inn, Hotel Listel Shinjuku, Hotel Sunroute Ikebukuro, and the Juraku Hotel (Ochanomizu).

The Inn Experience

There are over 100,000 *ryokan* inns still operating in Japan (which is about the size of the state of Montana in the U.S. and is so mountainous only about twenty percent of the

THE TRADITIONS OF HOSPITALITY   79

total area is inhabited). Of this immense number, some two thousand have been designated by the Japan National Tourist Organization as having facilities suitable for foreign guests, which usually means central heating, air-conditioning, Western style toilets, and private baths—for those visitors who choose not to let it all hang out in group baths.

The traditional Japanese inn encompasses most of the fine arts and crafts that are among the highest achievements of Japanese culture. It is designed to be aesthetically pleasing to the senses, tranquilizing to the mind and spirit, seductive in its image and feel, physically comfortable (Japanese-style comfort, of course), and both refreshing and invigorating.

The *ryokan* is made of natural materials that are totally compatible with the environment and its occupants, with wood being the main ingredient. The skill of the architect, the carpenter, and the landscape gardener are immediately evident.

As soon as you step into the *genkan* (gane-kahn) entrance foyer of an inn you go back in time—a hundred years, two hundred and fifty years, even half a millennium. The polished wooden porch and hallways, the *tatami* (tah-tah-me) reed-mat floors, the thick sliding wall panels and the thin rice-paper sliding doors, the *tokonoma* (toe-koe-no-mah) beauty alcove, the wall scrolls, the beautiful woods, the hot baths . . . all have remained basically unchanged for many generations.

Also unchanged is the lifestyle carried on within the inns. From the moment you step up on the entrance landing, minus your street shoes, your lifestyle is also changed. The first thing the newly arrived guest does is change into a *yukata* (yuu-kah-tah), the light cotton kimono-like robe that serves as casual wear as well as sleepwear. This is followed by tea, which is usually accompanied by tiny squares of sweetened beanjam.

The next traditional step is either the family-size hot bath or the *Oburo* (oh-buu-roe) or "big bath," which may accommodate anywhere from a dozen or so to twenty or thirty people (some combination inn/hotels have baths that will accommodate up to a hundred or more people at a time). For a detailed discussion of the pleasures and benefits of the Japanese bath, particularly mixed-sex bathing, see Chapter IX.

Back in your room following a scrub-down fore and aft and a good soaking in the pool (most inn baths can hardly be called "tubs"), you may have lunch or dinner, depending on the time of day, go out for a stroll if the weather is pleasant, have a party, or whatever.

The special ambience of the Japanese inn is a combination of its architecture, building materials, interior decoration, sparse, classically designed furnishings, and an intimacy that is totally lost in a Western-style hotel where the individual rooms are separated by solid walls and heavy doors that are usually kept locked. In contrast to the very private cell-like design and atmosphere of the Western hotel, the Japanese inn gives the feeling of shared intimacy, somewhat like one feels in a private home but much more intensely felt because you are sharing the intimacy with friends and strangers instead of family.

The sliding room-doors of the Japanese inn are never locked—they are not lockable. The interior room dividers—those made of white, almost gossamer-thin rice paper—are translucent and admit the slightest sound, including heavy breathing.

The intimacy of the Japanese inn is sensually exciting, and is a significant part of the pleasure of staying at an inn. Inn maids routinely enter rooms without knocking or calling out—not with any deliberate intention of catching you in a state of undress or engaged in any intimate activity, but simply because it is an age-old custom.

There is, in fact, no word for privacy in the Japanese language. The concept has not been totally alien in the Japanese culture, but it has had such a low order of priority there was obviously no need to name it. Whole families, extended families, and work-groups customarily lived in common rooms, the larger work-groups sometimes in barracks-like settings.

In present-day Japan there is a great deal of personal privacy in the homes of the more affluent, with parents having a private bedroom and children having their own rooms. But it is one of the prime tenets of Japanese business management that even ranking personnel are generally not isolated in private offices. Managers up to the *bucho* (buu-choe) class, which is the equivalent of a vice president in larger companies, share a large open room with everyone else in the division.

The Japanese contention is that it is natural and desirable for people to live and work in close intimacy because mutual understanding, close cooperation, and teamwork are the foundations of society. This belief, with all of its ramifications, especially applies to inns because they are regarded in the Japanese scheme of things as a major part of the pleasure trades (see Chapter XI, "Pleasures of the Night").

In other words, the inn is not just a place to sleep. It is a place to enjoy, to have fun—and then sleep to refresh yourself so you can have more fun the next day. If you think about this concept for a while, and fully understand it, you will be able to get a lot more out of your stay in a Japanese inn.

Western travelers, unfortunately, tend to compare the customs, facilities, and services of the Japanese inn with a Western hotel. The inn often gets low marks because they are comparing pears and apples. No matter how hard you strain, a pear is not going to taste like an apple. The point is to recognize the pear as a pear and savor its special taste and qualities to the fullest.

My best memories of Japan—and I would wager the best memories of most foreign residents and visitors alike—are of experiences that took place in Japanese inns—and not all of these experiences were in the prone position.

One of the most vivid of these memories took place in an inn overlooking the banks of a river near the small city of Seki in the foothills southwest of Nagoya. I was in Seki on a business trip and was invited to lunch by the cutlery manufacturer I was calling on. The inn we went to was several hundred years old. It was situated on a rise that was high enough to afford a view of the river, but not high enough to miniaturize the scene.

We where shown to a room that provided the best view of the river, and served drinks and fresh seafood. The setting was superb; the beauty of the inn was intoxicating; the service was classic Japanese; the food was delicious. For two hours we ate, talked, admired the scenery, and absorbed the total ambience of the experience to its fullest measure.

The only thing that could have improved on the experience would have been to share it with a female companion. But that is another story—or I should say, many stories.

Again unfortunately, many Westerners do not know how to fully let go and enjoy themselves. They are so conditioned to work and to regarding themselves and everything in the world seriously that they have lost the childlike ability to give their intellectual self time off, to suspend it actually, to let their human senses take over, to exercise and stretch themselves to their limits. The Japanese inn is designed for this kind of sensual pleasuring. It sets the mood and provides the place. You just have to recognize what it is offering you, and take advantage of it.

Some inns are much better for the resensualization of the body and spirit than others. Many have been built within urban areas, or have been encircled and closed in by cities, and have lost a significant part of their special attraction. I suggest that you select inns located in the mountains or high above the ocean (as in Atami), as far removed from the world of high technology as possible.

Technology is not sexy. Instead of appealing to the sensual side of a person (which our civilization misunderstands, misuses, and abuses) advanced industrial systems actually arouse certain primordial fears that are linked with loss of freedom and a sterile rather than the richly emotional existence so important to the human psyche. In fact, in recent years, behavioral scientists have become aware of a direct relationship between sexual maladjustment and so-called progress based on technology. Progress, in the current sense of the word, induces depression, which in turn produces sexual inadequacies. A few nights in a ryokan helps to relieve this depression and restore interest in the sensual side of life.

The traditional culture of Japan was erotic in principle, and it is this sensual orientation in Japanese inns that gave them a special role in Japanese history—a role they continue to play today to those who understand and take advantage of them.

Any visitor who comes to Japan on vacation and fails to spend a few days in a traditional Japanese ryokan is missing much of the point of the trip.

CHAPTER VII

Nihongo
A Little Language
Goes a Long Way

You *Can* Speak Japanese

Quite frankly, Japanese is a very difficult language to master unless you learn it naturally as a child. The reason for this difficulty is that there are several forms and levels of Japanese that are normally used in different situations, which are determined by the relative ages of the speaker and speakee, by their sex, by their social status, their business rank, whether it is a formal or informal occasion, whether the two are friends from their school years or afterward, and so on. There are at least half a dozen other situations that affect how the language is used.

All of the above has to do with the language in its spoken form. There are also several other distinct forms that are appropriate for formal speeches, for broadcasting the news on radio or television, and for writing the news in newspapers or magazines.

Of course, the newcomer to the language can simply forget about most of the above situations or forms of the

85

language because he or she is not going to start broadcasting news, make speeches, or be called on to respond in formal high-toned Japanese.

And, fortunately, there is one standard conversational form that is much easier to learn, including its polite form, and it is perfectly acceptable to the Japanese when used by anyone who speaks only a little of the language and is still in the early stages of learning.

In fact, this conversational form of Japanese (which has been called "mother's Japanese") is especially easy for English speakers to learn because the pronunciation is very similar to Spanish, and the grammatical structure of the language is such that you can communicate a broad range of concepts and ideas with a vocabulary of just a hundred or so words.

For example, the English sentence "I want to eat" is a rather complex grammatical structure with a subject, verb, and object. In Japanese you can express exactly the same thought or meaning with one word: *tabetai* (tah-bay-tie). If you want to say, "I don't want to eat," all you have to do is use the negative form of the verb meaning "to eat," i.e. *tabetakunai* (tah-bay-tah-kuu-nie).

This is true for literally hundreds of other thoughts. Another example: "I want to go"—*Ikitai* (ee-kee-tie). And the negative: "I don't want to go"—*Ikitakunai* (ee-kee-tah-kuu-nie).

The past and future tenses of these words are just as simple and in ordinary usage are the equivalent of saying a full sentence: "I ate (already)"—*Tabemashita* (tah-bay-mahssh-tah). "I will eat"—*Tabemasu* (tah-bay-mahss).

By memorizing or just reading the present, past, negative, and desiderative form of a hundred different words, you can express four hundred complete thoughts. That is enough to get you in or out of a lot of trouble. Add another hundred nouns, pronouns, adjectives, and adverbs to the above and you can qualify as a genuine linguist to your envious friends.

Japanese Made Easy

The Japanese language is made up of syllables based on only six sounds: a (ah), i (ee), u (ou / not yuu), e (eh), o (oh), and n (like the *n* in *bond*). The following pronunciation charts include all the sounds and syllables in the Japanese language, with their English-language phonetic equivalents. To pronounce the syllables correctly, all you have to do is read the phonetic sounds in English.

Japanese Pronunciation Chart #1
(In Japanese and Phonetically)

A	I	U	E	O
ah	ee	uu	eh	oh
KA	**KI**	**KU**	**KE**	**KO**
kah	kee	kuu	kay	koe
SA	**SHI**	**SU**	**SE**	**SO**
sah	she	sue	say	soe
TA	**CHI**	**TSU**	**TE**	**TO**
tah	chee	t'sue	tay	toe
NA	**NI**	**NU**	**NE**	**NO**
nah	nee	nuu	nay	no
HA	**HI**	**HU**	**HE**	**HO**
hah	he	who	hay	hoe
MA	**MI**	**MU**	**ME**	**MO**
mah	me	moo	may	moe

Japanese Pronunciation Chart #1 (Continued)
(In Japanese and Phonetically)

YA	I	U	E	YO
yah	ee	uu	eh	yoe
RA	**RI**	**RU**	**RE**	**RO**
rah	ree	rue	ray	roe

(Trill the *R's* a bit if you can)

GA	GI	GU	GE	GO
gah	gee	goo	gay	go

(As in "geese")

ZA	JI	ZU	ZE	ZO
zah	jee	zoo	zay	zoe
DA	**JI**	**ZU**	**DE**	**DO**
dah	jee	zoo	day	doe
BA	**BI**	**BU**	**BE**	**BO**
bah	bee	boo	bay	boe
PA	**PI**	**PU**	**PE**	**PO**
pah	pee	puu	pay	poe

Pronunciation Chart #2
(The following 33 syllables are combinations of some of those appearing above. Pronounce the two-part phonetic aids rather rapidly, "binding" the parts together. Pronounce other combinations as one syllable.)

RYA	RYU	RYO
re-yah	re-yuu	re-yoe

(Trill the *R's* a bit)

MYA	MYU	MYO
me-yah	me-yuu	me-yoe

NYA	NYU	NYO
ne-yah	ne-yuu	ne-yoe
HYA	**HYU**	**HYO**
he-yah	he-yuu	he-yoe
CHA	**CHU**	**CHO**
chah	chuu	choe
SHA	**SHU**	**SHO**
shah	shuu	show
KYA	**KYU**	**KYO**
q'yah	que	q-yoe
PYA	**PYU**	**PYO**
p'yah	p'yuu	p'yoe
BYA	**BYU**	**BYO**
b'yah	b'yuu	b'yoe
JA	**JU**	**JO**
jah	juu	joe
GYA	**GYU**	**GYO**
g'yah	g'yuu	g'yoe

Japanese You Can Use

Tabemasu *(tah-bay-mahss)*
I eat.
I will eat (now).
I do eat (it *or* that).

Tabetai *(tah-bay-tie)*
I want to eat.

Tabetakunai *(tah-bay-tah-kuu-nie)*
I don't want to eat.

Tabemashita *(tah-bay-mahssh-tah)*
I ate (already).
He, she, it ate.

Tabemasen *(tah-bay-mah-sin)*
I do not eat (that).
I'm not going to eat.
I did not eat *(if asked).*

Tabemasen deshita *(ta-bay-mah-sin desh-tah)*
I did not eat.

Tabemasho *(tah-bay-mah-show)*
Let's eat.

Tabete kudasai *(tah-bay-tay kuu-dah-sie)*
Please eat (it *or* now).

Tabemasu ka? *(tah-bay-mahss kah?)*
Are you going to eat?
Do you eat (it, that)?

Tabetai desu ka? *(tah-bay-tie dess kah?)*
Do you want to eat?

Nomimasu *(no-me-mahss)*
I drink.
I will drink (now).
I do drink (it *or* that).

Nomitai *(no-me-tie)*
I want to drink.

Nomitakunai *(no-me-tah-kuu-nie)*
I don't want to drink (now *or* it).

Nomimashita *(no-me-mahssh-tah)*
I drank (already).
He, she, it drank.

Nomimasen *(no-me-mah-sin)*
I do not drink.
I'm not going to drink.
I did not drink yet *(if asked)*.
He, she does not drink.

Nomimasen deshita *(no-me-mah-sin desh-tah)*
I did not drink.

Nomimasho *(no-me-mah-show)*
Let's drink.

Nonde kudasai *(noan-day kuu-dah-sie)*
Please drink (it *or* now).

Nomimasu ka? *(no-me-mahss kah?)*
Do you drink (that)?
Will you drink (something)?

Nomitai desu ka? *(no-me-tie dess kah?)*
Do you want to drink (something)?

Ikimasu *(ee-kee-mahss)*
I go.
I am going.
I will go.

Ikitai *(ee-kee-tie)*
I want to go.

Ikitakunai *(ee-kee-tah-kuu-nie)*
I don't want to go.

Ikimashita *(ee-kee-mahssh-tah)*
I went.
He, she, it went.

Ikimasen *(ee-kee-mah-sin)*
I do not go.
I am not going.
I did not go *(if asked)*.

Ikimasen deshita *(ee-kee-mah-sin desh-tah)*
I did not go.

Ikimasho *(ee-kee-mah-show)*
Let's go.

Itte kudasai *(eat-tay kuu-dah-sie)*
Please go.

Ikimasu ka? *(ee-kee-mahss kah?)*
Are you going?
Is he, she going?

Ikitai desu ka? *(ee-kee-tie dess kah?)*
Do you want to go?

Moraimasu *(moe-rye-mahss)*
I will receive (it).
I will accept (it).

Moraitai *(moe-rye-tie)*
I want to receive (take) it.

Moraitakunai *(moe-rye-tah-kuu-nie)*
I don't want to receive (accept) it.

Moraimashita *(moe-rye-mahssh-tah)*
I received it.

Moraimasen *(moe-rye-mah-sin)*
I didn't receive it.

Moraimasen deshita *(moe-rye-mah-sin desh-tah)*
I did not receive it.

Moraimasho *(moe-rye-mah-show)*
I'll receive (take) it.
Let's receive (take) it.

Moratte kudasai *(moe-rot-tay kuu-dah-sie)*
Please receive (take) it.

Moraimasu ka? *(moe-rye-mahss kah?)*
Will you take (receive) it?

Moraitai desu ka? *(moe-rye-tie dess kah?)*
Would you like to receive/take it?

Kaimasu *(kie-mahss)*
I will buy (it).

Kaitai *(kie-tai)*
I want to buy (it/that).

Kaitakunai *(kie-tah-kuu-nie)*
I don't want to buy it/that.

Kaimashita *(kie-mahssh-tah)*
I bought it.
He, she bought it.

Kaimasen *(kie-mah-sin)*
I'm not going to buy it.
I didn't buy it *(if asked)*.

Kaimasen deshita *(kie-mah-sin desh-tah)*
I did not buy (it).

Kaimasho *(kie-mah-show)*
I'll buy it.
Let's buy it.

Katte kudasai *(kot-tay kuu-dah-sie)*
Please buy it.

Kaimasu ka? *(kie-mahss kah?)*
Are you going to buy it?

Kaitai desu ka? *(kie-tie dess kah?)*
Would you like to buy it?

Kikimasu *(kee-kee-mahss)*
I hear.
I can hear *(if asked)*.

Kikitai *(kee-kee-tie)*
I want to hear.

Kikitakunai *(kee-kee-tah-kuu-nie)*
I don't want to hear.

Kikimashita *(kee-kee-mahssh-tah)*
I heard (it).

Kikimasen *(kee-kee-mah-sin)*
I don't hear it.
I didn't hear it *(if asked)*.

Kikimasen deshita *(kee-kee-mah-sin desh-tah)*
I did not hear (it).

Kikimasho *(kee-kee-mah-show)*
Let's listen?

Kiite kudasai *(keet-tay kuu-dah-sie)*
Please listen.

Kikimasu ka? *(kee-kee-mahss kah?)*
Are you going to listen?

Kikitai desu ka? *(kee-kee-tie dess kah?)*
Would you like to hear?

Kimasu *(kee-mahss)*
I am coming.

Kitai *(kee-tai)*
I want to come.

Kitakunai *(kee-tah-kuu-nie)*
I don't want to come.

Kimashita *(kee-mahssh-tah)*
I came.
He, she, it came.

Kimasen *(kee-mah-sin)*
I am not coming.
He, she, it is not coming.

Kimasen deshita *(kee-mah-sin desh-tah)*
I, he, she did not come.

Kimasho *(kee-mah-show)*
Let's come.

Kimasu ka? *(kee-mahss kah?)*
Are you, he, she coming?

Kitai desu ka? *(kee-tie dess kah?)*
Do you want to come?
Does she, he want to come?

Mimasu *(me-mahss)*
I see.
I will see.

Mitai *(me-tie)*
I want to see (it, that).

Mitakunai *(mee-tah-kuu-nie)*
I don't want to see (it, that).

Mimashita *(me-mahssh-tah)*
I saw (it, him, her).

Mimasen *(me-mah-sin)*
I don't see (it).

Mimasen deshita *(me-mah-sin desh-tah)*
I didn't see (it).

Mimasho *(me-mah-show)*
Let's see (it).

Mite kudasai *(me-tay kuu-dah-sie)*
Please look (at it).

Mimasu ka? *(me-mahss kah?)*
Do you see (it)?
Will you see (it)?

Mitai desu ka? *(me-tie dess kah?)*
Do you want to see it?

Yomimasu *(yoe-me-mahss)*
I read (it).

Yomitai *(yoe-me-tie)*
I want to read.
I want to read it.

Yomitakunai *(yoe-me-tah-kuu-nie)*
I don't want to read.
I don't want to read it.

Yomimashita *(yoe-me-mahssh-tah)*
I read it.

Yomimasen *(yoe-me-mah-sin)*
I do not read.

Yomimasen deshita *(yoe-me-mah-sin desh-tah)*
I did not read (it).

Yomimasho *(yoe-mah-show)*
Let's read.

Yonde kudasai *(yoan-day kuu-dah-sie)*
Please read.
Please read it.

Yomimasu ka? *(yoe-me-mahss kah?)*
Are you going to read it?

Yomitai desu ka? *(yoe-me-tie dess kah?)*
Would you like to read (it)?

Arimasu *(ah-ree-mahss)*
There is (something exists; I have something).

Arimashita *(ah-ree-mahssh-tah)*
There was (I had something; it was there).

Arimasu ka? *(ah-ree-mahss kah?)*
Do you have some?
Do you have it?
Are there any?

Arimasen *(ah-ree-mah-sin)*
I don't have it.
There isn't any.

Arimashita ka? *(ah-ree-mahssh-tah kah?)*
Did you have it?
Was there any?

Kakimasu *(kah-kee-mahss)*
I write.
I will write.

Kakitai *(kah-kee-tie)*
I want to write.

Kakitakunai *(kah-kee-tah-kuu-nie)*
I don't want to write.

Kakimashita *(kah-kee-mahssh-tah)*
I, he, she wrote.

Kakimasen *(kah-kee-mah-sin)*
I, he, she do not write.

Kakimasen deshita *(kah-kee-mah-sin desh-tah)*
I, he, she did not write.

Kakimasho *(kah-kee-mah-show)*
Let's write.

Kaite kudasai *(kite-tay kuu-dah-sie)*
Please write.

Kikimasu ka? *(kah-kee-mahss kah?)*
Do you write?
Will you write?

Kakitai desu ka? *(kah-kee-tie dess kah?)*
Do you want to write?

Haraimasu *(hah-rye-mahss)*
I will pay.

Haraitai *(hah-rye-tie)*
I want to pay.

Haraitakunai *(hah-rye-tah-kuu-nie)*
I don't want to pay.

Haraimashita *(hah-rye-mahssh-tah)*
I paid.

Haraimasen *(hah-rye-mah-sin)*
I do not pay.
I will not pay.

Haraimasen deshita *(hah-rye-mah-sin desh-tah)*
I did not pay.

Haraimasho *(hah-rye-mah-show)*
Let's pay.

Haratte kudasai *(hah-rot-tay kuu-dah-sie)*
Please pay.

Haraimasu ka? *(hah-rye-mahss kah?)*
Are you going to pay?
Will you pay?

Haraitai desu ka? *(hah-rye-tie dess kah?)*
Would you like to pay?

Yarimasu *(yah-ree-mahss)*
I will do it.

Yaritai *(yah-ree-tie)*
I want to do it.

Yaritakunai *(yah-ree-tah-kuu-nie)*
I don't want to do it.

Yarimashita *(yah-ree-mahssh-tah)*
I did it.

Yarimasen *(yah-ree-mah-sin)*
I do not do it.

Yarimasen deshita *(yah-ree-mah-sin desh-tah)*
I did not do it.

Yarimasho *(yah-ree-mah-show)*
Let's do it.

Yatte kudasai *(yaht-tay kuu-dah-sie)*
Please do it.

Yarimasu ka? *(yah-ree-mahss kah?)*
Will you do it?

Yaritai desu ka? *(yah-ree-tie dess kah?)*
Would you like to do it?

Kaerimasu *(kie-ree-mahss)*
I will return.
He, she will return.

Kaeritai *(kie-ree-tie)*
I want to return.

Kaeritakunai *(kie-ree-tah-kuu-nie)*
I don't want to return.

Kaerimashita *(kie-ree-mahssh-tah)*
I returned.
He, she returned.

Kaerimasen *(kie-ree-mah-sin)*
I will not return.
He, she will not return.

Kaerimasen deshita *(kie-ree-mah-sin desh-tah)*
I did not return.
He, she did not return.

Kaerimasho *(kie-ree-mah-show)*
Let's return.

Kaette kudasai *(kite-tay kuu-dah-sie)*
Please return.

Kaerimasu ka? *(kie-ree-mahss kah?)*
Will you return?
Will he, she return?

Kaeritai desu ka? *(kie-ree-tie dess kah?)*
Do you want to return?

Personal Pronouns

Personal pronouns *(I, we, you, he, she, they)* are not used as often in Japanese as they are in English. Well over half of the time, the appropriate pronoun is "understood" because the meaning is more or less built into the verb used, or it is understood from the context of the sentence—as demonstrated by the single-word "sentences" above.

There are, however, many occasions when it is not only proper but necessary to use the personal pronouns. Here they are:

I   **watakushi** *(wah-tock-she)*
we   **watakushi-tachi** *(wah-tock-she-tah-chee)*
you   (singular) **anata** *(ah-nah-tah)*
you   (plural) **anata-tachi** *(ah-nah-tah-tah-chee)*

he   **anohito** *(ah-no-ssh-toe)*
she   **kanojo** *(kah-no-joe)*
they   **anohitotachi** *(ah-no-ssh-toe-tah-chee)*
    There are some other forms of several of these words, but they are not necessary for basic communication, and can be ignored for the time being.

How to Use Numbers

Numbers are one of the most important foundations for communicating. In Japanese there are two numbering systems from one through ten, but only one system from eleven on. The first system, which is only for one through ten, is native Japanese, while the other complete system is imported from China. The first system is used for counting some things but not others. The same goes for the second system when the things to be counted are one through ten.
    Here is the first system:

one   **hitotsu** *(he-tote-sue)*
two   **futatsu** *(fuu-tot-sue)*
three   **mittsu** *(meet-sue)*
four   **yottsu** *(yote-sue)*
five   **itsutsu** *(eet-sue-t'sue)*
six   **muttsu** *(moot-sue)*
seven   **nanatsu, nana** *(nah-not-sue, nah-nah)*
eight   **yattsu** *(yaht-sue)*
nine   **kokonotsu** *(koe-koe-note-sue)*
ten   **to** *(toe)*
    When counting things (1 through 10) that, like hamburgers, are not specifically flat or cylindrical, the above system is used—*hambaaga futatsu* (two hamburgers); *donatsu muttsu* (six donuts), etc.
    When denoting "one person" and "two persons," *hitotsu* and *futatsu* are combined with a compound that means

"person": *hitori* (one person); *futari* (two persons). From three on, the Chinese system is used. Here is the Chinese system:

one   **ichi** *(e-chee)*
two   **ni** *(nee)*
three   **san** *(sahn)*
four   **shi** *(she)*, Yon *(yoan)*
five   **go** *(go)*
six   **roku** *(roe-kuu)*
seven   **shichi** *(she-chee)*
eight   **hachi** *(hah-chee)*
nine   **ku** *(kuu)*
ten   **ju** *(juu)*

From 11 to 99, all you do is combine the numbers above: 11 is ten plus one or *ju-ichi;* 12 is ten plus two or *ju-ni;* 19 is ten plus nine or *ju-ku.* Twenty is made up of two tens: *ni-ju;* 21 is *ni-ju-ichi;* 22 is *ni-ju-ni,* and so on to thirty, which is three tens or *san-ju.* Forty is *yon-ju;* fifty is *go-ju;* and so on. Ninety-nine is *kyu-ju-kyu* (nine tens plus nine). The spelling change from *ku* to *kyu* (que) is done for ease in pronunciation.

The word for 100 is *hyaku* (he-yah-kuu). From 100 to 199 follows exactly the same pattern as above: 101 is *hyaku-ichi;* 102 is *hyaku-ni;* 150 is *hayku-go-ju;* and so on to 199, which is *hyaku-kyu-ju-kyu.* Two hundred is *ni-hyaku,* which also follows suit (*Ni-hyaku-ichi, ni-hyaku-ni,* etc.).

The rest of the hundreds are: *sambyaku* (sahm-be-yah-kuu), *yon-hyaku* (yoan-he-yah-kuu); *go-hyaku* (go-he-yah-kuu); *roppyaku* (rope-p'yah-kuu—note euphonic change); *nana-hyaku* (nah-nah-he-yah-kuu); *happyaku* (hop-p'yah-kuu); *kyu-hyaku* (que-he-rah-kuu).

There is another word for "thousand": *sen* (sin). Once again, 1,001, 1,002, etc., are combinations of the word for thousand plus the other appropriate numbers: 1,050 = *sen-go-ju;* 1,260 = *sen-ni-hyaku-roku-ju;* 1,500 is *sen-go-hyaku.* Two thousand is *ni-sen;* 3,000 is *san-sen* (which is changed to *san-zen* for clarity in pronunciation).

This system goes up to 10,000, for which there is again a special word: *man* (mahn). Ten thousand is *ichi-man;* 10,500 is *ichi-man-go-hyaku;* 20,000 is of course *ni-man;* 50,000 is *go-man,* and so on up to one million, which is 100 *man* or *hyaku-man;* 2,000,000 is *ni-hyaku-man;* 5,000,000 is *go-hyaku-man,* etc. Ten million is *ichi-oku* (e-chee-oh-kuu).

Ordinal Numbers

To change the cardinal numbers to ordinal, just add *bamme* (bahm-may) to each of the numbers: 1st = *ichi-bamme;* 2nd = *ni-bamme;* 10th = *ju-bamme;* 21st = *ni-ju-ichi-bamme.*

Counting Other Things

There is a special class of words in Japanese (called numeratives in English) that are used when counting specific things like people, animals, flat things, round things, birds, cups or glasses of liquids, books, etc. Altogether there are about thirty of these class-words, but the most common half dozen will get you in and out of Japan with style. They are:

Nin *(neen),* for person or people: five people = *go-nin;* ten people = *ju-nin.*

Hiki *(he-kee),* for animals, fish, and insects (with euphonic changes): one animal = *ippiki* (eep-pee-kee); five animals = *go-hiki.*

Wa *(wah),* used to count birds—*ichi-wa; ni-wa; sam-ba* (euphonic change); *shi-wa.*

Satsu *(sot-sue),* used for counting books or magazines: *is-satsu; ni-satsu; go-satsu; ju-satsu.*

Hon *(hoan)*, used for counting long, round things, like pencils, fingers, rope, poles, etc.: *ippon; ni-hon; sam-bon* (euphonic change); *yon-hon; go-hon; juppon* (jupe-poan).

Mai *(my)*, for counting flat things, like paper, sheets, boards, trays, etc., i.e. *ichi-mai; ni-mai; san-mai; hachi-mai; ju-mai.*

Hai *(hie)*, for counting cups or glasses of liquids: *ippai; ni-hai; sam-bai* (euphonic change); *yon-hai; ku-hai; jippai* (jeeppie).

How to Tell Time

Time, in the sense of "what time is it?" is expressed in Japanese by the word *ji* (jee). "What" is *nani* (nah-nee) or in this case, *nan* (nahn). So: "What time is it?" = *Nan ji desu ka?* (nahn jee dess kah?).

Here is the time system:

1 o'clock   **ichi ji** *(ee-chee jee)*
2 o'clock   **ni ji** *(nee jee)*
3 o'clock   **san ji** *(sahn jee)*, etc. Just add *ji* to the proper number.

Han (hahn) is the word for "half," so 6:30 is *roku ji han;* 12:30 is of course *ju-ni ji han.*

To say "It is 3:30," just say *san ji han desu* (sahn jee hahn dess).

The Days of the Week

You cannot get very far in life these days without knowing the days of the week. This is especially important while traveling. The days of the week in Japanese are:

Monday   **getsuyobi** *(gate-sue-yoe-bee)*
Tuesday   **kayobi** *(kah-yoe-bee)*

Wednesday	**suiyobi** *(sooey-yoe-bee)*
Thursday	**mokuyobi** *(moke-yoe-bee)*
Friday	**kinyobi** *(keen-yoe-bee)*
Saturday	**doyobi** *(doe-yoe-bee)*
Sunday	**nichiyobi** *(nee-chee-yoe-bee)*

Periods of the Day/Week

today	**kyo** (k'yoe)
tonight	**komban** (kome-bahn)
tomorrow	**ashita** (ahssh-tah)
day after tomorrow	**assatte** (ah-sot-tay)
tomorrow morning	**ashita-no asa** (ahssh-tah-no ah-sah)
tomorrow night	**ashita-no ban** (ahssh-tah-no bahn)
yesterday	**kino** (kee-no)
last night	**yube** (yuu-bay)
day before yesterday	**ototoi** (oh-toe-toy)
morning	**asa** (ah-sah)
this morning	**kesa** (kay-sah)
this afternoon	**kyo gogo** (k'yoe go-go)

The Months

January	**ichigatsu** (ee-chee-got-sue)
February	**nigatsu** (nee-got-sue)
March	**sangatsu** (sahn-got-sue)
April	**shigatsu** (she-got-sue)
May	**gogatsu** (go-got-sue)
June	**rokugatsu** (roe-kuu-got-sue)
July	**shichigatsu** (she-chee-got-sue)
August	**hachigatsu** (hah-chee-got-sue)
September	**kugatsu** (kuu-got-sue)
October	**jugatsu** (juu-got-sue)
November	**juichigatsu** (juu-ee-chee-got-sue)
December	**junigatsu** (juu-nee-got-sue)

Other important words that you can use to get across relatively complex thoughts:

Good morning	**Ohaiyo goazaimasu** *(oh-hie-yoe go-zie-mahss)*
Good afternoon	**Konnichi wa** *(koan-nee-chee wah)*
Good evening	**Komban wa** *(koam-bahn wah)*
Thank you very much	**Arigato gozaimasu** *(ah-ree-gah-toe go-zie-mahss)*
Excuse me	**Sumimasen** *(sue-me-mah-sin)*
When?	**Itsu?** *(eet-sue)*
Where?	**Doko?** *(doe-koe)*
What?	**Nani?** *(nah-nee)*
Mine	**Wataskushi-no** *(wah-tock-she-no)*
Yours	**Anato-no** *(ah-nah-tah-no)*
Enough	**Jubun** *(juu-boon)*
Expensive	**Takai** *(tah-kie)*
Cheap	**Yasui** *(yah-sue-ee)*
Big	**Okii** *(oh-kee)*
Small	**Chiisai** *(chee-sie)*
Delicious	**Oishii** *(oh-ee-shee)*
Hot	**Atsui** *(aht-sue-ee)*
Cold	**Samui** *(sah-muu-ee)*
Warm	**Atatakai** *(ah-tah-tah-kie)*
Hurry!	**Hayaku!** *(hah-yah-kuu)*
Slowly	**Yukkuri** *(yuke-kuu-ree)*
Goodby	**Sayonara** *(sah-yoe-nah-rah)*

You can see from the foregoing that learning how to use a great deal of Japanese is not a major undertaking. If you would like to considerably expand your choice of words and sentences, I recommend my *Japanese in Plain English* (Passport Books), which contains some 1,200 of the most common words in the Japanese language, with example sentences (all phoneticized) for practical daily use.

CHAPTER VIII

Gochiso-Sama!
Pleasuring the Palate

Overcoming Gastrophobia

The travel industry discovered a long time ago that the most important thing in whether or not people enjoy themselves when they are away from home is how well they eat. People will put up with almost anything if the food is really outstanding. This particularly applies to traveling abroad, because visitors are regularly subjected to new and unusual experiences that are often upsetting.

When we are home eating our familiar diet, we spend very little time thinking about the psychology of food or how it affects us physiologically. But when we are asked to eat food we are not familiar with, everything changes. We are immediately interested in the ingredients, what it looks like, how it smells, and finally how it tastes—and this is when our cultural conditioning, especially our biases, really shows. If it is our first experience with a particular cuisine, we also soon discover that some unfamiliar foods have an immediate and sometimes serious physical effect on our bodies.

I began eating a Japanese diet on a daily basis in the early

1950s, when I was a student in Tokyo, because I couldn't afford meat dishes or other dishes that were similar to the American food I had been raised on. Subsisting primarily on rice and noodles, I almost always felt hungry (and produced a lot more gas than usual). I do not recommend that visitors go this far.

I also recall that when the Japanese first started traveling abroad in the early post-war period, the majority of them would be ill by about the third day from eating meals with lots of meat and butter. In some cases, the illness was so severe they returned to Japan before finishing their trip.

But visitors to Japan today need have no reservations or fears about being able to eat a diet that is compatible with their system and pleasing to their palate. Japanese cuisine has come a long way since the early 1950s—not that all of what is now available in Japan is necessarily the healthiest kind of food to eat, but there are dozens of meat, seafood, poultry, and vegetable dishes that are outstanding gastronomic experiences, and will not make you ill or leave you feeling famished.

Again, the primary factor is not a lack of good food but reluctance on the part of many visitors to try dishes that look and sound unfamiliar. Many first-time visitors to Japan allow their conditioned responses to control them in what they eat. And I'm not talking about raw fish or dried octopus or any of the other uncooked or uncommon foods that are considered gourmet treats by the Japanese but evoke responses that range from caution to disgust among many Westerners.

There are, in fact, a few Japanese foods that one generally has to grow up with to be able to eat with any degree of satisfaction, much less develop a taste for. These include (for me, anyway) uncooked *mochi* (moe-chee), *natto* (nottoe, and a couple of varieties of sea slugs.

Mochi is a glutinous mass made from cooked rice that

has been kneaded and pounded until it has the consistency and taste of a very heavy paste. I don't mind it at all when it is fried, but raw or boiled is another matter. Natto is fermented beans, which, as the Japanese readily admit, look bad, smell bad, and taste bad. But it is a traditional dish that is highly regarded by most older Japanese (the younger set often prefers cowboy beans or French fries).

In addition to dozens of dishes that might be described as Japanized versions of popular Western foods, there are an equal number of dishes that are traditional, or have been developed over the past several decades, that are pleasing to most palates at first taste. Some of these are dishes of true gourmet quality that would not be out of place in the finest restaurants in the U.S. or Europe.

The Best Dishes of Japan

The following list of Japanese dishes are ones that I regularly recommend to foreign friends and guests visiting Japan, and which have proven to be the most acceptable to the majority of people over a period of many years:

Mizu-taki *(me-zoo-tah-kee)*—A recent informal survey found that mizu-taki was the most popular wintertime dish in Japan. It consists of small pieces of chicken, leeks, Chinese cabbage, vermicelli, and tofu boiled in an earthen pot containing a stock made from water and dried fish-shavings. Other vegetables may be added to taste. Each piece is dipped in a spicy sauce before eating.

Suki-yaki *(sue-kee-yah-kee)*—People who like meat generally love suki-yaki. It consists of thin slices of beef boiled in a slightly sweetened shoyu-sake stock with mushrooms, leeks, Chinese cabbage, vermicelli, and chunks of tofu. Aficionados dip the meat (and the other ingredients as well) into a stirred raw egg dip before eating—with rice.

Nabe-mono *(nah-bay moe-no)*—Literally "earthenware pot things," nabe-mono refers to a number of popular hot-pot dishes made up of different ingredients. *Chiri nabe* (chee-ree nah-bay) consists of fish (usually cod) boiled with cabbage, leeks, carrot slices, mushrooms, and tofu, dipped in a spicy sauce before eating. *Dote nabe* (doe-tay nah-bay) is made up of oysters, leeks, tofu, edible chrysanthemum leaves, and chunks of carrot in a casserole that includes sweetened miso paste. A raw egg is usually served as a dip. Another nabe-mono version, *yose nabe,* (yoe-say nah-bay) has both chicken and fish as its main ingredient.

Tempura *(tim-puu-rah)*—One of the most popular of all Japanese dishes, tempura consists of selected seafoods and vegetables coated in a special batter and deep-fried. Among the items most commonly found in tempura: shrimp or prawns, whitefish, eggplant, green peppers, onions, a slice of sweet potato, string beans, a square of nori, and beefsteak plant. A light, delicate dip, in which each piece is dipped before eating, is served on the side. Seasoned tempura eaters mix a bit of grated horseradish into the dip before using. Tempura is served with a bowl of rice, soup, and small chunks of pickles.

Tonkatsu *(tone-kot-sue)*—A pork filet or roast steak breaded in a flour-egg batter and deep-fried, tonkatsu is a typical Japanese dish that most visitors thoroughly enjoy the first time they try it. It is served with shredded cabbage (and in some restaurants, potato salad), soup, and rice. Experienced gourmets put a kind of steak sauce on their tonkatsu, and shoyu on the shredded cabbage.

Okonomi-yaki *(oh-koe-no-me-yah-kee)*—This is the quiche of Japan. It is a pancake (thick or thin, depending on the style of the vendor or restaurant) made from a batter containing chopped vegetables, meats, seafoods, and eggs. Street-stand vendors usually have only one thin version. In specialty restaurants, you can usually specify if you want beef, chicken, or seafood as the main ingredient. The more expensive thick versions can be a full meal.

Shabu Shabu *(shah-buu shah-buu)*—Another dish that is cooked on the diners' table, shabu shabu is thin slices of very tender beef, leeks, Chinese cabbage, and tofu boiled in a large copper or brass pot (with a chimney) filled with water or stock. The meat takes only seconds to cook. Before eating, each piece or bite is dipped in a sauce made of miso, sesame seeds, and shoyu, or in a second dip made of lemon juice and grated radish.

Teppan-yaki *(tape-pahn-yah-kee)*—This is the style of grill-cooking made famous in the U.S. by the Benihana restaurant chain. In the more expensive places that cater to visitors, guests are seated around large grills attended by individual chefs. A selection of vegetables that usually includes onions, green peppers, bean sprouts, and mushrooms, along with chunks of beef or pork, are grilled to the guests' specifications. In less expensive places, the grills are built into tables (often booth-style), and the guests do their own cooking. Many teppan-yaki houses grill the meat in chopped-up garlic and oil.

Udon Suki *(uu-doan ski)*—Another hot dish that is a favorite in winter, udon suki includes chunks of chicken and sometimes shrimp or clams, leeks, mushrooms, chrysanthemum leaves, and white noodles boiled in a suki-yaki sauce.

Sushi *(sue-she)*—Almost everyone knows by this time that sushi is slices of raw fish and other seafood nestled on buns of lightly vinegared and sweetened rice. There are over a dozen commonly used sushi fish, along with clams, abalone, fish eggs, sea chestnut eggs, octopus, squid, and conger eel. If you are not already a sushi fan, it might be best to start out with tuna *(maguro),* since it does not have a fishy taste and is not tough or stringy. You can order the different kinds of sushi one at a time (just by pointing to them if you are at a sushi bar) to discover which ones you like best. Many shops place a small dab of greenish horse-radish *(wasabi /* wah-sah-bee) under the slab of seafood on some of their sushi. It is very hot and you may want to remove it or leave only a bit of it. If you don't want it there in the first place, just say *Sabi nuki* (sah-bee nuu-kee), which means "without horseradish."

Oyako Donburi *(oh-yah-koe doan-buu-ree)*—This is a bowl of rice covered with pieces of chicken and onions cooked in egg. It is a very simple and inexpensive dish that is available in most soba and udon noodle shops as well as general *(shokudo /* show-kuu-doe) restaurants. Unless the restaurant is really below par, the dish usually ranges from tasty to delicious, and it is filling.

There are dozens of other rice dishes, including many with toppings such as curry, beef-stew gravy, suki-yaki type meat, or tempura-style shrimp, along with several versions of fried rice (with chopped up vegetables, meats, chicken, shrimp or crab, and egg), plus the same or similar rice mixtures boiled together in a pot, and called *kama-meshi* (kah-mah-may-she) or "pot food," but generally speaking, one has to acquire a taste for these dishes, primarily be-cause the main ingredient is rice.

Yaki-tori—This worldwide favorite is nothing more than small chunks of chicken (and liver, if you want), green peppers, and onions (or leeks) on bamboo or metal skew-ers, grilled over charcoal. Just before serving, or during the process of grilling, they are salted or dipped into a shoyu-based barbecue sauce, depending on your choice. Yakitori is usually eaten as a snack rather than a full meal, especially when eaten at outside sidewalk vendors. In restaurants, a yaki-tori meal would include rice, soup, and probably pickles.

Adventures in Good Eating

There are dozens of well-known restaurants in Tokyo, Kyoto, Osaka, Kobe, and other large Japanese cities that are famous as specialty restaurants, noted for their steaks, crab-meat dishes, tempura, sushi, tofu dishes, teppan-yaki, baked eel, pot-boiled "stews," and so on, plus such ethnic restaurants as Chinese, French, German, Greek, Indian, Italian, Mexican, and Russian. These are the restaurants that advertise in English to the foreign community and to visitors from abroad, and generally range from good to excellent.

Many of these specialty restaurants, particularly the Japanese, are "experience places" with outstanding ethnic decor, and are an important part of the special pleasures of Japan. You won't have any trouble identifying or finding these places.

Eating Well for Less

If you are even a little bit adventurous—and want to economize on your food bills—you should also patronize the same restaurants as the average Japanese. These restaurants seldom if ever advertise and exist by the hundreds to the thousands in larger Japanese cities. They usually display plastic duplicates of the dishes they offer in showcases at the entrance. The duplicates are so realistic-looking that the uninitiated visitor to Japan often takes them for the real thing.

Both general and specialty restaurants utilize these plastic exhibits to advertise their wares, but to the foreign tourist they serve a second purpose as well. In addition to being graphic examples of the dishes available in individual restaurants, the dummy dishes are also a sign that the restaurant caters to the average local customer and is reasonably priced, since expensive restaurants, including restaurants that cater primarily to foreign residents and visitors, ordinarily do not display such plastic images.

Most general and specialty restaurants in Japan also have set breakfasts, lunches, and dinners, called *teishoku* (tay-e-show-kuu), that include a main course and side dishes. These set courses are invariably much cheaper than ordering a similar number of dishes à la carte (from one-half to two-thirds cheaper in many cases), so it is worthwhile to check them out. *Teishoku* meals are often displayed on trays (which is the way they are usually served).

General restaurants are known as *shokudo* (show-kuu-doe) or "places to eat" in Japanese, and are the Japanese equivalent of the typical American coffee shop, with breakfast, lunch, and dinner menus—the latter including several meat, chicken, and seafood dishes. While many of these dishes are prepared exactly the same way as in the U.S., the taste may differ somewhat because of the use of different condiments, and some of the side dishes may be a little different (an unfamiliar vegetable, for example). But you are getting a good, solid meal of meat, fish, or fowl with vegetables (and a dessert of ice cream, pie, cake, or fruit, if you like). In virtually all cases, you have a choice of a plate of rice or bread with the usual meal.

Shokudo are commonly found in department stores and office buildings; in, under, or near railway terminals, in shopping complexes, at airports, and along highways. (The coffee shops in Western-style hotels in Japan are *shokudo*, but they are usually quite a bit more expensive than outside restaurants and generally do not offer inexpensive set [*tei-shoku*] meals.)

Of course, you may eat solely in American-style fast-food restaurants while you are in major Japanese cities (McDonald's, Denny's, Wendy's, Anna Miller's, Victoria Station, etc.) at prices well below what one pays in hotel and "class" restaurants—but you should resort to these restaurants only in emergencies or to break a steady diet of unusual or exotic fare.

CHAPTER IX

Ofuro
When in Rome . . . !

The Traditions of Bathing

B athing regularly in hot water has been a solidly entrenched national custom in Japan since the beginning of recorded history. It probably dates back hundreds or even thousands of years earlier because bodily cleanliness is a paramount tenet of Shintoism, the native religion.

This practice alone was enough to distinguish the Japanese from the Chinese and Koreans and from most Westerners up until very recent times. When the first Westerners appeared in Japan, the Japanese could not stand to be near them very long because they smelled so.

Some foreigners, all of whom were men, who took up residence in Japan in the 1500s (before the government's exclusion policy) adapted rather quickly to the custom of regular bathing, not only because they discovered that it felt good to be clean and to not give off an offensive smell, but also because men and women bathed together, thus giving them a chance to see women in the nude.

But the first Western missionaries to reach Japan (the first one arrived in 1549) were shocked at the Japanese custom of bathing—first that they bathed regularly, and second, that they bathed together. Of course, it was the mixed-sex bathing that most upset the sex-obsessed missionaries, who saw the human body as an instrument of the devil, and themselves divinely charged to get the devil out of every damned soul they encountered.

Japanese converts to the Christian religion were prohibited from bathing more than once a week, while the missionaries themselves stayed as far away from water as possible (which could have been one of the reasons why they eventually failed to turn Japan into a Christianized nation—or at least I like to think so!).

Western missionaries were finally expelled from Japan just before the beginning of the 1600s because of their interference with internal political affairs and the threat that their activities would result in their home countries invading Japan—not because of their attitudes toward the Japanese custom of bathing.

Over two hundred and fifty years later, when missionaries were once again allowed to enter Japan, they very quickly demonstrated that they had not learned anything in the intervening centuries. They once again prohibited daily bathing and railed continuously against the Japanese custom of mixed-sex bathing.

Western missionaries still today have not succeeded in Christianizing Japan (and never will, of course), but their efforts did eventually play a major role in Japan's legally banning mixed-sex bathing in public bath facilities during the American military occupation of Japan.

I remember it as though it were yesterday. Bathhouses were given a grace period during which they were to build walls separating the baths into male and female sections. For several months prior to starting construction, many bathhouse operators strung a rope across the large common pool, with the portion on the left designated for men, and the right side for women.

Later, when the first solid partitions were put up, many of them separated only the washing area and the large soaking pool and about half of the undressing area. The operator on duty (who collected the small fee) was situated on a raised podium between the male and female sections. When you were standing beside the podium to pay your fee, you had a clear view of the female section of the bath-house. It was not until years later that the two sections were completely separated in most bathhouses in the city areas.

With the coming of affluence in Japan and the construction of Western-style homes and apartments with built-in baths and showers, the number of public bathhouses dwindled. Well over half of the people in Japan now have their own private bathing facilities. Among my own circle of foreign friends who live in Japan, there are a few who still go to the local neighborhood bathhouse several times a week—daily, in fact, unless they have to work late. They follow the old custom because it adds a very special dimension to the routine of staying clean. It is a social experience, pleasing to both the mind and the body.

Mixed bathing in homes in Japan is still a common practice—although many of the tubs are so small they will accommodate only one person at a time. One of the nicest things about bathing with someone is that you have someone to scrub your back. What a wonderful feeling!

The Ritual of the Bath

The normal routine in a public bath or in a bath at a hot-spring spa is to carry any clean underclothing you intend to put on later with you to the bath, leave it and your *yukata* robe or other clothing in a plastic or wicker basket provided for that purpose in a dressing area outside of the bath proper, then enter the bath carrying your own soap and a *tenugui* (tay-nuu-gooey), a small combination washcloth and hand towel.

As you probably have heard by this time, you do not bathe in a Japanese bath. You scrub on the outside of the bath and then enter it to leasurely soak and chat with friends or fellow bathers. Washbasins, small buckets for ladling water out of the tub (or in larger places, hot and cold water spigots), along with low stools to sit on, are provided for bathers to douse themselves with hot water, scrub down, and rinse before climbing into the bath.

Bathing etiquette calls for both men and women to cover themselves discreetly with small hand towels when standing up and moving about in the bath. Women, of course, make no attempt to cover their breasts, since exposing them while bathing is not regarded as lewd or licentious in Japan.

Besides being much more sanitary and aesthetically pleasing to wash outside the tub you are going to soak in, mixed bathing provides many benefits that have been lost or downgraded in most Western societies. One of the greatest banes of Western civilizations is the hangup about human sexuality. There is a basic contradiction between the Western views of sexuality and reality, i.e., human needs, which results in friction, frustrations, and conflicts that have plagued our societies since cave days.

Mixed bathing does not solve all of these problems, but when done regularly from infancy by everyone it certainly eliminates many of the sources of sexual hangups, and reduces others. As a result of influence from the West, the Japanese custom of mixed bathing is unfortunately being eroded.

It is still common, however, to see scenes of mixed bathing regularly on national television, but again the scenes are invariably at hot-spring spas. On these televised programs both men and women cover their sex organs with small hand towels, so we are not talking about total frontal nudity on public TV. The TV scenes frequently show young bare-breasted women getting in and out of the pools, and sometimes exposing their breasts while they are in the water. But generally speaking, older women are not filmed unless their breasts are covered by a small towel or water. The rationale here is probably an arbitrary decision made by the TV people that the breasts of older women are not going to appeal to their audience.

Recently I watched a Sunday afternoon TV special on hot-spring spas in which the host was an attractive young woman. She was shown repeatedly in the nude, with only the little *tenugui* towel covering her pubic area, as she joined different groups of people, including men, in a variety of baths at different spas. In a number of cases, the only other bathers were men. She joined them with enviable savoire faire while carrying on a spritely commentary for the benefit of the viewing audience.

Now that is the kind of thing I would like to see on American television!

Taking the Plunge

I recall my own first experience in a mixed bath in Japan. It occurred in the latter part of the 1940s when I was a teen-aged member of the Occupation forces. The setting was a hot-springs spa in the foothills about two hours north of Tokyo. This, mind you, was shortly after the end of World War II when many Japanese in rural areas had never seen a Westerner in person, much less in the nude.

Just by luck, the bath that I chose to enter at that time

and in that place was fairly full—of females. There were three elderly women and about a dozen girls ranging in age from seventeen or eighteen down to five or six.

At that time, I understood only basic Japanese. My entrance caused a flurry of chatter and giggling among the younger girls, while the older women bowed and accepted me without so much as a raised eyebrow. They did, however, look me over.

I must admit that this first introduction to the institution of mixed bathing took a degree of courage I probably would not have had in my own country and culture. I knew mixed bathing was an accepted practice in Japan, and that my entering the bath was only unusual because I was a foreigner, not because I was a male. I knew there would be no objections or embarrassment on their part, and that whatever trepidations I felt were my own hangups—which I was determined to overcome.

After I had scrubbed and entered the pool, the older women immediately began trying to talk to me. Within a matter of seconds, I was completely at ease and relaxed. None of my earlier fears of sexual arousal and that sort of thing materialized. This is not to say, of course, that such things never happen or that they didn't happen on some other occasion, but my baptism was both painless and pleasurable, and I became a devotee.

You can make the transition from hungup neophyte to an experienced mixed-sex bather just as easily. It's all in your head, as the saying goes. The best time and place, as in my own case, is a hot-spring spa *(onsen)* where everyone goes knowing that "anything goes" at *onsen*. All you have to do is accept the fact that it doesn't make any real difference what strangers might think of you, that their opinions or judgments will not affect you in any way whatsoever.

The challenge is to come to terms with yourself; to accept yourself as you are without worrying about what others think. This, of course, is the message that psychiatrists preach to people having a wide variety of coping problems, particularly self-image and sex-related problems.

If you can accept yourself to the extent that you are not bothered at all by the thought or practice of mixed bathing, you are not likely to have any problems that would require psychiatric counseling. So put a hot-spring spa on your itinerary, and take the plunge.

CHAPTER X

Funiki Wo Suiageru
Soaking Up the Atmosphere

Strolling the Ginzas of Japan

Tokyo's *Ginza Dori* (gheen-zah doe-ree), which bisects the famous shopping and entertainment district known as "The Ginza," was the first street in Japan to be paved, the first to have Western-style streetlights, and the first to have buildings made of brick.

As a result of this early "international" development, Ginza Street became a magnet for Japanese and foreign residents alike before the end of the nineteenth century. Hundreds of thousands of people from Tokyo as well as adjoining cities and prefectures flocked to the Ginza on weekends and holidays to see the new Western-type buildings and streetlights, to shop for imported merchandise, and to eat and drink in the restaurants and bars that sprang up between the shops and department stores and on the backstreets of the area.

Ginza ni ikimasho! (gheen-zah nee e-kee-mah-show) or "Let's go to the Ginza," very quickly became one of the most commonly heard phrases in Tokyo. The custom of going to the Ginza just to stroll up and down the main thoroughfare and the backstreets became institutionalized as *Ginbura* (gheen-buu-rah) or "strolling the Ginza," and was something virtually everyone did on a regular basis well into the 1960s.

It used to be said that if you wanted to meet someone during this period—anyone, Japanese or foreign—all you had to do was go to the intersection of Ginza and Hibiya Streets (which used to be known as Owari-cho because laborers from the district of Owari were used to reclaim the land in the area), and wait. From 1952 until the early 1960s, the favorite rendezvous spot was the southwest corner in front of the Sanai Shop (now a high-rise building with a rounded front). While I waited there for a date one time in 1956, my high-school Latin teacher came by.

Really Old Japan Hands will recall that the Matsuya Department Store on the northeast corner of the Ginza-Hibiya Streets intersection was the main Tokyo PX during the American military occupation of Japan, and that one of the most popular GI hangouts in the city was the snack bar in the Wako Department Store on the northwest corner. Another flashback about this extraordinary era in U.S.-Japan relations: the Isetan Department Store in Shinjuku was used as billets by the Occupation forces. GIs by the hundreds used to sit on the brass rails that still ring the building and ogle the girls passing by.

Tokyo's Ginza was certainly not the only popular strolling street to develop in Tokyo or in Japan following the opening of the country to the West. It just happened to be the first one that was Westernized. In fact, "strolling streets" have been an integral part of Japanese life since the beginning of urbanization.

Many cities in Japan began as the sites of castles, temples, or shrines. There was always one main thoroughfare leading to the castle, the temple, or the shrine. Tradesmen invariably built their shops along these thoroughfares, since people going to and from the castles, etc., would pass by their storefronts. Virtually all traveling in Japan up to the 1860s and 1870s was by foot, so there was an almost constant stream of passersby.

All of the hundreds of post-station towns resulting from the institution of the "Processions of the Lords" (Chapter III) began as inns and shops lining both sides of the roads they were on, turning all of these "main avenues" into strolling streets.

Festivals and other festive occasions have traditionally been very common in Japan. Some were associated with shrines or temples, others with more commercial sponsorship. These events always attracted large numbers of people into the streets. Since Japanese homes have always been small and crowded, people spent a lot of time out in the streets, socializing and enjoying the pageantry of the passing crowds, with the great Processions of the Lords among the regular attractions during the long Tokugawa dynasty.

Japan's large cities today are made up of what used to be dozens of towns and villages that likewise grew up around shrines and temples, and in the case of Tokyo, around the mansions of the provincial feudal lords who were required to maintain their families in Edo during the last 247 years of the reign of the Tokugawa Shoguns. These former towns and villages are easily discernible in present-day Tokyo, Osaka, and other major cities in Japan. In Tokyo they include the well-known districts of Shinagawa, Akasaka, Ueno, Shinjuku, Nihonbashi, Ikebukuro, and so on.

The point is that each of these districts today has its own main thoroughfare and shopping/entertainment center where strolling remains a major form of recreation. Besides housewives walking or riding bikes to these shopping streets on a regular and often daily basis, families customarily take walks in their own neighborhoods on weekends and holidays—just to get out of the house and enjoy a bit of exercise and fresh air.

But the shopping, dining, and entertainment centers that have developed around important commuter transportation terminals in Japan's large cities remain the most popular strolling areas. Each of these areas is a microcosm of Japan—filled with humanity, jammed with every conceivable kind of retail store, restaurant, and night-spot, and ablaze at night with a jungle of neon signs that turn the areas into fantasylands.

Getting Off the Tourist Trails

Decades ago when I worked for the Japan Travel Bureau, I learned that the best way to ensure that visitors had a good time while they were in Japan was to take them into the backstreets of one or more of these shopping-entertainment districts and simply let them walk around and absorb the sights and sounds, stopping at places that caught their eyes, and letting them take time to investigate, to satisfy their curiosity.

I found that just one or two hours is not enough to get the full impact of this kind of experience. It requires a whole evening, say from 7 to 11 P.M. or later, depending on the age and stamina of the visitors. The idea is to go slow, look at everything, stop around 7:30 for dinner, go somewhere else for dessert, a third place for coffee, and then continue the stroll.

Around 10:30, again depending on the age and proclivities of the visitors, many choose to stop in briefly at one or more nightspots, which include bars, beer gardens, nightclubs, and cabarets.

Japan's thousands of cabarets are special in that they

employ large numbers of attractive female hostesses to sit with, cater to, and otherwise entertain male customers. Foreign women occasionally go to cabarets with male escorts, but they are designed for and almost exclusively reserved for men. (See Chapter XI, "Pleasures of the Night.")

Finally, one of the best ways to close out a night of getting acquainted with this side of the "real Japan" is to stop at a *yatai* (yah-tie), or street vendor, selling various kinds of snack food. Among the popular dishes available at *yatai* are *oden* (oh-dane), a kind of stew that includes vegetables and seafood; *okonomi-yaki* (oh-koe-no-me-yah-kee), a kind of egg-and-vegetable pancake, and baked sweet potatoes.

Some of these wheeled *yatai* food carts, particularly those selling oden, provide stools for five or six customers. The others are usually stand-up or take-away operations. *Yatai* selling hot food are especially popular during the colder winter season, and mostly come out at night in the entertainment districts. In summer, *yatai* can be found during the day on weekends and holidays, as well as at night. Daytime *yatai* may offer anything from ice cream to *yaki-tori* (yah-kee-toe-ree) or tidbits of chicken barbecued on wooden skewers.

Mixing with the Natives

A great many professional people in the travel industry (as well as in academia, the government, and elsewhere) labor under the misconception that observing another society as an outsider is enough—that you really don't have to get down with the natives to understand and appreciate a culture. As you know by this time, I'm a firm believer in going native.

There are several aspects to a culture—spiritual, intellectual, emotional, physical, and so on. If you really want to absorb even a piece of foreign culture you have to experience it; you have to participate in the lifestyle of the people so that it becomes a part of you.

As a short-time visitor to Japan, you are naturally limited in what you can do and how long you can do it. But you can at least get a taste of Japanese culture by meeting as many people (other than tourist guides and hotel staff) as possible, and I propose that you program in one or more days to be devoted solely to meeting and communicating (to whatever degree possible) with ordinary Japanese.

You can do this with structured home-visits arranged by a Japanese travel agency. You can make an effort to get advance introductions to Japanese individuals, through business or social channels. You can ask for help from travel agents, airline or hotel staff, or tourist information centers operated by the Japan National Tourist Organization. They *will* be interested in what you want to do and *will* try to help you.

Many Japanese will enthusiastically go out of their way to have a chance to meet and spend a few to several hours with foreign visitors—either out of a pure sense of hospitality or because they want to expose themselves to foreigners, to practice their English, to demonstrate goodwill, and to help make sure the visitor gets a good impression of Japan.

The Japanese take these things personally and seriously. It is therefore not so far out to suggest that you *can* make contact with private individuals after you arrive in Japan. One of the connections that works especially well is through schools. If a school in your own area does not have any kind of relationship with Japanese schools, you can have someone in Japan call a nearby school and tell them you would like to visit the school in order to learn something about the Japanese educational system so you can share the knowledge with your own school system when you return home.

This invariably gets you the invitation you are seeking, and often is expanded into a major experience that goes beyond the first meeting. Such impromptu meetings have, in fact, led to student exchanges and family visits.

If you live in or near a city that has a sister-city relationship in Japan it is very easy to go through this connection to arrange private meetings with one or more Japanese families. If you are a member of the Kiwanis Club or the Lions Club or the Masons, these organizations have thousands of members in Japan who can be contacted through their international headquarters. Members of these clubs are especially interested in direct person-to-person contact with foreigners.

While much smaller and more exclusive, Japanese members of the Young Presidents Club are another connection that can be used. The YMCA and YWCA organizations are very active in Japan, and are also excellent contact points for individual programs during visits to Japan.

One technique more affluent visitors sometimes use is to hire vacationing students (who are studying English) to act as their guides and companions while they are in Japan. This can be a marvelous way to really get acquainted with a typical Japanese, and often to make a lifelong friend. (This approach doesn't have to be limited to the school vacation periods. Japanese university students are very casual about attending classes, having only to pass the periodic examinations.)

Visitors who come to Japan via one of the Japanese airlines can begin the process of learning about the people and culture by first interacting with the airline flight attendants en route, and with everyone else they meet in the process of traveling. (I have noticed over the years that most travelers, particularly those in groups, have a tendency to spend most of their time abroad talking with each other, often virtually ignoring the local scene. This is not the way to learn about a foreign country.)

You should begin to use your Japanese-language ability as early as possible and on every occasion that presents itself. This is another area in which Americans in particular are very weak. Many Americans live abroad for ten or more years and do not learn to speak the local language. There is no excuse for this kind of extreme provincialism—and the world can no longer afford to indulge this kind of cultural myopism.

In addition to the mutual responsibility people have to understand and communicate with each other, the simple fact is that is what makes traveling abroad both fun and educational.

CHAPTER XI

Yoru No Asobi
Pleasures of the Night

The "Hot" Water Business

Most visitors to Japan get just a glimpse of a side of
Japanese life that is much more important to the
understanding of the people (and a lot more interesting to
learn) than what one might imagine. This other side of
Japan—which the Japanese do not talk about but otherwise do not hide—is known in Japanese as *mizu shobai* (me-
zoo show-bye), or "water business."*

While the *mizu shobai* originally included theatrical and
other types of entertainment, it is now primarily used in
reference to the huge world of bars, nightclubs, cabarets,
soaplands (massage-bath houses), and sometimes to a special category of hotels known as "lovetels," which specialize
in renting rooms by the hour (although all-night rates are
available) to couples seeking a private place for a short
time.

---

*For a detailed discussion of this fascinating side of life in Japan, see the
author's *Japan at Night—A Guide to Leisure and Recreation in Japan* (Passport Books).

The size of Japan's nighttime entertainment industry is astounding to the newcomer. It is in fact one of the largest industries in the country, and plays a far more important role in the economy and society than similar businesses abroad. One of the major reasons for the importance of the *mizu shobai* in Japanese life is that entertaining friends or guests at home is very rare, and is mostly limited now to the few who have become Westernized, and have larger than usual homes.

The Japanese are frequently visited in their homes by relatives, but when it comes to friends and business associates, particularly where entertainment is concerned, virtually all such meetings take place in coffee shops, restaurants, hotels, bars, clubs, or cabarets.

Home entertainment did not develop in Japan because houses were very small, very fragile, and very cold in the winter. The only form of heat was small *hibachi* (he-bah-chee) charcoal braziers, set on the floor, or in a covered floor-pit that people sat around with their feet and legs under the cover). Private homes were also acutely susceptible to fires from the *hibachi* used for heating and cooking.

While Japanese homes and apartments built in recent decades are constructed of much sturdier materials that are far less susceptible to flames, and much more effective methods of heating are now commonplace, they are generally still so small that the only "public" area in a typical home is a "living room" that is often no more than ten by twelve feet, with a number of furnishings that further reduce the open space.

Another factor in the immense size and importance of the nightime entertainment trades is that social etiquette in Japan was traditionally very detailed and very strict. About the only time one could "dispense with etiquette" was when drinking, during which time almost any kind of behavior was acceptable. The *mizu shobai* thus served as a giant stress-remover for the Japanese, allowing them to throw off their inhibitions and relieve their frustrations.

Yet another important element in the *mizu shobai* today is that businessmen have developed the custom of wining and dining prospects and customers (and themselves) in the bars, clubs, and cabarets that make up the key parts of the industry. This practice is regular and systematic, and accounts for much of the billions of yen that annually changes hands between the business community and the *mizu shobai*.

The visitor to Japan must know about the *mizu shobai*, how it works and why it is important, in order to have any in-depth insight about the country. But learning about the *mizu shobai* can be both expensive and painful if you do not follow some basic guidelines.

Cabarets, patronized almost exclusively by businessmen on expense accounts, normally do not have set prices, and are very expensive. Foreign patrons of cabarets are either highly placed executives with substantial entertainment budgets, or the guests of Japanese business associates. There are, however, a collection of cabarets in Tokyo, Osaka, Kobe, and a few other cities that cater to foreign customers, with posted prices that are well below what is usually charged Japanese patrons. These cabarets advertise in the English-language guide-type publications available in these cities (*Tokyo Weekender, Tour Companion, Tokyo Journal* in Tokyo, *Kansai Time-Out* in the Osaka-Kobe-Kyoto area).

Generally speaking the foreign community in Japan patronizes the beer gardens, hotel lounges, bars, nightclubs (which have hostesses but do set and post prices), discos, pubs, and restaurants that have various forms of entertainment, including live shows. Some, of course, also frequent the notorious soaplands, where the services run the gamut in the sensual arena.

Visitors in Japan have no problem finding a wide variety

of nightspots to explore. There are more than twenty-five thousand in Tokyo alone. The Ginza district in downtown Tokyo boasts 3,200 of these *mizu shobai* bars and clubs (along with its department stores and hundreds of boutiques and restaurants), which employ approximately 36,000 hostesses to serve and otherwise cater to their male clientele.

The travel industry in Japan, particularly Japan Gray Line, offers nighttime entertainment tours that include one or more cabaret stops (where they have special set prices for the tours). This is the easiest and most economical way to experience the typical nightspot scene. Among the half dozen night tours Japan Gray Line runs in Tokyo is one that includes a sukiyaki dinner, a geisha party, and a nightclub show. Another version of this tour offers a kabuki show in place of the nightclub stop.

The visitor to Japan generally will not go too far wrong by patronizing the nightspots that advertise in the English-language press. They are seeking foreign clientele, almost always operate under a Western system of pricing and paying, and can also be expected to have English-speaking staff or hostesses.

It is generally only the exclusive Japanese-style hostess places (whether they are called clubs or cabarets) that do not follow the Western pricing system, so one can usually go into any other kind of club or bar without worrying about being ripped off.

The Real World of the Geisha

There are perhaps half a dozen Japanese words known to most educated foreigners around the world. One of these words is *geisha* (gay-e-shah), which means "skilled person"—in this case women skilled in playing traditional Japanese musical instruments, in Japanese-style dancing, singing, and in catering to men more or less as personal waitresses and companions during eating and drinking parties.

Geisha have a long and mostly honorable history in Japan, going back several hundred years. The institution developed during the early decades of the Tokugawa Shogunate (1603–1868). During the first generations, the women were basically prostitutes, but as the practice grew into a profession, the status of the women went up.

Eventually the training of the geisha, along with their constant exposure to businessmen, political leaders, and the other elite of the country, made them into the best-educated, most experienced, and often most talented women in the country.

By the time internal and external pressures were undermining the long reign of the Tokugawa shoguns in the early part of the 1800s, the more talented and ambitious geisha themselves were high on the social scale in Japan. Famous geisha were ardently courted by leading businessmen and politicians, and often became their wives.

One young imperial prince fell in love with a geisha who already had a patron, and ended up having to borrow the money (from a madam in the *mizu shobai*) to ransom her. The young prince, who then married the geisha, was Hirobumi Ito, who went on to become one of the leading Japanese statesmen of his times, with a career that spanned more than fifty years.

With the downfall of the Tokugawa Shogunate in 1867–68, the status of the geisha lost some of its luster—primarily because the Japanese quickly learned that Westerners hid their extramarital affairs from public view, and that women of the pleasure world were looked down on. In their rush to emulate Westerners, the Japanese began to be more discreet about their recreational activities in the "willow world."

The profession of the geisha did not die, however, and despite having shrunk considerably in postwar Japan (because of competition from hostesses in cabarets, along with other forms of nightlife), it survives and thrives today in a pattern that has changed very little since Tokugawa days.

Perhaps the biggest change in the geisha world is that the cost of their services has become so high that only very successful businessmen and the highest-ranking bureaucrats and political officials (who are authorized to spend tax money on their entertainment) can afford them. The host of an evening that includes geisha can expect to pay anywhere from a thousand dollars—for a very small, very short party—to ten thousand dollars or more.

Much to the surprise and possible disappointment of many foreigners, the "geisha house" in the sense meant is a figment of their imagination. Except in outlying provincial areas, geisha generally do not live and work on the same premises. They live in apartments or other accommodations, and work in *ryotei* (rio-tay), which are inn-restaurants. The *ryotei* call them in when they have booked a party that wants the services of the geisha.

In earlier years it was common to see geisha being transported to and from *ryotei* in jinrikisha (generally lacquered black), but one is lucky to see this sight more than a few times a year now.

The *ryotei* utilizing the services of geisha are almost always clustered in areas that are known as "geisha districts." Among the more famous of these districts in Tokyo today are Akasaka, Shimbashi, and Yanagibashi. The Akasaka area, just down a hill from Japan's Diet Building and other government offices, is favored by the political leaders of the country.

Geisha *ryotei* do not cater to the general public. They are available only by reservation, and most of them require recommendations from known patrons before they will accept reservations. Parties are served in private Japanese-style rooms. Most of guests leave the *ryotei* at the end of the evening, but overnight lodging can be provided for those who desire it.

With few exceptions, the only foreigners who go to geisha *ryotei* today are the guests of Japanese hosts. There are several dozen inn-type restaurants in Tokyo, Osaka, Kyoto, and elsewhere which cater to foreign clientele and have "geisha" waitresses. Few if any of these *geisha* are members of the Geisha Association and they are unlikely to have gone through the professional training required by the association of members in good standing.

Of course, the foreign visitor generally cannot tell the difference between a professional licensed *geisha* and one who is unlicensed and lacks the traditional training. These "amateur" *geisha* can invariably sing and dance and often play the *shamisen* (sha-me-sane) as well. Virtually every Japanese girl-woman in the country knows how to interact well enough with male guests to satisfy that requirement.

If you want the genuine *geisha* experience, you need a guarantor and a fat wallet. I recommend you settle for cabaret hostesses. They are almost always far more attractive than *geisha,* cost far less, and you can have a lot more fun with them. The other choice is to patronize one of the foreign-oriented inn-restaurants that provide unlicensed *geisha* for their guests. See the local English-language guide publications for names and addresses of these establishments.

CHAPTER XII

Shoppingu-No Charenji!
The Shopping Challenge!

Strategies for Smart Shopping

Shopping has traditionally been one of the major attractions of foreign travel because it provides an opportunity for the ultimate consumer to cut out some of the middlemen and get much closer—if not directly—to the source of many popular, sought-after products, with substantial savings in cost.

The cost benefit is no longer a primary consideration in shopping in Japan, however. In fact there are many Japanese-made products that can be bought at cheaper prices abroad than they can in Japan itself. The reason for this is the current high disparity between the relative value of Japanese yen versus the dollar and other foreign currencies.

The cost of pearls, high-tech electronics, cameras, lenses, and other Japanese-made items that are now popular around the world has not changed significantly as far as their yen price is concerned, but the price of *yen* has more than doubled in recent years.

When yen was pegged at 360 per dollar, a ¥36,000 string

142 DISCOVERING CULTURAL JAPAN

of pearls was a bargain at $100. Now that same string of pearls costs well over $200. Again, the price of the pearls was not raised. The cost of yen went up.

The disparity between the yen and the U.S. dollar is now such that many prices in Japan are simply outrageous from the American viewpoint. A cup of coffee, for example, ranges from $3 to $5. In a hotel, a glass of orange juice ranges from $4 to $6. An American-style breakfast in a hotel (which was $5 to $10 dollars until the mid-1980s), now costs from $15 to $30. These same extremes apply across the board when one converts dollars or some other weak currency to yen, whether we're talking about something to eat, wear, or enjoy.

There are, however, many ways to avoid these price extremes while in Japan, especially where food prices are concerned, and still be able to satisfy the urge to bring back gifts and souvenirs of the trip. Of course, you will have to go out of your way to achieve these savings because you will not find budget prices in hotels.

Where dining is concerned, the secret is simply to eat in ordinary Japanese restaurants, particularly those that feature set breakfasts, lunches, and dinners, which usually cost less than half of what you pay when ordering à la carte or in hotel restaurants.

Another gambit is to stop in at neighborhood markets and buy a two- or three-day supply of fresh fruits and possibly other items as well. Tangerines, apples, pears— especially the *niju-seki nashi* (nee-juu-say-kee nah-she) or "twentieth century pears"—persimmons, and bananas make excellent snacks. Eating an inexpensive and delicious tangerine (*mikan* / mee-kahn) is certainly an excellent substitute for a $4 or $5 glass of orange juice.

It is easy enough to go even further in saving on your food bills, if you are willing to do a bit of additional shopping. Western-style lunch meats, condiments, and a variety of outstanding breads are available in Japanese supermarkets, providing all the makings needed for a good old-fashioned sandwich.

Hotel Shopping Arcades

All of the luxury-class and most of the first-class hotels in Japan have shopping arcades on the premises—some of them with as many as two dozen or more stores, offering a variety of the products for which Japan is famous.

The prices in these shops are generally higher than those located outside of hotels simply because of the cost of the space. Furthermore, hotel arcade shops generally do not offer discounts or bargains of any kind. Their biggest attraction is that they save the shopper a lot of time and inconvenience because you can commute to and from them by elevator. They also offer a fairly large selection of the most popular gift and souvenir items under one very comfortable roof. If this convenience outweighs the cost factor, shopping for most of the things you might want to buy in Japan is very easy indeed.

The Tax-Free Shops

Several hundred shops in Japan, congregated in airports and downtown locations, are licensed by the government to sell tax-free gift and souvenir items to visitors and non-Japanese residents in possession of passports. The original purpose of the shops was to offer a price advantage to tourists to encourage shopping.

Tax-free shops still offer savings of ten to twenty percent off the regular retail price of various kinds of merchandise, particularly items classified in the luxury class. Another advantage of shopping at tax-free stores is that they stock a number of items that are popular with foreign visitors, have staff who speak English, and usually offer packing and shipping services.

But tax-free shops are few in number, and offer only a limited selection of merchandise, much of which is likely to be the same made-in-Japan products that can be bought abroad for less money. The best approach is to patronize these shops *when* they are convenient and when you have no better option, such as discount shops or discount districts where the prices are often substantially lower than those in tax-free outlets.

Discount Shopping

Discount shopping has always been popular in Japan but is even more extensive today because prices in Japan are high by any standards (in this case, in relation to how much the Japanese earn). In addition to regular bargain days and special sales at specialty stores, variety stores, and department stores, there are year-around discount shops and shopping areas in Tokyo and other cities that are known by virtually every Japanese.

The largest and most famous of these areas is the *Akihabara* (ah-kee-hah-bah-rah) district in Tokyo, a few minutes from the downtown area, where household appliances, electrical items and components, and a wide variety of electronic products are the main attractions.

Prices in Akihabara range from twenty to fifty percent or more below retail prices in regular stores, but because of the yen-dollar disparity, they are often not bargains for visitors. Often, now, only hard-to-find electrical or electronic parts are actually price bargains in Japan.

Reordering Your Shopping Priorities

The best approach to shopping in Japan today is to shop only for things not readily available abroad, such as specialty handicraft items, including such traditional things as garden lanterns (in metal or stone), interior decoration items such as *andon*-style lighting fixtures, a style of chinaware that is especially attractive, or art objects and other unusual items with a value (to you) that is not specifically related to their dollar cost.

All of Japan's prefectures and many of its cities have what is referred to as *meibutsu* (may-e-boot-sue) or "famous products," meaning products that have been made in their area for generations and are representative of the district. These products range from folding fans, teapots, wooden dolls, lacquerware, particular kinds of pottery and stoneware to bamboo utensils. (See Chapter 13 for a more complete listing.)

These local famous products, which are representative of traditional Japan and often not exported, make the best kind of gift and souvenir, since they are distinctive as well as rare. Among them are things that you can treasure for a lifetime. If you are going to be traveling to various cities and prefectures in Japan, you should take advantage of the opportunity to check out their *meibutsu*. The prices are generally much lower there than they are in tourist shops in Tokyo or Kyoto, for example.

The main point is that Japan is no longer the place to shop for strictly utilitarian products or equipment, and that the only real bargains in Japan today are traditional products that have intangible value. If you make up your shopping list with this in mind, you are much less likely to be disappointed with either prices or what you end up buying.

CHAPTER XIII

Mingeihin

Souvenirs with Soul

The Master-Apprentice System

Like many cultures around the world, the early industrial civilization of Japan was based on the production of tools, utensils, and other necessities by individuals who developed their skills to a high degree and then passed them on to assistants or apprentices.

In Japan the master-apprentice system was institutionalized in the society at a very early stage of its development, but masters from Korea and China also played a major role in the final flowering of the process. Beginning in the fifth century A.D. skilled craftsmen coming to Japan from the mainland changed from an occasional occurrence to commonplace, resulting in a renaissance of development in virtually every field of human endeavor.

Prior to these early contacts with the Asian mainland, Japan had no system of writing. Culture and civilization were transmitted by word of mouth, example, and on-the-job training. The Korean and Chinese masters who came into Japan had also been trained in the master-apprentice system, and found fertile ground for their knowledge and skills among the Japanese.

By the eighth century, the Japanese had imported and synthesized virtually the whole gamut of Chinese culture, adapting it to fit their distinctive philosophy. The output of the thousands of masters and skilled apprentices turned the lifestyle of the ruling class in Japan into a highly sophisticated existence that equaled or surpassed that in any of the great civilizations of Asia or Europe.

As this system continued for generation after generation, and the years of apprenticeship increased to decades instead of years, the level of skill required to achieve journeyman status became higher and higher, and eventually virtually every master craftsman was an artist. The finest craftsmen were master artists whose work achieved a classic style and beauty that today would win them fame and fortune—yet their work was so commonplace that only fairly affluent people could afford to buy it for ordinary use in their homes without attributing any special significance to it.

The poorest farmers and townspeople used pottery, lacquerware, and other handcrafted items that were the products of a proud tradition of quality that extended down to the lowest level.

When the first Japanese-made handicrafts reached Europe in the sixteenth century, their classic style and beauty made a tremendous impression on royalty and gentry alike. Many products that were simple kitchen utensils in Japan became treasured collectors' items to their new owners.

Much of the charm of modern Japan is bound up in the traditional products still being produced today by its master craftsmen, and Japan owes much of its popularity as a travel country to the men and women who have carried on the skills of their distant ancestors.

Further, the high standards of design and quality that are characteristic of most of Japan's contemporary high-tech products, from portable tape recorders and video cameras to cosmetics and watches, have their antecedents in the handicraft traditions of the past—and are now formidable factors in the efforts of American and European manufacturers to sell their goods in Japan.

These same traditions are responsible for the extraordinary inroads Japanese designers are making in the international fashion world, and are very likely to carry them to the forefront of this multibillion-dollar-a-year industry.

Because of significant differences in climate, in the availability of raw materials, and in the particular occupations that developed in early Japan, regions developed different product specialties. Farmers in the northern snowbound regions of the Tohoku district, noted since prehistoric times for its beautiful forests, became carvers of distinctive wooden dolls called *kokeshi* (koe-kay-she).

Iron ore was also found in surface deposits in the Tohoku region. Craftsmen in this area become known for their superb cast-iron bells and teapots. By the middle years of the long Tokugawa Shogun dynasty (1603–1868), virtually every region and province in Japan had its noted *meibutsu* (may-e-boot-sue) or "famous products," and travelers visiting these areas made a special point of buying them.

The Famous Things

Here is a selected list of the most famous products of some of Japan's leading city areas:

Tokyo: woodblock prints, toys, fans, cameras, electronic items, silverware, books, cloisonné, brocades, handmade paper, and pearls.

Kyoto: silk brocades from the Nishijin district, lacquerware, screens, dolls, scrolls, antiques, woodblock prints, damascene, cloisonné, and curios.

Osaka: silks, toys, antiques, art, and curios.

Kobe: bambooware, tortoiseshell ware, silk, and silk goods.

Nagoya: lacquerware, porcelain, chinaware, fans, cloisonné, and curios.

Kanazawa: kutani-yaki porcelains, silk, dolls, and lacquerware.

Nikko: woodenware, lacquerware, and curios.

Timeless Treasures

As we learned earlier, the pleasure trades in Japan are known as *mizu shobai* (me-zoo show-by) or "water business." I like to think that part of the reason for this unusual name is that pleasure is an ephemeral thing that evaporates like water—and the higher the climax of pleasure the more rapidly it fades after the peak.

Since a trip abroad is something like the "water business," in that the pleasures fade quickly once you return home, it is very important to acquire a number of tangible, permanent reminders of your trip—besides photographs.

The best kind of timeless treasures to take home from Japan are examples of its handicraft arts. I recommend a few choice ceramic, pottery, or lacquerware pieces that you thereafter keep as decorations, to be placed on a stand or shelf (the Western version of the *tokonoma*), where they can be seen and enjoyed for the rest of your life. Of course, hanging scrolls, Hakata dolls, kokeshi dolls, ironware, etc., can also serve the same purpose.

In addition, I suggest that you buy some lacquerware and chinaware for regular use (especially when you have visitors). Both wares are very distinctive and add a special allure to any setting. You will also be directly reminded again and again of your experiences in Japan. The memories will remain alive, and just as the tea host reserves the last measure of pleasure for himself, you will be able to make your memories of Japan a permanent part of your life.

Sayonara
("If It Must Be So")

It is easy to determine if people really enjoyed a visit to Japan. All you have to do is ask them, just before they leave, if circumstances permitted would they readily extend their visit by several days, and would they like to come back and stay longer the next time.

The answers you get are revealing about the travelers as well as about the efficiency and effectiveness of the travel industry. Travelers who are very positive about their experiences, and are enthusiastic about returning to Japan at the first opportunity, frequently express regret, however . . . about what they failed to do. Their biggest complaint is that they spent too much time sightseeing in "old Japan," and not enough time getting acquainted with the Japan of today, particularly the people.

If you have followed most of the advice in this book, that is much less likely to happen to you, and the Japanese word of farewell, *sayonara* (sah-yoe-nah-rah), literally "if it must be so," will have new meaning.

Your new familiarity with the language, the food, the customs, and the lifestyles of Japan will also add a new dimension to your everyday affairs, and the memories will stay with you for life.